Shakespeare's Pagan World

The Roman Tragedies

J. L. Simmons

University Press of Virginia
Charlottesville

THE UNIVERSITY PRESS OF VIRGINIA
Copyright © 1973 by the Rector and Visitors
of the University of Virginia

First published 1973

ISBN: 0-8139-0488-9
Library of Congress Catalog Card Number: 73-80126
Printed in the United States of America

For Fleur

Preface

I TAKE IT as an auspicious sign that this season, at Stratford-upon-Avon, the Royal Shakespeare Company is performing Shakespeare's Roman plays as a group for the first time anywhere. It is the thesis of this study that Shakespeare's conception of the Roman world and its place in universal history generated a particular and distinctive kind of tragedy in the three major Roman plays and that they can profitably be considered as a group. One can agree with Kenneth Muir in his address to the British Academy (1958) that each of Shakespeare's tragedies is *sui generis*, and at the same time recognize that certain basic patterns and attitudes recur—or, rather, develop. I certainly do not want to suggest that, as an infant, Shakespeare received a static impression of the pagan world at the font of Holy Trinity Church. Only in the late *Coriolanus* do we get the clearest and most fully developed rendering of Shakespeare's idea of Rome and its ethos. And it is for this reason that I begin at the end of the series, after outlining my thesis in an introductory chapter. The perverse clarity of *Coriolanus*, however, could be achieved only after years of dynamic reflection, following the writing of *Julius Caesar* and *Antony and Cleopatra*. Shakespeare's vision of the Roman tragedy, moreover, began to come into focus only after his triumphs in the comedy of English history.

My apparent neglect of *Titus Andronicus* may be mitigated, for those who admire it, by the fact that this earliest Roman play is the subject of the final paragraphs of my Conclusion. *Titus Andronicus* is certainly a tragedy full of potentialities, some of which conflict with others. Unmistakably, one such potentiality is the tragedy of Rome in general and that of *Coriolanus* specifically. I trust this will speak for itself by the time the reader reaches the final pages.

Work on this book was made possible by generous grants from the Tulane Council on Research, from the Henry E. Huntington Library, and from the Folger Shakespeare Library. I also want to acknowledge permission to use material that appeared in earlier versions in *Tulane Studies in English, ELH*, and *Shakespeare Survey*. Throughout this study all references to Shakespeare's plays are from the edition of Peter Alexander.

Other debts are extensive and of long standing. I wish to thank Professor Richard C. Harrier for giving me the initial impulse to pursue Shakespearean studies. Professor Fredson T. Bowers directed an earlier version of this book in the form of a dissertation and has steadfastly influenced me with his radiant sympathy and critical power. Professor David M. Bevington, who also helped to direct my dissertation, continues to inspire me with his wisdom and to honor me with his friendship. I am especially indebted to my friend Professor E. C. Bufkin, who gave this manuscript a detailed and sensitive reading; but such a debt can no more be accounted than the one to my mother and father or the one expressed in the dedication.

J. L. SIMMONS

New Orleans, Louisiana
October 9, 1972

Contents

Shakespeare's Pagan World

The Roman Tragedies

I

Introduction

A World Elsewhere

THE JUSTIFICATION for grouping *Julius Caesar*, *Antony and Cleopatra*, and *Coriolanus* as Shakespeare's Roman tragedies is undeniable. The label insists only upon their common setting, although their relationship is reinforced by a common derivation from Plutarch. When A. C. Bradley found that these three plays failed to meet his "standard of pure tragedy," he bequeathed to us a commonly accepted value judgment that further isolated the plays, in a category considerably below the exalted Great Four. Shakespearean criticism since 1904, however, has questioned this judgment. As an indication of critical revaluation, L. C. Knights, in his essay "*King Lear* and the Great Tragedies" for the Pelican *Age of Shakespeare* (1955), omitted without comment *Hamlet* and *Othello* and added *Antony and Cleopatra* and *Coriolanus* to form, as it were, a new Great Four. It is therefore interesting that, despite the significant reappraisal given to *Antony and Cleopatra* and *Coriolanus* and to the problematic nature of *Julius Caesar*, the only integral relationship generally recognized in the three Roman tragedies—as opposed to the rather more superficial matters of setting and source—turns out to be the very reason for which Bradley excluded them, "their historical character."[1]

On the basis of this historical character, M. W. MacCallum justified his pioneering work, *Shakespeare's Roman Plays and Their Background* (1910): "Shakespeare's Roman plays may be regarded as forming a group by themselves, less because they make use of practically the same authority and deal with similar subjects, than because they follow the same method of treatment, and that method is to a great extent peculiar to themselves. They have points of contact with the English histories, they have points of contact with the free tragedies, but they are not

---

[1] *Shakespearean Tragedy* (London: Macmillan, 1904), p. 3.

quite on a line with either class. It seems, therefore, possible and desirable to discuss them separately."[2]

In the next book (1961) devoted exclusively to the three plays, Maurice Charney insists that they do not "constitute a well-defined group" in the sense of the problem plays or the late romances. While the question of relationship is not really pertinent to his critical intent, his concluding remarks, in the appendix to which he relegates the matter, are in accord with MacCallum's differentiation: "The importance of political ideas in the Roman plays extends into the dramatic action, for each of these plays presents a tragic conflict between the individual and the state."[3]

Derek Traversi, in the third and latest book on the Roman plays (1963), expresses surprise that no more than the two previous studies exist, but the distinguishing factor he sees in the group does not essentially differ from MacCallum's view and would not of itself justify a new study: "The plays, by bringing together into a mutually enriching unity two of the principal themes of Shakespeare's mature work—those expressed respectively in the historical chronicles and in the series of great tragedies which followed them—constitute one of the undoubted peaks of his achievement."[4] The political and historical aspect of the plays extends Shakespeare's concerns in the English histories; the focus on an individual of "a single exalted nature" reflects the preoccupation of the tragedies. Thus the generally accepted attitude toward the Roman plays, as J. C. Maxwell summarized it in his essay on twentieth-century criticism, "involves recognition of their affinities with the history plays, but it has not meant treating them [as Bradley and even MacCallum did] as necessarily prevented by those affinities from being fully tragic."[5] This paradoxical reversal in critical attitude leads us to the question that a study of the Roman plays must answer: in what positive way does their historical character create a special kind of tragedy while, at the same time, imposing distinctive limitations?

I purpose to suggest that *Julius Caesar*, *Antony and Cleopatra*,

[2] *Shakespeare's Roman Plays and Their Background* (London: Macmillan, 1910), p. vii.

[3] *Shakespeare's Roman Plays: The Function of Imagery in the Drama* (Cambridge, Mass.: Harvard Univ. Press, 1961), pp. 207, 217.

[4] *Shakespeare: The Roman Plays* (London: Hollis & Carter, 1963), p. 9.

[5] "Shakespeare's Roman Plays: 1900–1956," *Shakespeare Survey*, 10 (1957), 1. I am generally indebted to Maxwell for these opening remarks.

and *Coriolanus* are indeed essentially different from Bradley's Great Four and that the most important factor in their integral relationship is the historically pagan environment out of which each tragedy arises. In all three of these dramas, a kind of problem play stands between the critic and the tragedy because the conflict of opposing sides does not, as in Bradley's Four, involve the struggle between characters associated with the clarifying absolutes of good and evil. There are no villains—no Macbeth, Claudius, Iago, Goneril, Regan, or Edmund. And there are no characters whose goodness intimates absolute and transcending value. As John F. Danby has noted in relation to *Antony and Cleopatra*, no Cordelia appears in these Roman plays; "the Christian core" is undramatized: "Both *Antony and Cleopatra* and *Coriolanus* [and I should urge *Julius Caesar* as well] follow North's Plutarch without benefit of clergy."[6]

Hamlet, Othello, King Lear, and *Macbeth* take place in a world where a concentration of evil and disorder aligns itself against a clearly defined opposition. Despite the rich intermixture of good and evil—as in Hamlet or in Claudius—fair is fair unmistakably, and foul is foul. Although Macbeth or Othello may be tragically deceived, the audience is given no cause for doubt. But in the Roman plays—in the characters of Brutus, Caesar, Antony, Cleopatra, and Coriolanus—the audience discovers that fair, disconcertingly, can be foul and foul be fair. Volumnia's rebuke to Coriolanus typifies a perplexing moral environment peculiar to Shakespeare's pagan world:

> You are too absolute;
> Though therein you can never be too noble
> But when extremities speak.
>
> (III.ii.39–41)

Although these plays deal with the conflict of extremities, the extremities are not those of good and evil. Neither side offers an absolute that can establish our moral perspective.

Critical commentary gives evidence of this moral uncertainty. In fact, the polarities in the criticism of the three plays signal their common and essential relationship. A glance at the criticism of *Julius Caesar*, though a familiar picture, reveals a dialectic such as arises in the commentary on the two later Roman plays. The dialectic in *Julius Caesar* has doubtlessly been agitated by the appeal that the conflicting extremities make to still quite topical ideologies. Not surprisingly, Brutus provokes the most

---

[6] *Poets on Fortune's Hill* (London: Faber, 1952), p. 149.

sympathy, Caesar little more than scorn. Probably the growth of fascism in the twentieth century was partly responsible for the climax of this tendency, John Dover Wilson's Cambridge edition in 1949. For Wilson the play's theme is tyranny versus freedom, and if similar commentators did not press the idea "that the main issue of the play is not the conspirators' fate but the future of Rome, of liberty, of the human race," they agreed in spirit upon the moral nature of the conflict.[7] A theatrical consequence of this tendency was Orson Welles's modern-dress production (1937) with Caesar as Führer. And in 1962, demonstrating the mercurial nature of political left and right, a projected Broadway production had Caesar dressed as Fidel Castro. It was mercifully aborted.

The alternative, to side with Caesar, is no more attractive. If we recall that German criticism in the years preceding the Second World War did for Caesar just what the Allied forces did for Brutus,[8] changing sides as either a critical or a political reaction proves merely ironic. There were supporters for a heroic Caesar all along—MacCallum, for example, in 1910; historical critics generally found it difficult to support a conspirator rather than a figure of one-man rule. To represent this critical opposition, one can cite Sir Mark Hunter's insistence that Shakespeare viewed the murder of Caesar as "the foulest crime in secular history."[9] T. S. Dorsch, editor of the New Arden edition in 1955, was therefore by no means the first to encourage a rehabilitation of Caesar; but his interpretation was the first of recent date to be conjoined with a thorough dressing-down of the sentimental Brutus.[10] Since then Gordon Ross Smith has taken us as far as possible from sympathy with Brutus, having made of him, with a Freudian diagnosis, a fairly ugly neurotic.[11] As for the practical result, Roy Walker assures us that a production at Stratford-upon-Avon, in which the titular hero was the sympathetic and dramatic center, afforded magnificent theater.[12]

Happily the critical attitude toward this play can no longer be naive. Irving Ribner, it is true, has gone back to the Dover

[7] *Julius Caesar* (Cambridge: Cambridge Univ. Press, 1949), p. xx.
[8] See the references in Charney, p. 228, n. 24.
[9] "Politics and Character in Shakespeare's *Julius Caesar*," *Trans. Royal Soc. Lit.*, 10 (1931), 109–40; see also James E. Phillips, *The State in Shakespeare's Greek and Roman Plays* (New York: Columbia Univ. Press, 1940), pp. 174–88.
[10] *Julius Caesar*, Arden Shakespeare (London: Methuen, 1955), pp. xxvi–lxi.
[11] "Brutus, Virtue, and Will," *SQ*, 10 (1959), 367–79.
[12] "Unto Caesar: A Review of Recent Productions," *Shakespeare Survey*, 11 (1958), 128–35.

Wilson line; but instead of comparing Caesar with modern tyrants, he reaches his conclusions with the historical method he applied to the English history plays. Caesar can only be termed a tyrant, not a king, because he is without the absolute and divine right that only God can give. "An ordinary man, no matter how great, could not aspire to kingship; he could only aspire to tyranny, and this is precisely what Brutus fears."[13] Such simplistic historicism, however, only presents more problems. If, in the English history plays, there is almost always a tension working against orthodoxy, how much more so when the location is Rome. Ribner also ignores any distinction to be made between Shakespeare's approval of monarchy for metaphysical reasons and his approval for political ones. The orthodox rationale for monarchy was based not only on the order of God's creation but on the efficacy of the institution. Finally, one cannot overlook the likelihood that many members of Shakespeare's audience, influenced by a very common historical imprecision, considered Caesar to be a king, the first in the most famous line. We have the eye-witness account of one such member, Thomas Platter, a Swiss traveler who saw the play at the Globe in 1599: "After lunch on September 21st, at about two o'clock, I and my party crossed the river, and there in the house with the thatched roof we saw an excellent performance of the tragedy of the first Emperor Julius Caesar."[14] Ribner's conclusions, then, are based on a not entirely acceptable premise.

Ernest Schanzer was the first to synthesize diametrically opposed attitudes toward the conflict in the play by recognizing that Caesar's moral ambivalence is a "deliberate dramatic device." The medieval view of Caesar as one of the Nine Worthies and the Renaissance view of him as a proud and aspiring tyrant are both structurally incorporated into the play, not only in the direct representation of Caesar but also in the indirect and divergent representations made of him by the other characters. Schanzer urges that *Julius Caesar* belongs to his newly defined category of problem play, the problem being twofold: "the psychological problem of the nature of the 'real' Caesar; and, hinging upon this, the moral problem of the justifiability of the murder."[15]

[13] "Political Issues in *Julius Caesar*," *JEGP*, 56 (1957), 13.
[14] The translation and the original German (first published in *Anglia*, 22 [1899], 458) are in Dorsch, pp. vii and 166.
[15] *The Problem Plays of Shakespeare* (London: Routledge & Kegan Paul, 1963), p. 70. Schanzer's argument first appeared in "The Problem of *Julius Caesar*," *SQ*, 6 (1955), 297–308.

The acceptance of such a view involves two more problems. First, critical synthesis quickly dissolves, at least in this case, into a factitious critical skepticism, as revealed in a recent article: "The outcome of a close examination of *Julius Caesar* is the discovery that no theory of the meaning of the play or of its major characters can unify the dissident elements." Objecting even to Schanzer's resolution, the critic continues: "It is more convincing to say that *Julius Caesar* is not a problem play, but a play about a problem: the difficulty—perhaps the impossibility—of knowing the truth of men and of history."[16] Second, and more significantly, Schanzer does not organically relate his "problem" to what he considers "the play's main moral issue, the rival claims of personal relations and the *res publica*."[17] In spite of Schanzer's important contribution to our understanding of *Julius Caesar*, we are finally short-circuited back to Bradley's complaint, that the historical character of events works against, or is at least disassociated from, the really tragic potential.

This critical circle, as I have drawn it, is viciously simplified; but it does, I think, circumscribe the difficulties generated by the play's moral conflict. The same problematic opposition of moral extremities is in *Antony and Cleopatra*, an opposition also synthesized in Schanzer's problem category. Notoriously the play has been read as a severe rebuke of lust and as an almost religious hymn to transcendental love. Surprisingly, no one has suggested the inclusion of *Coriolanus* in the amorphous category of the problem play, but this final Roman tragedy presents a nightmare of moral relativity. The dramatic appeals in the play perplex us in our search for some acceptable mode of action or point of view. No other Shakespearean tragedy ends with the helpless resignation—really the dismissal—proposed by the Volscian lord: "Let's make the best of it" (V.vi.147). It might seem that we are back in the darkly satiric world of *Troilus and Cressida*, as O. J. Campbell assures us. But if one does not feel that Coriolanus is being ridiculed, one feels even less certain that a norm and a purpose for the satire lie in "political teaching."[18] D. J. Enright has shown dissatisfaction with the classification of *Coriolanus* because "tragedy" is for him too honorific a designation. He does not insist on redubbing it a "debate";

---

[16] Mildred E. Hartsock, "The Complexity of *Julius Caesar*," *PMLA*, 81 (1966), 61.

[17] Schanzer, p. 65.

[18] *Shakespeare's Satire* (London: Oxford Univ. Press, 1943), pp. 198–217.

he does insist on the play's inferior status when considered in the list of Shakespearean tragedy.[19]

It is interesting that *Coriolanus* should be so magnificently perverse and ironic not only because it is Shakespeare's last tragedy but also because it carries to a grimly logical extension fundamental aspects of those tragedies that preceded it. Coriolanus's experience even calls up dissonant recapitulations of the tragic experiences in the Great Four. Like Hamlet, Coriolanus is called upon to act in the fulfillment of a public and private duty, and that action will almost inevitably involve him in a corruption alien to his virtuous nature. Like Othello, he is an easy victim for those who see good only through the eyes of evil. Like Lear, he is ejected from his proper world and experiences the horror of becoming the nameless, unaccommodated man. Like Macbeth, he denies his humanity and faces death in a morally idiotic relationship to the rest of the world. Generally, like all four of these heroes, Coriolanus is a regal figure whose social stature is commensurate with his moral force and greatness. Other men are dwarfed by him. Yet he is terrifyingly vulnerable: in some tragic way, the imperfections of the world expose his limitations and combine with them to overthrow him. And the world is tragically weakened by his loss.

To juxtapose Coriolanus with Hamlet, Othello, Lear, and Macbeth is, however, merely to beg again the problematic nature of *Coriolanus* and the need to see it in the mode of the Roman tragedies, not in the kind of the Great Four at all. The fundamental distinction between these two broad classes of Shakespearean tragedy is most apparent in the final Roman play; even more crucially than *Julius Caesar* and *Antony and Cleopatra*, *Coriolanus* demands critical recognition of a pagan environment seen in the light of Christian historiography. The ironies and the perversities of the play serve to expose Rome's ultimate tragic plight.

The antedating of Christian revelation is the most significant historical factor in these historical tragedies, and in this sense they are more genuinely Roman than is usually recognized.[20]

---

[19] "*Coriolanus:* Tragedy or Debate?" in *The Apothecary's Shop* (London: Secker & Warburg, 1957), pp. 32–53. The essay first appeared in *Essays in Criticism*, 4 (1954), 1–19.

[20] Cf. Harold S. Wilson, *On the Design of Shakespearian Tragedy* (Toronto: Univ. of Toronto Press, 1957), pp. 3–15. Wilson makes a basic distinction between those tragedies that "invoke Christian assumptions" (*Romeo and Juliet, Hamlet, Othello, Macbeth*) and those in which "references to a Chris-

Shakespeare could scarcely have escaped this particular historical point of view. North's Epistle Dedicatory to Queen Elizabeth offers Plutarch to the reader with the didactic implications of what was an Augustinian commonplace:

How many examples shall your subiectes reade here, of seuerall persons, and whole armies, of noble and base, of young and old, that both by sea and land, at home and abroad, haue strayned their wits, not regarded their states, ventured their persons, cast away their liues, not onely for the honor and safetie, but also for the pleasure of their Princes? Then well may the Readers thinke, if they haue done this for heathen kings, what should we doe for Christian Princes? If they haue done this for glorie, what should we do for religion? If they haue done this without hope of heauen, what should we do that looke for immortalitie?[21]

Shakespeare accurately represents Rome as a pagan world in which the characters must perforce operate with no reference beyond the Earthly City. All attempts at idealistic vision by the tragic heroes, all attempts to rise above the restrictions of man and his imperfect society, are tragically affected by the absence of revelation and the real hope of glory. Implying this historical distinction, Shakespeare views his Roman world with the cosmic irony of what that world could not know.[22]

The Roman heroes do not have access to St. Augustine's Heavenly City. Hamlet, Othello, Lear, and Macbeth—according to Arthur Sewell—"address themselves to a metaphysical world in such a way that we feel them to be citizens of that world as much as of this."[23] Brutus, Caesar, Antony, and

tian way of thought do not appear" (*Julius Caesar, Coriolanus, Troilus and Cressida, Timon of Athens, Antony and Cleopatra, King Lear*). The distinction in each case is historically accurate. For comment on the special case of *King Lear*, see my remarks later in this chapter.

[21] *The Lives of the Noble Grecians and Romanes* (London, 1595). Throughout this study I cite the second edition rather than the first (1579). As Ernest Dowden noted in his copy (now in the Folger Shakespeare Library), the second edition is "the one used by Shakespeare in all probability." I am indebted to the important essay by J. Leeds Barroll, "Shakespeare and Roman History," *MLR*, 53 (1958), 327–43. Barroll quotes North's dedication on pp. 333–34. North is echoing *The City of God* V.xviii.

[22] I use the phrase "cosmic irony" with reference to David Worcester, *The Art of Satire* (Cambridge, Mass.: Harvard Univ. Press, 1940), pp. 127–37. The most obvious example is the laughter of Troilus at the conclusion of Chaucer's work.

[23] *Character and Society in Shakespeare* (Oxford: Clarendon, 1951), p. 77.

Coriolanus are definitively Romans. The pressures and the exigencies of Rome conflict with vision even as the city helps to generate aspiration. The shifting glories and degradations of Rome are always involved in the tensions of the plays, sometimes supporting the heroes' greatness, sometimes thwarting it. The Roman hero cannot live "a private man in Athens" (*Ant.* III.xii.15) or "under the canopy" (*Cor.* IV.v.38). For Shakespeare to have shown Coriolanus on the open field between Rome and Antium would have been to give us another tragic world altogether, a kind of garbled *Lear*. When Bradley and MacCallum speculate on this undramatized lapse of time and Coriolanus's "decision" to return to Rome,[24] they miss the most tragic point of the play:

> Despising
> For you the city, thus I turn my back;
> There is a world elsewhere.

> (III.iii.135–37)

The first sentence wrenches both language and identity in its destructive irony: there is no other world for Coriolanus. He must return to Rome, for only Rome can tell him who he is:

> "Coriolanus"
> He would not answer to; forbad all names;
> He was a kind of nothing, titleless,
> Till he had forg'd himself a name i' th' fire
> Of burning Rome.

> (V.i.11–15)

Rome having failed his vision of Rome, he must now confirm Sicinius's charge—"depopulate the city and / Be every man himself" (III.i. 264–65). Coriolanus must become Rome.

Yet Rome is doomed. This certainty is shaped by more than the Elizabethan consciousness of mutability. In the Christian adaptation of the theory of the four monarchies, Rome was identified with the last world empire to rise before the establishment of the fifth, the eternal kingdom of Christ.[25] At the time of

[24] A. C. Bradley, "*Coriolanus*," in *A Miscellany* (London: Macmillan, 1929), pp. 90–92; MacCallum, pp. 611–16.
[25] See Barroll, pp. 330ff.; J. W. Swain, "The Theory of the Four Monarchies," *Classical Philology*, 35 (1940), 1–21; and W. M. Green, *Augustine on the Teaching of History*, Univ. of California Publications in Classical Philology, 12 (1944), 315–32. For further aspects of the Augustinian and Christian historiography see my discussion of *Coriolanus* in the following chapter. That the mythos of a Christianized Rome could support, in contradistinction to

Christ's birth, the watershed in universal history, Rome will have reached its zenith under Augustus and will have begun the decline. The Christian view of classical history, established most influentially by Augustine and Orosius, had been anti-Roman from the start. Augustine wrote his *City of God* to absolve Christianity from what he saw as the inevitable decline and fall of the Earthly City. But the Augustinian view is not entirely negative: while exposing the essential carnality of the Roman ethos and the fraud of the Roman gods, Augustine began a tradition of admiration for these pagan heroes who were exemplary according to their lights and of sympathy for their ultimate tragic failure. He granted sufficient substance to the Roman *virtus* to justify God's giving the city the power of domination for the purposes of divine providence. Orosius in his *Seven Books of Histories Against the Pagans* stressed Rome's providential role in unifying the world so that Christ could be born in the time following the events of *Antony and Cleopatra:*

> The time of universal peace is near.
> Prove this a prosp'rous day, the three-nook'd world
> Shall bear the olive freely.
>
> (IV.vi.5–7)

For some fascinating reason Shakespeare chose to thwart, dramatically, this providential Roman peace with the unhistorical skirmish between the Rome of Augustus and the Britain of Cymbeline. But *Cymbeline* happily and inevitably concludes with an allusion to the grand cosmic irony:

> Never was a war did cease,
> Ere bloody hands were wash'd, with such a peace.[26]
>
> (V.v.482–83)

In his Roman tragedies Shakespeare is at one and the same time recreating the historical reality of the glory that was Rome and perceiving that reality in a Christian perspective. In order to achieve the former, Shakespeare develops the Christian point of view by a technique of implying affirmative statement through irony. In the tragic world of Rome, that is, an outright positive statement is impossible. This technique and perspective

the pervasive influence of Augustine, the dream of Rome's political and ecclesiastical eminence is shown by Charles Till Davis, *Dante and the Idea of Rome* (Oxford: Clarendon, 1957). But that idealization, certainly after the Reformation and in England, was not the main Christian tradition.

[26] See Robin Moffet, "*Cymbeline* and the Nativity," *SQ*, 13 (1962), 207–18.

infuse *Coriolanus*, for example, with the grand but tragic irony of Rome as the truly Eternal City:

> You may as well
> Strike at the heaven with your staves as lift them
> Against the Roman state; whose course will on
> The way it takes, cracking ten thousand curbs
> Of more strong link asunder than can ever
> Appear in your impediment.
>
> (I.i.65–70)

Here, as MacCallum noted, is epitomized "the Idea of Rome";[27] and from Shakespeare's vantage point that Idea is even grander than Plutarch, for all his admiration, could perceive. Plutarch could not know either the ultimate tragedy of Rome's decline and fall or the aura of magnificence that antiquity radiates. Strangely enough, even MacCallum failed to see that the Idea of Rome does not triumph over the paradoxes in the play. In this most ironic of tragedies, Menenius's confident assertion to the mob is the ironic and tragic crux: the tragedy both for Coriolanus and for Rome lies in the mutability of all earthly cities. When Coriolanus is exiled, his parting words historically forecast what Shakespeare's audience would recognize post facto, the general decay of Roman *virtus* and the invasion of the Goths:

> Let every feeble rumour shake your hearts;
> Your enemies, with nodding of their plumes,
> Fan you into despair! Have the power still
> To banish your defenders, till at length
> Your ignorance—which finds not till it feels,
> Making but reservation of yourselves
> Still your own foes—deliver you
> As most abated captives to some nation
> That won you without blows!
>
> (III.iii.127–35)

Near the end of the play, Menenius again assumes the immutability of Rome in an ironic comparison with the absolute Coriolanus:

See you yond coign o' th' Capitol, yond corner-stone? . . . If it be possible for you to displace it with your little finger, there is some hope the ladies of Rome, especially his mother, may prevail with him.

(V.iv.1ff.)

[27] MacCallum, pp. 547–48.

But Coriolanus, as we already know, has failed in his attempted immutability; and the Roman Capitol will also become, archetypally, the ruins of time. Coriolanus's tragic demand for an Eternal City, not necessarily implied in Plutarch's political account, tacitly assumes the Christian critique of pagan Rome's place in universal history, generating in the texture of the play what Henry James called operative irony. The situation inevitably begs "the possible other case," the ideal against which "the actuality is pretentious and vain." This actuality represents, in James's most appropriate words, "a campaign, of a sort, on behalf of the something better (better than the obnoxious, the provoking object) that blessedly, as is assumed, *might* be."[28] The audience can understand and sympathize with Coriolanus's aspiration for immutability. It can sanction his lonely and desperate certainty that events will defeat the ideal. But the audience rises critically above the Roman's limitations by looking at those events after the Christian fact: the dissolution of Rome will owe as much to what Coriolanus represents—the Roman ethos itself—as to the internal dissensions.

To anticipate briefly how this operative irony works in the less political *Antony and Cleopatra*, we note the first exchange between the lovers:

> *Cleo.* If it be love indeed, tell me how much.
> *Ant.*   There's beggary in the love that can be reckon'd.
> *Cleo.* I'll set a bourn how far to be belov'd.
> *Ant.*   Then must thou needs find out new heaven, new earth.
>
> (I.i.14–17)

Antony's resounding echo of St. John's Revelation—"And I sawe a new heauen, & a new earth: for the first heauen, and the first earth were passed away"[29]—if it cannot refer to the true transcendent dimension, initiates in the play what Robert Speaight has called "Antony's bungling quest of the Absolute."[30] As in the case of Coriolanus, to see this glittering aspiration as tragically impossible is more important than to see it, in the spirit of the Roman soldiers, as wrong. As if to clinch its significance

---

[28] *The Art of the Novel: Critical Prefaces*, ed. R. P. Blackmur (New York: Scribner, 1934), p. 222.

[29] Throughout this study I cite the Geneva Version, the version Shakespeare most often used, from *The Geneva Bible: A Facsimile of the 1560 Edition*, ed. Lloyd E. Berry (Madison: Univ. of Wisconsin Press, 1969).

[30] *Nature in Shakespearian Tragedy* (London: Hollis & Carter, 1955), p. 129.

for the play as a whole, the apocalyptic imagery returns at the conclusion, as when the guards enter to discover the half-dispatched Antony, whose "torch is out" (IV.xiv.46):

> *2 Guard.* The star is fall'n.
> *1 Guard.* And time is at his period.
>
> (ll. 106-7)

& there fell a great starre from heauen burning like a torche. (Rev. viii: 10)

And . . . time shulde be no more. (x: 6)

Therefore in those daies shal men seke death, and shal not finde it, and shal desire to dye, and death shal flee from them. (ix: 6)[31]

As Antony's untidy suicide is associated with the falling star and the end of the temporal realm, Cleopatra's regal death calls forth Charmian's ecstatic "O Eastern star!" (V.ii.306)—suggestive of the "morning starre" promised to the triumphant (ii: 28), as Ethel Seaton notes, and also of the sign of that nativity heralding the eternal in "the time of universal peace."

It is not, of course, self-evident what to make of this biblical imagery. G. Wilson Knight perhaps would see it as indicating a truly realized apocalypse, Love triumphant over Time.[32] Roy Battenhouse has recently employed the evidence to urge how far Antony and Cleopatra are from the ethics and dogma of medieval Christianity.[33] What I would choose to insist upon, however, is the operative irony of this imagery from Revelation working in an entirely and historically pagan world. A new heaven and a new earth, beyond that bourn that limits human aspiration, will come only when, according to the Geneva gloss, "all things shalbe renued and restored into a moste excellent and perfect estate," when "all things shalbe purged from their corruption." Yet all of the Roman heroes aspire to "a moste excellent and perfect estate." The paradoxical aspiration for the ideal and the corruption preventing its realization work both positively (*pace* Battenhouse) and negatively (*pace* Knight) to create the tragic and heroic world of man in his Earthly City.

As treated by Shakespeare, the aspirations of the Roman

[31] Ethel Seaton, *"Antony and Cleopatra* and the *Book of Revelation,"* RES, 22 (1946), 219-24. My references are to pp. 220 and 222. See also William Blissett, "Dramatic Irony in *Antony and Cleopatra," SQ,* 18 (1967), 151-66.
[32] G. Wilson Knight's study of *Antony and Cleopatra* is in *The Imperial Theme* (London: Oxford Univ. Press, 1931), pp. 199-326.
[33] *Shakespearean Tragedy: Its Art and Its Christian Premises* (Bloomington: Indiana Univ. Press, 1969), pp. 176-81.

heroes have the potentiality for absolute sanction when the proper relationship is revealed between the temporal and the divine. Without this proper relationship and the means of atonement, the Roman hero's vision is necessarily flawed. But the substance of that vision is never dramatically rejected even though in the tragic blindness of the human condition the virtue can only be paradoxical. To discard the vision would be to discard the aspiration in man that traditionally proved his essential alienation from the imperfections of the world and his distinction among the creatures: "Kingdoms are clay; our dungy earth alike / Feeds beast as man" (*Ant.* I.i.35–36).

Because of Rome's ultimate darkness and the inevitable qualification of vision, the insights of Brutus, Caesar, Antony, and Coriolanus into their own tragedies are severely limited in a way unlike those of the protagonists in Bradley's Great Four. Macbeth acknowledges the absolute of grace and the solidarity of Christian society that he has forfeited. He recognizes exactly where his way of life has brought him, and that awareness prevents him from becoming, for us, simply a monster. Like Othello, Macbeth understands the moral environment in which his soul and body have been ensnared. Hamlet, no matter how skeptical, is influenced from beginning to end by that possible world to come, and his final trust in providence prepares us for an expiatory death. In *King Lear* Shakespeare scrupulously created a historically pagan world without metaphysical certainties, but a world that has no hope except in its desperate prescience of Christian revelation. Despite the historical "darkness," the poles of good and evil were never more dramatically defined; the potentialities of the Christian eschatology—arising typologically from the level of nature—were never more crucially to the point. Lear's final agony to determine whether Cordelia lives shadows the metaphysical mystery of the play: if she lives, redemption is real. In the dramatic terms of poetry, situation, and character, here is a moral revelation that might illuminate for Lear all possibilities of affirmation or of negation. Cordelia is a type of Christ; but everything hinges upon whether, factually and realistically, Cordelia and Christ live. The answer to this ultimate mystery lies in silence.

Brutus, Antony, and Coriolanus do not have a moment or the possibility of recognition. Their vision never reaches the level of our moral perspective. They represent an extreme, an impossible absolute; they will permit no compromise with their vision of perfection. We can speak of Brutus's confusion in the last two acts, we can infer an accompanying disillusionment; but he does not see as much as we see. On such grounds he has been denied tragic status, but he is at one here with Antony and Coriolanus. Antony fluctuates between a condemnation of his effeminacy and a glorification of his love. He rejects neither attitude with finality, and his death can be seen as "a simple and positive unity,"[34] as an unquestioning moral affirmation, only by overlooking half of the play. Cleopatra in the fifth act gloriously tempers Antony's death in the fourth, but while we experience his death the pathetic is more pronounced than the tragic. At best, Antony resigns himself to his irreconcilable and mutually destructive desires. Though the range of his wavering gives Antony a tragic greatness, his vision at any given moment is fragmented and cannot cope with the totality of his experience. Coriolanus's reversal comes in the great scene with Volumnia, and it is marked by his baffled silence—not the silence of *King Lear* but of moral confusion. And in the final scene at Corioli we see that his experience has not changed him.

Because the focus is removed from the tragic insight of these protagonists, the Roman heroes do not have the stature of Hamlet, Othello, Lear, or Macbeth. If, however, Brutus does not have the stature of Hamlet, or Antony of Macbeth, the situations in the Roman plays tower over those in the other four. Hamlet transcends the events of a historically obscure Danish prince revenging the death of his father—though the objective correlative of fact is quite sufficient to support the character. Character and plot in the Roman plays are not so separable. The Roman heroes achieve their stature only by playing their parts in a famous historical event. Instead of appealing to a metaphysical realm, these heroes appeal to their vision for a world here and now.[35] They are isolated in the fame of their time and space. They are aware that they are taking part in the enduring poetry of history, and they show the appropriate exaltation and sense of responsibility. The House of Fame becomes the transcendent heaven here: the Roman heroes' lack of awareness is compensated for by their actions in situations of the greatest historical moment.

[34] Knight, p. 285.

[35] Arthur Sewell asserts that, because Antony and Coriolanus do not address themselves to a metaphysical world, "social and political judgments . . . [are] adequate to deal with them" (pp. 76–80), as with the heroes in the English history plays. But along with the loss of metaphysical certainties, social and political judgments have lost their absolute sanctions. For this fundamental difference between the English and the Roman histories, see the Appendix, "The Moral Environment in Shakespeare's English History Plays."

Macbeth gives significance to the murder of Duncan; the murder of Caesar gives significance to Brutus. The Roman hero, that is, does not rise above his history. It can contain and define his greatness because the responsibility for it rests on him. The tragic world draws in and destroys Hamlet, Othello, and Lear after the sudden, uninhibited release of evil. Beyond this moment is always the possible other case of what might have been in a nontragic world. Even Macbeth stands apart from the situation he has created: we see vividly, through his eyes, the world of charity and kindness that he destroys for himself. In their flawed natures these four tragic heroes have a responsibility for their fall, but the situations confronting them are not the result of the totality of their natures: good, as Bradley insists, is never the cause. The Roman plays differ fundamentally here. There is no possible other case for Brutus, Antony, and Coriolanus. Their ideal vision makes it impossible for them to be other than what they are. They have what is essentially a humanistic conviction of man's dignity and potentialities in this life; and the situations that destroy them proceed not from evil but from a heroic attempt to translate their vision into action, to impose their ideal upon the reality.

Because the protagonists are making history and earning their places in the House of Fame, the Roman plays are essentially historical tragedies. The state plays a dramatic role in the conflict in a way that cannot be argued for *Hamlet, King Lear,* and *Macbeth:* the hero's relationship to Rome establishes both his limitations and his greatness. In *Coriolanus* we find the basic pattern underlying the two earlier plays, and it is a pattern in which Rome is both protagonist and antagonist. Rome must reject the very heroes it has generated, the heroes who embody the city's glory. Brutus, like Coriolanus, is "whooped" out of the gates. Antony, whose case is complicated by the alternate, irreconcilable attraction of Egypt, finds himself excluded from the Rome of his past greatness when Octavius takes over the city. Rome, moreover, must not only reject; it must destroy. It cannot allow Antony to be a citizen of Egypt or "a private man in Athens." It can no longer tolerate Brutus and Coriolanus with their intractable ideals of perfection.

Exiled from Rome, the Roman heroes must therefore, in the falling action of their tragedies, confront their city. There is no world elsewhere. The tragic reconciliation in these plays is thus distinctive. From the hero's point of view, there is no reconciliation. He will not reject his vision, for it defines him. Nor can vision be transposed to a metaphysical sphere (the ambivalent power of Cleopatra is unique) because no such sphere exists for them and, as far as they are concerned, the visions are pointless if they are not realizable. This obstinacy therefore entails an ultimate lack of recognition and a continued degree of blindness. The hero meets his death with a consciousness of defeat, a world-weariness, as one disoriented and lost. Consequently the closing scenes of these plays, while satisfying our moral expectations, leave us more painfully aware than ever of the limited nature of the world. This is of course true in Shakespearean tragedy in general. But in the Roman plays there is no evil to purge; there are no villains to punish. Those remaining are themselves the destroyers of the noblest; but the noblest, with their impossible demands, take from the survivors "a great part of blame" (V.vi.146), as the Volscian lord concedes to Aufidius.

Although Rome finally destroys, it gives what immortality it can to the tragic hero: it can acknowledge, after his disruptive influence is over, the greatness of one who will not accept its limited terms. The fame of the one in fact depends upon the other: "These now, and other such like, in their bookes, how should they haue beene so knowne, and so famous, had not Romes Empire had this great and magnificent exaltation and dilatation? Wherefore that Empire, so spacious, and so continuant & renowned by the vertues of those illustrious men was giuen, both to stand as a rewarde for their merrites, and to produce examples for our vses."[36] Aufidius, whose name is lost in oblivion, reflects St. Augustine's point: "I would I were a Roman; for I cannot, / Being a Volsce, be that I am" (I.x.4–5). It is upon this mutually defining, paradoxical relationship between city and hero that Shakespeare constructs the tragic tension in his Roman plays. And this tragic relationship depends upon the complementary aspect—the operative irony—of the Augustinian comparison: "How farre the Christians should bee from boasting of their deedes for their eternall country, the Romaines hauing done so much for their temporall Citty." Christians "doe but that for gayning the society of the Angells, which the other did (or neere did) for their preseruing of the glory of the Romaines." Shakespeare's Roman heroes demand to be judged, with all of the tragic consequences, by the standards of "the society of the Angells," yet in the heroic terms of what they "neere did."

[36] *The City of God* V.xviii. I have used the text of *St. Augustine, of the Citie of God: with the learned comments of Jo. Lod. Vives*, trans. John Healey (London, 1610). This passage and the one following are on pp. 221, 223.

II

Coriolanus

The Graces of the Gods

THE TRAGEDY of Coriolanus is inherent in Shakespeare's earlier Roman plays. As I suggested in the introductory chapter, a pattern underlying *Julius Caesar* and *Antony and Cleopatra* emerges starkly in *Coriolanus*, and therefore I think it best to begin with this clearest and final statement of Shakespeare's idea of the Roman tragedy. Shakespeare focuses at last on a protagonist whose moral vision is unblinkingly the moral vision of Rome. Brutus represents only a part of Roman glory; he must be complemented by Caesar. Antony's Roman greatness is enhanced as well as destroyed by his vision of love. But in Coriolanus Shakespeare discovers a hero whose fate is the abstract of a larger tragedy, the tragedy of Rome itself. In this obscure episode near the fountainhead of Roman history, Shakespeare sees figured the nature of the times to come; in the conflict between Coriolanus and his city are the seeds that in the brood of time will bring Rome both greatness and destruction. Through compromise, Rome is to be longer-lived than Coriolanus. Indeed, Volumnia's final appearance, as she moves silently across the stage to the shouts of the people, is full of grandeur as well as irony. The temporizers will, after their fashion, try to hold the walls of the city together. But their nobility cannot survive "when extremities speak," and history will prove an endless conflict of extremities. The Idea of Rome in the last analysis is subject to the city of Rome; physical and temporal survival must be deemed the highest value. Yet physically and temporally the Earthly City cannot escape destruction in a world of flux and mutability. In the perspective of Christian historiography, Shakespeare perceives the peculiar greatness of the Roman Empire, the destiny of which is to rule the world and to destroy itself.

I

It is Coriolanus who embodies the glory that will become Rome. He has been nurtured in accordance with the city's definition of virtue: "Now in those dayes, valiantnes was honoured in Rome aboue all other vertues: which they call *virtus*, by the name of vertue it selfe, as including in that generall name, all other speciall vertues besides. So that *virtus* in the Latin, was as much as valiantnesse."[1] In this much-noted passage from Plutarch's "Life of Caius Martius Coriolanus," what must have struck Shakespeare most forcibly is the linguistic irony of valiantness as the all-inclusive virtue; for *Coriolanus* proves it to be quite exclusive, indeed life-denying. Nevertheless, the Renaissance accepted this *virtus*, exercised in a spirit of self-sacrifice, as the essence of Roman nobility, a virtue which, at least as a secondary cause, justified the providential emergence of Rome as conqueror and ruler of the world. The practical need to defend, expand, and maintain the Earthly City had been successfully idealized into an ethos designed to secure Rome truly as the Eternal City. In a world without divine revelation Rome itself defines the only approach to human excellence. So Cominius acknowledges to the Senate, echoing the passage in Plutarch:

> It is held
> That valour is the chiefest virtue and
> Most dignifies the haver. If it be,
> The man I speak of cannot in the world
> Be singly counterpois'd.
>
> (II.ii.81–85)

As a moral absolute the virtue that Coriolanus represents must not be questioned by the mutable and, in Roman terms, entirely "unvirtuous" populace. The humanistic virtue is as beyond the subhuman as heavenly virtue is beyond Rome's aristocratic apprehension, represented here by Volumnia:

> Cats that can judge as fitly of his worth
> As I can of those mysteries which heaven
> Will not have earth to know.
>
> (IV.ii.34–36)

Both Volumnia and Menenius, as patrician representatives, equate Coriolanus metaphorically with the cornerstone of the Capitol. Menenius assumes the permanence and immutability of both:

See you yond coign o' th' Capitol, yond corner-stone? . . . If it be possible for you to displace it with your little finger, there

---

[1] *Lives* (London, 1595), p. 236.

is some hope the ladies of Rome, especially his mother, may prevail with him. But I say there is no hope in't.

(V.iv.1ff.)

Coriolanus symbolizes, for Volumnia, the essential Rome rising above the base and vulgar:

> As far as doth the Capitol exceed
> The meanest house in Rome, so far my son—
> This lady's husband here, this, do you see?—
> Whom you have banish'd does exceed you all.

(IV.ii.39–42)

In order to bring about the identification of Coriolanus with "the fundamental part of state" (III.i.151), Shakespeare completely ignores the evidence in Plutarch that Coriolanus's political and personal failure was owing to the lack of a proper education:

A rare and excellent witte vntaught, doth bring forth many good and euill thinges together: like a fat soile bringeth forth herbes & weedes that lieth vnmanured. For this *Martius* naturall wit and great hart did maruellously sturre vp his courage to doe and attempt notable actes. But on the other side for lacke of education, he was so chollericke and impacient, that he would yeeld to no liuing creature: which made him churlishe, vnciuil, and altogether vnfit for any mans conuersation. . . . And to say truly, the greatest benefite that learning bringeth men vnto, is this: that it teacheth men that be rude and rough of nature, by compasse and rule of reason, to be ciuill and curteous, & to like better the meane state, then the higher. (pp. 235–36)

Civility and courtesy, the "rule of reason," the excellence of "the meane state"—these are positive values that Plutarch and Shakespeare can both appreciate, but they are not subsumed by the Roman *virtus*, the all-encompassing valiantness. Not accepting the implications of the Roman ethos so literally, Plutarch judges Coriolanus to be deficient even though he fully develops in valiantness; his unusual upbringing paradoxically has both good and bad results. But Shakespeare, with grim irony, urges Coriolanus not as a victim of neglect but as the epitome of Roman cultivation.[2] The virtue itself proves paradoxical.

[2] Roy Battenhouse argues that Shakespeare altered Plutarch to represent in Coriolanus "the tragedy of an ethos" (*Shakespearean Tragedy: Its Art and Its Christian Premises* [Bloomington: Indiana Univ. Press, 1969], p. 310). See also W. I. Carr, " 'Gracious Silence'–A Selective Reading of *Coriolanus*," *English Studies*, 46 (1965), 221–34; Matthew Proser, *The Heroic Image in*

Volumnia, instead of being (as in Plutarch) the passive bene-ficiary of her son's "notable actes," has actively and purposefully educated him for their performance:

> thou hast said
> My praises made thee first a soldier.
> (III.ii.107–8)

> Thy valiantness was mine, thou suck'dst it from me.
> (III.ii.129)

> Thou art my warrior;
> I holp to frame thee.
> (V.iii.62–63)

In relation to those who share the Idea of Rome, Coriolanus is not "altogether vnfit for any mans conuersation." He is "vnciuil" only to those who, not Romans by ideal definition, perversely exist in Rome, thwarting vision:

> I would they were barbarians, as they are,
> Though in Rome litter'd; not Romans, as they are not,
> Though calved i' th' porch o' th' Capitol.
> (III.i.238–40)

Shakespeare might easily have accepted—as no doubt Jonson or Chapman would have done—a Stoic Right Reason or "the meane state" as the violated moral norm for *Coriolanus*. But Shakespeare rejected that moral and dramatic possibility. Because his Coriolanus epitomizes Roman virtue, the voice of patrician Rome cannot find the moral terms to condemn him except to suggest, as does Menenius, that "his nature is too noble for the world" (III.i.255). Appropriately enough, it is Volumnia who stumbles upon the language of paradox that alone can handle Shakespeare's hero and the Roman plight. The passage serves admirably as epigraph to the bewildering moral environment:

> You are too absolute;
> Though therein you can never be too noble
> But when extremities speak.
> (III.ii.39–41)

Five Shakespearean Tragedies (Princeton, N.J.: Princeton Univ. Press, 1965), pp. 135–70; R. F. Hill, "*Coriolanus*: Violentest Contrariety," *Essays and Studies*, 17 n.s. (1964), 12–23; and especially Derek Traversi's fine essay in *An Approach to Shakespeare*, 2nd ed. (New York: Doubleday, 1956), pp. 216–34. For Traversi the tragedy of Coriolanus "represents a failure on the part of a whole society" (p. 233).

Significantly, Volumnia is oblivious of her paradox, even though it contradicts all her previous tutoring. When she must face the "extremities" of her son's exile, Coriolanus comforts her with the very precepts that she has just urged him to reject. The contradiction exposes Rome's moral incoherence:

> Nay, mother,
> Where is your ancient courage? You were us'd
> To say extremities was the trier of spirits;
> That common chances common men could bear;
> That when the sea was calm all boats alike
> Show'd mastership in floating; fortune's blows,
> When most struck home, being gentle wounded craves
> A noble cunning. You were us'd to load me
> With precepts that would make invincible
> The heart that conn'd them.
>
> (IV.i.2–11)

Although Volumnia conveniently forgets her precepts, Coriolanus does not. If principles must give way to "extremities," if virtue and value lie in the interpretation of time and occasion, they cannot exist at all. Coriolanus recalls the absolute and idealistic Troilus in the Trojan Council scene (II.ii),[3] except that what Coriolanus is committed to is unchallenged by any other positive value. The voice of patrician Rome offers Coriolanus no moral alternative. His party can only urge that he temporize. Volumnia demands that for the first time in his life he practice "policy" and dishonest role-playing:[4]

> I prithee now, sweet son, as thou hast said
> My praises made thee first a soldier, so,
> To have my praise for this, perform a part
> Thou hast not done before.
>
> (III.ii.107–10)

But Coriolanus cannot dissemble:

> I will not do't,
> Lest I surcease to honour mine own truth,
> And by my body's action teach my mind
> A most inherent baseness.
>
> (III.ii.120–23)

[3] See Richard C. Harrier, "Troilus Divided," in *Studies in the English Renaissance Drama*, ed. Josephine W. Bennett et al. (New York: New York Univ. Press, 1959), pp. 142–56.

[4] For a discussion of the theatrical imagery see Maurice Charney, *Shakespeare's Roman Plays: The Function of Imagery in the Drama* (Cambridge, Mass.: Harvard Univ. Press, 1961), pp. 170–76.

He agrees to "mountebank their loves" only when his mother angrily charges him with pride, ironically the same moral rebuke made by the Tribunes and scattered citizens. Volumnia's conception of pride is equally questionable. If Coriolanus is proud because he cannot have a Machiavellian disregard for the relationship between the public and the private man, the Roman conception of pride is as paradoxical as its conception of virtue. Pride is no more the key to Coriolanus's tragedy than is a violation of Right Reason or "the meane state." In confirmation of Aufidius's important evaluation (IV.vii.35–55), Coriolanus has a merit to choke the word *pride* in the utterance.[5]

In developing his hero's preoccupation with inner truth, Shakespeare transforms the conflict as Plutarch saw it. Shakespeare makes his Coriolanus heroically face one of the most torturous dilemmas of Christian humanism. This avatar of Rome, though of course he cannot know it, is caught up in the paradoxical tensions inherent in the wearisome condition of humanity. The conflict that man must endure in his allegiances to two worlds, the real and the ideal, makes Coriolanus and Rome finally incompatible. The ideals defining Roman virtue may be entirely of the Earthly City, but Coriolanus maintains and defends those ideals in a manner characteristic of one whose devotion is to the Eternal City.[6] This conflict—one which so bewilders both Coriolanus and Rome—is clarified by the Christian perspective in which Shakespeare views and dramatizes his pagan's moral plight.

After guarded praise of Roman discipline, fortitude, and self-sacrifice, St. Augustine condemned the pagans for having no higher motivation to practice virtue than the desire to receive honor and fame. Such a desire, to be sure, was more commendable than a lust for riches and bodily pleasure, and that relative superiority justified God's allowing Rome dominion over more carnally minded kingdoms. Although only a partial good, loyalty to the state established in the Roman a devotion

[5] That the word *pride* merely begs the question is suggested by comparing Willard Farnham (*Shakespeare's Tragic Frontier* [Berkeley: Univ. of California Press, 1950], pp. 207–64) with John Dover Wilson, ed., *Coriolanus* (Cambridge: Cambridge Univ. Press, 1960), pp. xxvii–xxxi. Although Farnham stresses the hero's "paradoxical nobility," he weighs the balance in favor of pride; Wilson, however, denies that Coriolanus is proud at all in any pejorative sense.

[6] Cf. M. W. MacCallum, *Shakespeare's Roman Plays and Their Background* (London: Macmillan, 1910), pp. 594–95: "He cherishes a transcendent idea of the state, and is wounded to the heart that its members fall short of it."

to some value beyond himself. The desire for honor at least instilled a desire for the prerequisite of virtue. Plutarch's hero, who "was neuer ouercome with pleasure, nor money" (p. 236), typifies precisely this limited idealism, Milton's "last infirmity," which Rome could not look beyond. The distinctive moral temperaments of Plutarch's pagan and Shakespeare's Augustinian *manqué* are clarified in their contrasting reactions to the ceremonies that climax in the nomination of Caius Martius as Coriolanus. Plutarch's hero gracefully responds to Cominius's praise and to the offer of the Volscian spoils and the prize horse:

Martius stepping forth, told the Consull, he most thankefully accepted the gift of his horse, and was a glad man besides, that his seruice had deserued his generalles commendation: and as for his other offer, which was rather a mercenarie rewarde, then an honorable recompence, he would haue none of it, but was contented to haue his equall part with other souldiers. . . . The souldiers hearing *Martius* wordes, made a maruellous great shoute among them; and there were more that wondred at his great contentation and abstinence, when they sawe so little couetousnes in him, then they were that highly praised and extolled his valiantnes. For euen they themselves, that did somewhat malice and enuie his glorie, to see him thus honoured, and passingly praysed did thinke him somuch the more worthie of an honorable recompence for his valiant seruice, as the more carelesly he refused the great offer made vnto him for his profitte: and they esteemed more the vertue that was in him, that made him refuse such rewards, then that which made them to be offered to him, as vnto a worthie person. (p. 240)

The passage exemplifies in action the Roman ideal of valuing and accepting "honorable recompence," a recompense which is appropriately increased when the dishonorable is rejected. Plutarch's hero is not at all discomforted or embarrassed by Cominius's commendation, the gift of the symbolic horse, the shouts of the soldiers, or, finally, the title Coriolanus. On the contrary, in such recompense lies the motivation for action.

In Shakespeare this scene, which in Plutarch contains not the slightest dramatic conflict, is the first to represent Coriolanus's tragic dilemma in his moral relationship with Rome. He is unable to accept the general's commendation:

Pray now, no more; my mother,
Who has a charter to extol her blood,
When she does praise me grieves me.
(I.ix.13–15)

Like Plutarch's hero, he easily rejects the Volscian spoils as dishonorable, "a bribe to pay my sword" (l. 38). But the applause
that his magnanimity earns from the soldiers provokes, in Shakespeare's scene, a response entirely foreign to the source. The
tense moment is so crucial that the stage direction urges exagger-
ation to emphasize the transaction and also, I suspect, to mark
the "honorable recompence" of applause as slightly absurd: "*A
long flourish. They all cry*, 'Marcius, Marcius!' *cast up their
caps and lances. Cominius and Lartius stand bare.*" In angry
frustration, Coriolanus brutally rejects civility:

> May these same instruments which you profane
> Never sound more! When drums and trumpets shall
> I' th' field prove flatterers, let courts and cities be
> Made all of false-fac'd soothing!
>
> (ll. 41–44)

The perversity of this response indicates Coriolanus's plight in
coping with the recompense that St. Augustine rigorously
deemed inimical to inner truth. As far as Coriolanus is concerned, the Roman phrase "honorable recompence" is oxy-
moronic: the distinction between the reward of material spoils
and the reward of fame is not one of kind; though they vary
in degree, they are in the last analysis both "carnal," both bribes
to pay the sword. Coriolanus must attempt to make virtue its
own reward; or, as Cominius expresses it, to reward his deeds
with doing them (II.ii. 125–26).

In effect, Coriolanus rejects the Roman idea of honor as severely as did St. Augustine in his critique: "For this glory that
they seeke, is the *good opinion of men concerning such or such.*
And therefore that is the best vertue, that standeth not vpon
others iudgements, but vpon ones own conscience, as the Apostle
saith: *Our glory is this, the testimony of our conscience:* and
againe: *Let euery man prooue his owne worke, and so shall
he haue glory in himselfe onely, and not in another.* So that
glory & honor which they desire so, & aime so after, by good
means, must not go before vertue, but follow it: for there is
no true vertue, but leuelleth at mans chiefest good."[7] It is essentially this moral rigor that leads Coriolanus to a blind end. He
obviously fears to prove his virtue "no true vertue" by seeking
or even accepting recognition, "the good opinion of men." But

---

[7] *The City of God* V.xii. *St. Augustine, of the Citie of God: with the
learned comments of Jo. Lod. Vives*, trans. John Healey (London, 1610),
p. 215. Augustine cites II Corinthians i:12 and Galatians vi:4.

because the martial virtue of Rome is in no way directed "at mans chiefest good" and has no relevance beyond the formalized needs of the Earthly City, it can entail neither an intrinsic nor a metaphysical reward. Coriolanus cannot reward his deeds with doing them. If he can "glory in himselfe onely," it will not be in satisfactory Pauline terms. St. Paul's idea that true glory is in "the testimony of our conscience"—the witness standing in the knowledge and the glory of Christ—cannot pertain. For the Roman, the virtue is merely civic and man's primary moral relationship is not to a witnessing conscience but to a witnessing public.

Even when the Renaissance found the Earthly and the Heavenly Cities interrelated by the Christian Magistrate, the tensions between an external and internal conceptualization of honor could not be eliminated. No one could pretend that Elizabeth was actually the Faerie Queene. Because Shakespeare sets his play in the archetypal Earthly City, the conflict stands out with impossible clarity, revealing why "the interiorizing of honour," as D. J. Gordon calls it, could never be complete.[8] Although Coriolanus's denial that true honor lies in the public voice appeals positively to the audience, such a denial can only operate paradoxically in the Roman moral environment. The primary moral relationship of the Roman to Rome subsumes the Roman's relationship to himself and eliminates any possibility of "glory in himselfe onely." Indeed, the Roman's relationship to himself becomes all but meaningless. At the end of the play, when Coriolanus is the hero-traitor to all men, when he has no certain fame or even name in either Rome or Corioli, the final testimony of his own conscience—the resounding "I"—is the assertion of one who has, in canceling all other relationships, all but annihilated himself:

> If you have writ your annals true, 'tis there
> That, like an eagle in a dove-cote, I
> Flutter'd your Volscians in Corioli.
> Alone I did it.
>
>   (V.vi.114–17)

[8] "Name and Fame: Shakespeare's *Coriolanus*," in *Papers Mainly Shakespearian*, ed. G. I. Duthie, Univ. of Aberdeen Studies 147 (Edinburgh: Oliver & Boyd, 1964), p. 51. For my discussion of honor I am indebted to Professor Gordon's essay. I feel, however, that he neglects the centrality of Augustinian absolutism in its relation to the pagan plight of Rome and to the tensions in the play. See also Curtis Brown Watson, *Shakespeare and the Renaissance Concept of Honor* (Princeton, N.J.: Princeton Univ. Press, 1960); and Norman Rabkin, "*Coriolanus*: The Tragedy of Politics," *SQ*, 17 (1966), 195–212.

Voices of praise no less than written annals establish a man's identity in human society. After the victory at Corioli, therefore, Coriolanus will have to compromise or the play cannot proceed—unless Shakespeare would eject his hero, like King Lear, among fools and madmen to discover who he is. Cominius argues that the recompense is "In sign of what you are, not to reward / What you have done" (I.ix.26–27). Without such a sign, Coriolanus's conscience, instead of being the true witness to his honor, will be "the grave of [his] deserving." In attempting to inhibit his "good report," Coriolanus is nothing less than suicidal and should therefore be treated like one who wants to destroy himself:

> Too modest are you;
> More cruel to your good report than grateful
> To us that give you truly. By your patience,
> If 'gainst yourself you be incens'd, we'll put you—
> Like one that means his proper harm—in manacles,
> Then reason safely with you.
>
> (ll. 53–58)

Thus the "good report," from Rome's point of view, is to be equated with the essential self. This attitude is not new to one like Coriolanus who "fear[s] / Lesser his person than an ill report" (I.vi.69–70). Yet to accept the good report "in token" (I.ix.60) is to accept payment for virtue, thereby calling into question the purity of his motives and therefore of the virtue. The tragic plight, as Norman Rabkin points out, is clarified and illuminated by the historical fact that Rome, at this moment, literally confers upon the hero the name that is his identity.[9]

Coriolanus very awkwardly and only temporarily compromises with the underlying moral confusion. But the Augustinian question remains: what reward motivates a man to perform vir-

---

[9] *Ibid.*, p. 203. In a perceptive discussion of the scene, Rabkin stresses that Coriolanus compromises his sense of honor when he accepts his name. Rabkin concludes that the moral situation in the play is hopeless; that, although the man of principle must inevitably be destroyed, there is no positive alternative. But I doubt that any spectator has ever been impressed with the pessimism that would correspond to such a view of man in his society. The play is infused with a dispassionate and objectifying irony for which Rabkin does not account. Although the play presents a hopeless situation, the operative irony offers the audience the alternative of true honor and brotherhood through *caritas*. See also James L. Calderwood, "*Coriolanus*: Wordless Meanings and Meaningless Words," *SEL*, 6 (1966), 211–24.

tuous actions?[10] In the opening scene Shakespeare poses the issue
in terms of payment:

> 2 *Cit.*   Consider you what services he has done for his country?
> 1 *Cit.*   Very well, and could be content *to give him good report*
>   for't but that *he pays himself* with being proud.
>   (I.i.28ff., italics added)

As underlined by the highly significant fiscal imagery throughout the play, the motivation to action involves the terms and
expectations of reward. Cominius's distinction between bestow-
ing gifts as sign and as reward is argumentative but scarcely
real. Rome gives Coriolanus his name, the "good report"; yet,
as Menenius insists, "not without his true purchasing" (II.i.132).
Rome's moral covenant is no less than a contract entailing the
reward of earthly honor for services rendered. Because these
ideals have been defined on the basis of political necessities,
"Rome must know / The value of her own" (I.ix.20–21) if
the city is to survive. And as Rome must recognize, so Coriolanus must accept that recognition if he is to be a Roman.

The Christian covenant, as St. Augustine insists, admits of
the same fiscal imagery as the Roman. If man lays up treasures
for himself in the Heavenly City, a system of reward—the expectation of true glory—still operates as a motivating force.
Self-sacrifice and selflessness are not at all required; what
selflessness the covenant appears to entail is paradoxically the
ultimate self-fulfillment. The point that St. Augustine makes—
echoed didactically in North's dedication of his Plutarch to
Queen Elizabeth—is that the moral contract for the Roman is
really infinitely more demanding than that for the Christian.
The Christian is not forced to consider virtue the highest good;
he can blatantly acknowledge his motivation to be the reward
of the highest good, the glory that is eternal life. "Why is it
then so much to despise all this worlds vanities for eternitie?"
Augustine asks: the Romans did what they did "for their temporall Citty, and for humaine glory."[11]

Besides the distinct disadvantage of ephemerality, the Roman
contract becomes even more self-defeating and morally incoherent by a contradictory stipulation that the reward be no *sum-
mum bonum*. For if the glory that Rome bestows is the highest

---

[10] Cf. Gordon, p. 41: "Honour as reward for virtue, as a motive for action,
is taken for granted." This statement, I should urge, needs careful and crucial
qualification.
[11] *The City of God* V.xviii. (*Vives*, p. 221.)

good, one might as well pursue it "by craft & false means."[12] It was certainly not only the Christian saint who recognized that "vertue is as much disgraced in seruing humaine glory as in obeying the pleasures of the body."[13] Augustine cited at least two advanced pagans, Horace and Cicero, who understood that the desire for glory is a vice; yet they had to consider the vice a limited virtue because of its appeal in motivating noble action for the state.[14] To the noblest pagan conception, therefore, the idea of honor, as Coriolanus perceives, is a tainted paradox: the man worthy of honor must shun even that reward, if only so that glory will pursue him the more.

This paradoxical, even incoherent, attitude toward honor, fame, and glory is the source of the moral tensions in the play. Volumnia, who has trained her son to be ambitious for fame, describes the simplistic heroic quest for honor that the finer conception hopelessly complicates:

When yet he was but tender-bodied, and the only son of my womb; when youth with comeliness pluck'd all gaze his way; when, for a day of kings' entreaties, a mother should not sell him an hour from her beholding; I, considering how honour would become such a person—that it was no better than picture-like to hang by th' wall, if renown made it not stir—was pleas'd to let him seek danger where he was like to find fame. To a cruel war I sent him, from whence he return'd his brows bound with oak.

(I.iii.7ff.)

Cominius, speaking to the Senate in praise of Coriolanus, concludes with reference to the more sophisticated Roman morality of scorning all reward. Rather than being concerned with pay, Coriolanus will "spend" the deeds themselves in performing them. There is no transaction, as it were; no motive beyond the act itself:

> Our spoils he kick'd at,
> And look'd upon things precious as they were
> The common muck of the world. He covets less
> Than misery itself would give, rewards
> His deeds with doing them, and is content
> To spend the time to end it.

(II.ii.122–27)

Coriolanus is invested with a fatal hubris, of course. But if he becomes the victim of pride in trying to break all bond and

[12] *Ibid.*, V.xii. (*Vives*, p. 215.)
[13] *Ibid.*, V.xx. (*Vives*, p. 226.)
[14] *Ibid.*, V.xiii. (*Vives*, p. 217.)

privilege of nature, he does so only when it is evident that Rome can be neither his Eternal City without nor his paradise within. The tragedy is essentially that Coriolanus is not in Lear's world: Coriolanus can only turn to Rome to ask that salvific question, "Who is it that can tell me who I am?" Out of the answer "Nothing" can then come new creation; beyond the limitations of the public world, the potentialities of spiritual glory are, in *King Lear*, at least intimated if not realized. Away from Rome, Coriolanus also becomes nothing:

> "Coriolanus"
> He would not answer to; forbad all names;
> He was a kind of nothing, titleless,
> Till he had forg'd himself a name i' th' fire
> Of burning Rome.
>
>   (V.i.11–15)

Only in the fire of Rome can he discover a new identity. Coriolanus is, anomalously, a public hero without a public.

Because Coriolanus cannot know himself except in the applause of others, he is propelled toward the highest reward, the new name of Consul. Yet his insight into the nature of true nobility, an insight that in Rome is nothing less than a tragic burden, makes him genuinely reluctant. It is Volumnia, happily assuming honor to be a proper motivation and reward for action, who urges him on:

> I have lived
> To see inherited my very wishes,
> And the buildings of my fancy; only
> There's one thing wanting, which I doubt not but
> Our Rome will cast upon thee.
>
>   (II.i.188–92)

Volumnia's wishes epitomize the Roman ethos. With no difficulty she accepts what the Christian tradition saw as evil in the partial good of honor and fame, the fact that as external valuations they need not reflect inner truth:

> I would dissemble with my nature where
> My fortunes and my friends at stake requir'd
> I should do so in honour.
>
>   (III.ii.62–64)

The concept of honor that Coriolanus and St. Augustine oppose could not be better represented. Because Roman honor lies in the voices of the people, it is an honorable action for Coriolanus to dissemble for those voices. From Volumnia's point of view, the testimony of his own conscience, his inner truth, not only becomes irrelevant; the Roman lady quite agrees with the Citizen that, when Coriolanus makes an obstacle of such testimony, he can only be guilty of pride.

II

Coriolanus's moral reservation is ominous:

> Know, good mother,
> I had rather be their servant in my way
> Than sway with them in theirs.
>
> (II.i.192–94)

Their way involves accepting the actualities of Rome and the political necessities that those actualities impose. Coriolanus's concept of virtue, already compromised, is strained beyond endurance the moment he must ask for reward. The contractual arrangement for "honorable recompence," which Coriolanus must accept despite his finer moral intuitions, breaks down completely. In relation to ideal Rome, embodied for Coriolanus in the Senate, the virtuous man performs and the city recognizes freely by translating performance into the terms and titles of praise. The integrity of Rome depends upon this reciprocity and upon the propriety, the decorum, between the public language of praise and the true worth of the man, between the designating word and the thing designated. As soon as the virtuous man must ask for this recognition, the inherent contradictions and incoherencies of the system, already intuited by Coriolanus, are forced into the open. Moreover, Coriolanus must ask not the patrician body of ideal Rome but the many-headed beast for its favorable identification. Herein lies Shakespeare's most drastic change in Plutarch's account of events and in the arrangement of the plot. Not surprisingly, the episode becomes both the structural and the thematic crux.

Neither Plutarch nor his Coriolanus evinces any trepidation over the power of the people to have the final voice in approving the Senate's choice for consul. We can assume that Coriolanus stands before the people in his gown of humility without protest, because Plutarch does not render what he must have considered an unremarkable scene. In making this event precipitate the turning point in the plot, Shakespeare reveals in action the

Augustinian critique of Roman morality, its honor and political life. According to St. Augustine, the electioneering process whereby the candidate was obliged to ask for the people's voice contradicted any claim that the quest for virtue was sufficient in itself to motivate the honorable man. Cato, for example, although "he shunned glory" in his quest for virtue, nevertheless had to sue for the honor of office, a contradictory action the moral nature of which is best left unexamined: "the honors that *Cato* required he should not haue required, but the city should haue returned him them, as his due desart."[15] Juan Luis Vives, in his sixteenth-century commentary on *The City of God*, appropriately cites Plutarch's observation that Rome, especially in its moral decline, should rather have "bought" such a man as Cato for a magistrate; indeed, Cato was "more fit to bee forced vnto dignities" than to be required to crave what Coriolanus calls "the hire which first we do deserve" (II.iii.111).[16] And Cato, like Coriolanus, suffered the even greater ignominy of being refused.

The dilemma that Shakespeare invents out of Plutarch's account expresses the fundamental plight of man in his moral relationship to society, a relationship that transcends the specifically political. The severe Augustinian attitude cannot satisfactorily resolve the problem. As far as St. Augustine in concerned, there is a hostile duality between "inner truth" and "the opinion of men."[17] When confronted with the testimony of one's conscience as witness to the Heavenly City, Roman glory at its best is vainglory. St. Augustine thus established most influentially the absolute that Christian humanism could only wrestle with; for in this instance man could not be counseled to perfection. Man cannot be entirely of the Heavenly City if he is to be a part of civil society. He must be named, identified, and defined by the public testimony of language. Yet Coriolanus, after the victory at Corioli, has exhibited essentially this Augustinian rigor that does not allow for a positive attitude toward external honor. Coriolanus would say with Augustine that "that

[15] *Ibid.*, V.xii. (*Vives*, p. 215.) Again, seeing the influence of Augustine on the play, I disagree with Gordon (p. 49) that normatively "in the city honour is not given, the deed is not named without request." When the request is required, Coriolanus like Augustine recognizes the anomaly.

[16] *Vives*, p. 217.

[17] For the significance of the word *opinion* in this context, see Peter Ure, "A Note on 'Opinion' in Daniel, Greville and Chapman," *MLR*, 46 (1951), 331–38.

vertue is as much disgraced in seruing humaine glory as in obeying the pleasures of the body."

As we have seen, Coriolanus has been forced to compromise with this absolute. He must accept the humanist's view of honor best represented for the Renaissance by Cicero. Vives, in his commentary, cites this most worthy pagan to qualify and extenuate Augustine's definition of glory as merely "the opinion of men." Vives's amplification in itself is a revealing commentary not on Augustinian absolutism but on Renaissance Christian humanism in confrontation with that absolutism. "Opinion," Vives optimistically explains, is "glory in generall," glory as is vulgarly understood; it will satisfy only the man more concerned with ambition than with virtue: *"but the true glorie is a solid and expresse thing* (saith *Tully) no shadow: and that is the vniforme praise of them that are good, the vncorrupted voice of such as iudge aright of vertues excellence."*[18] This honor comes freely and unrequested from those who are capable of judging because they are themselves virtuous and because they are incorruptible. Their judgment, therefore, is more than opinion. Only under such conditions, as Sir William Cornwallis (1601) urged in echo of Cicero and Seneca, can external evaluation be respected as of moral value: "For opinion—whose is it but the multitude's, and shall Vertue's goodlinesse dresse her selfe in the puddle? Let them learne to iudge, and I will feare their censure; but so long as they can say nothing but 'My opinion is thus,' I will not bring my actions to be seene and allowed, but my conscience and the presidents of other times shall be my directors."[19]

In order for the conferred honor to be judicious and worthy, it must be controlled by decorum. Cicero's metaphors for true glory distinguish between the judgment and the man judged,

[18] *Vives,* p. 217. Vives is citing *Tusculan Disputations* III.ii. For another humanistic and misleading extenuation of Augustine, see the concluding section of Petrarch's *Secretum:* in this dialogue between Petrarch and St. Augustine over the value of fame and glory, Augustine's last word allows for the Ciceronian compromise: "I will never advise you to live without ambition; but I would always urge you to put virtue before glory. You know that glory is in a sense the shadow of virtue." *Petrarch's Secret; or the Soul's Conflict with Passion: Three Dialogues Between Himself and S. Augustine,* trans. William H. Draper (London, 1911), p. 182. Cited by Curtis Brown Watson, p. 54.

[19] "Of Fortune and her Children," *Essayes by Sir William Cornwallis, the Younger,* ed. D. C. Allen (Baltimore: Johns Hopkins Press, 1946), p. 232. Cf. Seneca, *Epistulae morales* CII.

but while the two are not identical they are nevertheless, in
metaphoric terms, inseparable: glory *"answeres vertue like an
Eccho, and followeth it like a shadow."*[20] The criterion indicates
why the Ciceronian doctrine of decorum influenced morals and
manners so strongly not only in Rome but in Renaissance England. Rhetorically, the ideal of decorum requires the word to
echo the thing, the manner to shadow the matter. By extension,
the rhetorical ideal permeates all aspects of civil life, all the manners and means by which a man communicates his parts to
others. The response that his public makes, completing the act
of communication, must also ideally suit the word to the thing,
the manner to the matter. If language reflects reality, public
praise will reflect the inner truth of the man appropriately. The
word is not the thing any more than the shadow is the body;
but the moral nature of decorum (in Nicholas Grimald's translation "what beecommeth," "comelynesse") is such "that from
honesty it cannot bee sundred."[21] The word *honesty*, it should
be observed, has reference here not to moral rectitude but simply
to that which is—the reality free from fraud. Of course moral
rectitude is presupposed, given the Ciceronian ethics based upon
what is appropriate to man's nature. The word *honest* nevertheless keeps this potential duality, as in Shakespeare's most famous
usage: the overwhelming irony of "honest Iago" is not that Iago
lies but that, more insidiously, he is not what he appears to be.
He could, that is to say, be an honest villain. This breakdown
of decorum—when men are not seen for what they are, when
the word cannot therefore be appropriate to the thing—leads as
easily to moral confusion in the public as in the private life.

St. Augustine, with his focus on the life of the inner man and
the silent reality, demands absolute moral distinction between
word and thing. He recognizes no difference between judgment
and opinion; both are extrinsic and therefore irrelevant to the
only reality that matters. Furthermore, praise almost inevitably
evokes fallen man's pride. Coriolanus also instinctively rejects
the moral possibility of decorum, but his attempt to do so is
incoherent and hopeless. It is a compromise for him to accept
the reward "in sign" of what he is, even though the sign is judi-
ciously formed by the honorable Cominius. Later, with Cominius before the Senate, Coriolanus again rejects hearing his deeds

---

[20] *Vives*, p. 217. Vives continues with his reference to *Tusculan Disputations*
III.ii.

[21] *Marcus Tullius Ciceroes three bookes of duties*, trans. Nicholas Grimald
(London, 1596), sig. F^v (I.xxvii).

translated into the oration of praise, even though that gratification, freely given by the noblest men in Rome, strives for decorum between the manner (the oration) and the matter (Coriolanus's valiantness)—"to thank and to remember / With honours like himself":

> He cannot but with measure fit the honours
> Which we devise him.
>
> (II.ii.45–46, 121–22)

Coriolanus is nevertheless "disbenched." But once more, unless he is to be "the grave of [his] deserving," he must accept the identification that names him Consul, the noblest Roman of them all. And he willingly does so "by the suit of the gentry to him / And the desire of the nobles" (II.i.228–29). According to the custom, however, Coriolanus must "entreat" the people, and in this exchange even the moot distinction between sign and reward totally disappears:

> To brag unto them "Thus I did, and thus!"
> Show them th' unaching scars which I should hide,
> As if I had receiv'd them for the hire
> Of their breath only!
>
> (II.ii.145–48)

"Their breath" can be neither Cicero's inextricable shadow nor inevitable echo. At the last moment, Roman honor depends upon, and indeed becomes, the opinion of men who cannot judge because they are neither uniformly good nor incorruptible. Their voices are meaningless, mere breath.

In what might well be the ironic touchstone for Shakespeare's vision, Plutarch sanctions this elective process because it was "that time when the golden and vnfoiled age remained yet whole in iudgement at Rome" (p. 242). Plutarch would, of course, describe vividly the later degeneracy of the system at the end of the Republic; but Shakespeare discovers no Golden Age even at this early stage of Roman history. Such a time might have existed, implies Coriolanus, before the exigencies of politics corrupted it, the corruption being specifically this elective "custom" that "might well / Be taken from the people" (II.ii.143–44):

> Custom calls me to't.
> What custom wills, in all things should we do't,
> The dust on antique time would lie unswept,
> And mountainous error be too highly heap'd
> For truth to o'erpeer.
>
> (II.iii.114–18)

In ironic evocation of Montaigne, Coriolanus identifies the Idea of Rome with some original natural truth. The philosophical implication of these lines assumes a Golden Age prior to the slavery of custom, the error that arises from the opinion of men.

Plutarch's admiration for the early "golden" Rome and his optimism regarding the plebeians' political maturity indicate how far Shakespeare's Rome is removed from the source:

> For offices of dignitie in the citie were not then giuen by fauour or corruption. It was but of late time, and long after this, that buying and selling fell out in election of officers, and that the voices of the electours were bought for money. . . . Therefore me thinkes hee had reason that said: hee that first made banckets, and gaue money to the common people, was the first that tooke away authoritie, and destroyed commonwealth. But this pestilence crept in by litle and litle, and did secretly winne ground still, continuing a long time in Rome, before it was openly knowne and discouered. For no man can tell who was the first man that bought the peoples voices for money. (p. 242)

This passage has an important negative influence on the tragedy; for Shakespeare, with a critical Elizabethan eye toward democracy, would be quite capable of informing Plutarch why "no man can tell who was the first" to corrupt the people's voice. The potential for corruption is inherent in the very form, unless indeed one posits a golden, prelapsarian age. Shakespeare's Coriolanus is therefore prophetic when he infuses the elective process with the language of beggary and bribery, two transactions that demean and pervert the already intolerable fiscal terms of Roman morality:

> *Cor.* No, sir, 'twas never my desire yet to trouble the poor with begging.
> *3 Cit.* You must think, if we give you anything, we hope to gain by you.
> *Cor.* Well then, I pray, your price o' th' consulship?
> *1 Cit.* The price is to ask it kindly.
>
> (II.iii.68ff.)

The First Citizen certainly makes the better showing; but for Coriolanus, in his extremity, kindness is nevertheless a price—a price that many, we know, promise to pay with suspicious readiness. St. Augustine, whose absolutism is ultimately the source for Coriolanus's rigor, observes the moral danger in the imagery that is Shakespeare's objective correlative: "The report of the people's mouths, and deeds known to men, carry along with them a most dangerous temptation from the love of praise: which, for the advancing of a certain private excellency of our own, collects men's votes as a beggar craves alms."[22] Coriolanus echoes Augustine's severity with the same contemptuous image: "There's in all two worthy voices begg'd. I have your alms."

Perhaps no scene in Shakespeare more challenges the judgment and sympathy of the audience than that in which Coriolanus stands before the people in the gown of humility. We must not, first of all, discount the strangeness of the antique form itself. Even an age of electioneering has not dulled the dramatic grotesquerie of the situation. The custom is palliated no more for us than for Coriolanus when Menenius assures the *candidatus* that his predecessors have accepted it. From Plutarch's bland report, Shakespeare creates as it were an emblematic representation of Coriolanus's moral plight, generating for the tragic victim the sympathy one wins merely from being forced into an impossible situation. It is impossible, to be sure, especially for Coriolanus; but one cannot imagine any of Shakespeare's noble characters meeting this test morally unscathed. Yet many critics have assumed Coriolanus's perversity to be quite intolerably reprehensible.

The scene exposes not only aristocratic inflexibility but democratic instability and ineffectiveness. The people on their own are clearly incapable of making the election meaningful. It is obvious why this custom, before the establishment of the Tribunes, has been no threat to the aristocratic status quo. To say that the people are incapable is not exactly to charge them with ignorance or to insist upon an Elizabethan view of democracy. Although later ages have struggled idealistically to ward off such doubts, the Third Citizen in his naiveté succinctly acknowledges the impotence of the individual:

We have power in ourselves to do it, but it is a power that we have no power to do.

Are you all resolv'd to give your voices? But that's no matter, the greater part carries it.

(II.iii.4ff., 35ff.)

The individual, not without justification, feels neither responsible for nor capable of affecting "the greater part." Only the leadership of the Tribunes brings about any meaningful ac-

---

[22] *St. Augustine's Confessions,* with an English translation by William Watts (1631), ed. W. H. D. Rouse (London: Heinemann, 1912), II, 193 (X.xxxviii).

tion—action that, however, Sicinius and Brutus entirely determine and control.

There is nevertheless an indication that the custom of granting
the people their voice at least assumes, in spite of evidence to
the contrary, a "golden age." The ideal form of the election
is intended to proclaim the worthiest. The Third Citizen understands that the custom is, or hitherto has been, controlled by
a perfect decorum that would prevent idiosyncratic breaches.
The people's voice, the language of public honor, must sound
an exact representation of the candidate's worth:

> If he show us his wounds and tell us his deeds, *we are to put
> our tongues into those wounds and speak for them;* so, if he tell
> us his noble deeds, we must also tell him our noble acceptance
> of them.
>
> (italics added)

In the cluster of wound-mouth-tongue imagery, the word and
the thing are literally at one. The communal action attempts
a ritual in which the outward sign transubstantiates the inner
grace. This action, in which the hero must show his wounds
in the spirit of humility and self-sacrifice, begs with tragic operative irony the blessed "other case"—mankind's accepting, and
therefore participating in, the benefits of Christ's Passion. As
the acceptance of that noble sacrifice is mankind's nobility,
so here the Citizens' voice will be a "noble acceptance." The
communion allows both to share the honor: "For he that sancti-
fieth, & they which are sanctified, are all of one: wherefore he
is not ashamed to call them brethren" (Hebrews ii:11). But such
typological allusiveness as the political situation and imagery
generate only anticipates the ultimate limitation of Rome and
its morality. In Shakespeare's pagan world the image is not sacra-
mental but grotesque. Nevertheless, all aspects of civil life must
normatively assume that language mirrors reality; and that
the people will name the best man is all that Rome has assumed.

But Coriolanus cannot accept the inevitability of decorum.
For him the form of the election is itself indecorous, and the
indecorous, being dishonest, cannot yield what is honest. The
custom thrusts upon Coriolanus a role for which he is ridicu-
lously ill-suited:

> It is a part
> That I shall blush in acting.
>
> (II.ii.142–43)

Out of the literal situation Shakespeare's favorite metaphor emerges effortlessly, that all the world's a stage, all men and women merely players. But the action, words, and even costume assigned to Coriolanus are, he feels, absurdly indecorous, creating an insidious discrepancy between the role and his natural capacities. Coriolanus will therefore fail, both as actor and as man, to meet the standard for decorum that Cicero himself urged by theatrical analogy: "For that beecommeth each man, which is most of all each mans owne. Let euerie man therefore know his owne disposition . . . least plaiers may seeme to haue more discreation then wee. For they dooe choose not the best Enterludes, but the fittest for themselues."[23] Coriolanus would give a perfectly decorous performance to reflect his essential self: "Rather say I play / The man I am" (III.ii.15–16). But Volumnia, in her advice to the stubborn player, allows for a dishonest relationship between the man and the part, between matter and manner. For her the theatrical metaphor affirms not Ciceronian decorum but Machiavellian deceit:

> now it lies you on to speak
> To th' people, not by your own instruction,
> Nor by th' matter which your heart prompts you,
> But with such words that are but roted in
> Your tongue, though but bastards and syllables
> Of no allowance to your bosom's truth.
>
> (III.ii.52–57)

But Coriolanus cannot make the separation between heart and tongue sufficient to create the actor's illusion of reality. He plays the part not of a humble petitioner, a beggar, a harlot, or a mountebank but of an actor playing these parts. To shield himself in the compromising situation, he mocks both his performance and his audience. In the process his theatrical irony disorients the people by corrupting language and action. Distrusting the public form, he assures the breakdown of form.

There is another reason for Coriolanus to doubt the decorum of his role. Unlike his part in the moral contract between him and the Senate, his role in the market place requires that he "tell . . . his deeds"; and language is removed from the essential matter of the deeds themselves. The people will respond to his language, not to his virtuous action. Furthermore, the telling falsifies the deeds and the purity of their motivation, because

[23] Nicholas Grimald, sig. G 2 (I.xxxi).

the telling is inescapably an asking. His initial perverse response
to the Citizens goes to the heart of the matter:

> Cor. You know the cause, sir, of my standing here.
> *3 Cit.* We do, sir; tell us what hath brought you to't.
> Cor. Mine own desert.
> *2 Cit.* Your own desert?
> Cor. Ay, not mine own desire.
> *3 Cit.* How, not your own desire?
> Cor. No, sir, 'twas never my desire yet to trouble the poor
> with begging.
>
> (II.iii.61ff.)

In the last retort Coriolanus takes refuge in irony because he
cannot straightforwardly answer the question. He knows that
ideally one should not have to sue for "his due desart," as St.
Augustine observed in regard to Cato's political career; and even
while forcing himself to go through the motions, Coriolanus
refuses to admit that his virtuous deeds were not the end in
themselves, the end which should make him deserving of reward
freely given, without his ambitious seeking and asking. The
Third Citizen, however, cleverly spots the contradiction: to ask
is to desire. The people are certain that the end of his virtue—his
desire—must be the reward, no symbolic identification as far
as they are concerned but a very real position of political power.

Coriolanus's greatest justification for rejecting the decorum
of the elective process is that the custom allows the people's
breath the formal power to determine worth. It therefore imposes a value upon what has no value. Their voice can only
be opinion—the result, says Cicero, of "all the mob combining
in a general tendency to error."[24] Cicero's view of the mob, ultimately derived from Plato, governs Coriolanus's attitude toward the plebeians from the first of the play. In the opening confrontation the implications of opinion underlie all the hero's
invective:

> What's the matter, you dissentious rogues
> That, rubbing the poor itch of your opinion,
> Make yourselves scabs?
>
> (I.i.162–64)

---

[24] *Tusculan Disputations*, with an English translation by J. E. King (London:
Heinemann, 1945), p. 227 (III.ii). See also pp. 529–31 (V.xxxvi): "Can anything
be more foolish than to suppose that those, whom individually one despises
as illiterate mechanics, are worth anything collectively?"

The rationale of Shakespeare's attitude toward the mob lies in the inimical nature of this opinion.[25]

No member of Shakespeare's audience would deny Coriolanus's philosophical and political belief that the people, collectively, epitomize instability and mutability. It is not to the point to show Shakespeare's undeniable affection for individuals or the certain glimmers of insight among the members. Any such democratic defense in fact misses the force of the epithet "many-headed": the richer the diversity of voices, the more unpredictable the concerted voice. Even if the mob will sometimes act correctly, it is never for the right reason. Sir William Cornwallis can again be cited as reflecting the traditional attitude, one that allows for glimmers of wisdom and permits a patronizing affection:

> For who knowes not the diuers formes of men's imaginations (as different almost as their faces), which showes them easily separated; and their forces being strong no longer than whiles together incorporated (being so subiect to be seuered—nay, they going against Nature if holding a continued vnion), what can issue from this confidence but danger? Their natures, but by the pleasure of nature and their education, is left ignorant, which impotencie leaues a wauering disposition easily seduced and as easily reformed, apt to beleeue a faire tale and as apt to beleeue weake reasons strong.[26]

The Third Citizen approves the mob's traditional reputation as the "many-headed multitude":

> not that our heads are some brown, some black, some abram, some bald, but that our wits are so diversely colour'd; and truly I think if all our wits were to issue out of one skull, they would fly east, west, north, south, and their consent of one direct way should be at once to all the points o' th' compass.
>
> (II.iii.18ff.)

Fortunately the nature of the mob prevents its acting in "continued vnion," and therefore the people do not wield power effectively and can be controlled by firm and punitive law. Unfortunately, however, the mob exists as a potential weapon for the demagogue to seize. It should be remembered that a chief reason for the fear of democracy was that its inevitable declension

---

[25] For Shakespeare's attitude toward the mob, see the discussion and references in C. A. Patrides, "'The Beast with Many Heads': Renaissance Views on the Multitude," *SQ*, 16 (1965), 241–46.

[26] "Of Popularitie," *Essayes by Sir William Cornwallis, the Younger*, p. 102.

was to tyranny. The mob's voice, according to Plutarch, will be instrumental in destroying the commonwealth when the age is no longer golden. But Shakespeare already foresees that eventuality.

Besides being worthless and politically dangerous, the voice of the people corrupts men into the enticing labor "not to obtaine trueths, but opinions warrant."[27] Coriolanus's syllogism is only slightly strained: "Who deserves greatness / Deserves your hate" (I.i.174–75). In Thomas Twyne's translation of Petrarch's *De remediis utriusque fortunae*, Reason cautions Joy, who falsely relishes "the opinion of Vertue," that "almost whatsoeuer the common people doth prayse, is rather woorthy of reprehension." At the climax of the dialogue all qualification vanishes: "Whatsoeuer the multitude thinketh, is vayne, whatsoeuer they speake, is false, whatsoeuer they dislyke, is good, whatsoeuer they like, is euyll, whatsoeuer they commende, is infamous, whatsoeuer they doo, is foolyshe."[28] Opinion not only lacks moral value, it emblematizes the mutability that defeats man's aspiration for truth and order. In Cornwallis's traditional image, one that the literal situation in the play activates, opinion "liueth vpon the breath of the vulgar."[29]

When the people speak, decorum between language and reality breaks down and with it the decorum of civil life. When Coriolanus is named traitor instead of consul, the state is thrown into moral chaos. This dramatic issue is quite foreign to the source because Plutarch did not grimly represent Coriolanus as the epitome of Roman *virtus* or indicate any significance to his loss of the election. In Shakespeare, when the people are given the power to judge and reject Coriolanus, the crisis strikes the cornerstone of the Capitol, the moral foundation on which Rome was founded and by which it has developed and maintained itself:

> Your dishonour
> Mangles true judgment, and bereaves the state
> Of that integrity which should become't,
> Not having the power to do the good it would,
> For th' ill which doth control't.
>
>   (III.i.157–61)

[27] William Cornwallis, *Discourses upon Seneca the Tragedian* (1601), intro. by Robert Hood Bowers (Gainesville, Fla.: Univ. of Florida Press, 1952), sigs. B 4–B 4ᵛ.
[28] *Phisicke against Fortune* (London, 1579), sigs. B 7ᵛ–B 8.
[29] "Of Opinion," *Essayes by Sir William Cornwallis*, p. 54.

III

Shakespeare wrote many plays about heroes, but only *Antony and Cleopatra* and *Coriolanus* are distinguished by heroic appeals that are exclusively and definitively aristocratic.[30] Coriolanus and Cleopatra, for all their differences, share an unyielding horror of being scrutinized and judged by a vulgar audience. When the queen of Egypt contemplates her dishonor at the hands of Octavius, her most terrifying thought is the vulgarization of her nobility in a dramatic representation for a popular Roman audience:

> *Cleo.*   Now, Iras, what think'st thou?
> Thou an Egyptian puppet shall be shown
> In Rome as well as I. Mechanic slaves,
> With greasy aprons, rules, and hammers, shall
> Uplift us to the view; in their thick breaths,
> Rank of gross diet, shall we be enclouded,
> And forc'd to drink their vapour.
> *Iras.*   The gods forbid!
> *Cleo.*   Nay, 'tis most certain, Iras. Saucy lictors
> Will catch at us like strumpets, and scald rhymers
> Ballad us out o' tune; the quick comedians
> Extemporally will stage us, and present
> Our Alexandrian revels; Antony
> Shall be brought drunken forth, and I shall see
> Some squeaking Cleopatra boy my greatness
> I' th' posture of a whore.
>
> (V.ii.206–20)

Cleopatra dazzlingly holds up a mirror to the world of the Globe playhouse. Her speculation about a Roman play reflects the actual dramatic event of Shakespeare's Roman play: the Roman populace looks exactly like the London populace crowded around her open stage; Cleopatra is in fact being boyed by some incredible young master and often, no doubt, in the exaggerated posture of a whore; the Alexandrian revels have already generated the laughter to encloud the Globe with the vapor of garlic. In other words, the heroic couple have already been exposed to the dramatic humiliation that the noble Cleopatra dreads; and they have deserved it to the extent that their aspiration has been punctured comically by the reality.

[30] I have discussed this phenomenon as Shakespeare's response to the Jacobean political and theatrical climate in *"Antony and Cleopatra* and *Coriolanus,* Shakespeare's Heroic Tragedies: A Jacobean Adjustment," *Shakespeare Survey,* 26 (1973), 95–101.

Cleopatra's mirror image, however, is one-dimensional. The Roman performance will merely be grotesque caricature rendered with crude dramaturgical techniques and inspired by an even cruder moralism. Such a play might well have been in the popular repertory of the 1580s, something like a Roman *Famous Victories*. The appeal to the Roman populace, Cleopatra insists, will obliterate the dignity of heroic tragedy and the glory of heroic love.[31] Shakespeare's Cleopatra, by implication, thus denies the varletry of censuring London a simplistic moral response to her tragedy: *Antony and Cleopatra* is obviously so much more than Cleopatra's projected Roman play, more than what the Roman populace could appreciate. At the same time, her trepidation—her dramatic vulnerability—points to the lovers' failure to realize their heroic vision in action. Those mechanic slaves with their rules represent a legitimate measurement that Shakespeare's comprehensive point of view incorporates.

The famous passage in *Antony and Cleopatra* anticipates precisely the crucial dramatic scene in *Coriolanus*. In both cases the image of public display—Cleopatra exhibited as the prize of Caesar's triumph, Coriolanus standing for election in the market place—dissolves effortlessly into the image of a demeaning theatrical performance: "It is a part / That I shall blush in acting." More insidiously, the breath of the people, which Coriolanus despises as much as Cleopatra, has the power to determine the value of his performance, his moral worth and his fame.

Explicitly in *Coriolanus* Shakespeare brings aristocratic and heroic appeals into tension with a popular and unheroic world. The noblest Roman of them all does not wish to perform for the breath of those who, because they are not themselves noble, have no understanding of nobility. The people's imagistic association with materialism stigmatizes them as opposed to the ideal.[32] They are "the voice of occupation," "of craft," and their nature is subdued to what it works in. When they fight, the reward they seek is limited by values so crude that they cannot judge even a dishonorable recompense:

[31] For the semantic confusion behind "heroical love," a confusion that encouraged the belief that only the great are subject to this overwhelming passion, see John L. Lowes, "The Loveres Maladye of Hereos," *MP*, 11 (1914), 491–546.

[32] The finest discussions of the imagery in *Coriolanus* are to be found in G. Wilson Knight, *The Imperial Theme* (London: Oxford Univ. Press, 1931), pp. 154–98; Maurice Charney, "The Dramatic Use of Imagery in Shakespeare's *Coriolanus*," *ELH*, 23 (1956), 183–93; and his later amplification in *Shakespeare's Roman Plays*, pp. 142–96.

See here these movers that do prize their hours
At a crack'd drachma! Cushions, leaden spoons,
Irons of a doit, doublets that hangmen would
Bury with those that wore them, these base slaves,
Ere yet the fight be done, pack up.
                                                    (I.v.4–8)

In response to this action, Coriolanus scathingly refers to "the common file" as "our gentlemen" (I.vi.43), and thematically his sarcasm is apt. Roman gentility demands a total disregard for material reward; even the idea of an "honorable recompence" compromises the highest sense of Roman honor. The people's association with money and trade therefore hopelessly vulgarizes them. Although within the gates, they are beyond the pale of Rome's acknowledged values. Volumnia can be cited once more for the aristocratic Roman attitude, still another disposition that Coriolanus is shocked to find altered by events:

I muse my mother
Does not approve me further, who was wont
To call them woollen vassals, things created
To buy and sell with groats; to show bare heads
In congregations, to yawn, be still, and wonder,
When one but of my ordinance stood up
To speak of peace or war.
                                                    (III.ii.7–13)

The most revealing symptom of their inhumanity is their inability to comprehend the nature of patrician authority and nobility. Like savages or children they can only admire, with a brief span of concentration, what is beyond their ken. By a happy rhetorical trope the people lose their humanity in their main activity: from human beings who buy and sell they become things to be bought and sold.

For Coriolanus, the pursuit of the people's voice taints him with their gross materialism. If the breath of the people must be "the hire" for his service, he is reduced to the lowest social level in desiring payment from such employers. He becomes the beggar craving alms, "an ostler, that for th' poorest piece / Will bear the knave by th' volume" (III.iii.32–33). Because the role requires him to counterfeit, he sinks even beneath the level of honest servants and beggars to become the cheat, the mountebank (III.ii.132). Because he is selling his integrity, he is guilty of prostitution. The transaction deviates from the moral norm of trade, which involves the exchange between two parties of that acknowledged to be of approximately equal value. If one party questions the value of what is offered by the other or is unable to appreciate that value, the basis of honest trade is undermined, just as the coin of the realm is debased and corrupted by the counterfeit.

Ironically Coriolanus must insist upon absolute integrity in trade because in the last analysis the morality governing fiscal transactions is the morality governing Roman honor, a morality that does not, as St. Augustine insisted, rise above the carnal. Although the most refined pagan sensibilities urged a rejection of even "honorable recompence," such high-mindedness was impracticable unless one posited, like Cicero in *Somnium Scipionis*, a heaven to recognize service to the state.[33] But since neither virtue itself nor heaven can offer the reward, the integrity of Rome depends upon the purity of a contract between two parties: the honorable recompense that Rome gives must exactly—decorously—match the Roman's virtue. There must be a "true purchasing." Coriolanus adopts this quantitative system in his consideration of the people: "I love them as they weigh" (II.ii.72). His images of beggary, prostitution, bribery, and fraud metaphorically condemn his "exchange" with the weightless mob as a perversion.

Of all deviations from the norm of contractual exchange, however, none is so dangerous as extortion. Extortion brings the threat of force into play and therefore bodes violence and disorder. Furthermore, value can no longer be, in such circumstances, a consideration. Coriolanus therefore objects vehemently to the gift of free corn to the people. It is not recompense because they have not paid for it either in money or in service. They buy simply with threats:

> They know the corn
> Was not our recompense, resting well assur'd
> They ne'er did service for't.

> (III.i.120–22)

Coriolanus objects to the gift of the Tribunes on the same principle. The establishment of the Tribunes no less than the free distribution of corn gives the people something they have not earned except through their physical power to blackmail the city. There is no "true purchasing."

[33] The purpose of the work, as Macrobius explains it, is "to teach us that souls of those who serve the state well are returned to the heavens after death and there enjoy everlasting blessedness." *Commentary on the Dream of Scipio,* trans. William Harris Stahl (New York: Columbia Univ. Press, 1952), p. 92.

This forced innovation activates the power of the people's voice into a new political force. The approval that the people customarily extended to the Senate's choice had heretofore confirmed the meaninglessness of the form and, paradoxically, demonstrated decorum. The noble Senate selected—or, ideally, recognized and acknowledged—the noblest Roman. The voice of the people then echoed the worth of the man: "So, if he tell us his noble deeds, we must also tell him our noble acceptance of them." Theoretically, the voice was not simply "the voice of occupation" but the communal voice of Rome, one real and indivisible city. In order to sound the voice, the *candidatus* and the people had to be at one. As in the image that grotesquely and ironically recollects Christ's Passion, the hero's wounds spoke with the tongues of the people.

The aptness and ideal significance of the image are garbled by what is necessary to activate mouth and tongue into voice— breath. The breath must be entirely the people's, and therefore the ideal communion is spoiled because breath is mere opinion, extrinsic and irrelevant to real value. The breath becomes insidiously relevant to political power, however, when the Tribunes are established "to defend their vulgar wisdoms" (I.i.213). Breath is given the power to determine and declare value. As the old formality springs to political life and takes on meaning, this breath destroys the communal and ritualistic image of decorum and sets up another in its place. The wounds are no longer the mouth through which the people speak. The Tribunes become both "the tongues o' th' common mouth" (III.i.22) and, a few lines later, the mouths for the common tongues. In this metaphoric confusion mouth, tongue, and breath achieve a monstrous communion entirely separate from the matter of Rome, the thing the voice must signify. The voice of Rome is now purely "the voice of occupation." The political action of the people confirms the aristocratic prejudice against the people's unsavory breath—as abhorrent to patrician sensibilities as an association with trade:

> You have made good work,
> You and your apron men; you that stood so much
> Upon the voice of occupation and
> The breath of garlic-eaters!

> (IV.vi.96–99)

The objection against the mob's breath, so commonly charged in the popular drama, transcends fastidiousness and merges with the desire to protect noble ideals from enclouding opinion. It is this desire that provokes Cleopatra's horror of "thick breaths, / Rank of gross diet."

From the opening scene of *Coriolanus*, imagery and structure work together to climax in the odorous cries that "whoop" Coriolanus from Rome. As that cry of the "rank-scented meiny" (III.i.66) conjoins the images of breath and "gross diet," so the opening insurrection, motivated by hunger, anticipates that crisis by feeding and activating the power of breath: "They say poor suitors have strong breaths; they shall know we have strong arms too" (I.i.57). The people extort not only their Tribunes but, as we later learn, the free distribution of corn. When the Tribunes revoke Coriolanus's election, the two issues of food and breath are forced into conjunction:

> *Bru.* The people cry you mock'd them; and of late,
> When corn was given them gratis, you repin'd;
> Scandal'd the suppliants for the people, call'd them
> Time-pleasers, flatterers, foes to nobleness.
> *Cor.* Why, this was known before.
> *Bru.*   Not to them all.
> *Cor.* Have you inform'd them sithence?
>
> (III.i.42–47)

This angry exchange allows Coriolanus to repeat his great diatribe against the "frank donation." Structurally, the opening and middle episodes are thus linked causally by the hero's vehement recapitulation. Thematically, the imagery of the earlier issue is used morally to characterize the new voice of Rome that will smack of the majority's "gross diet":

> You are plebeians,
> If they be senators; and they are no less,
> When, both your voices blended, the great'st taste
> Most palates theirs.
>
> (III.i.101–4)

When Coriolanus fails in his effort to keep the Roman voice free from the taste and breath of the people, the city has become uninhabitable. His departing exultation loathingly gathers up the strands of the imagery:

> You common cry of curs, whose breath I hate
> As reek o' th' rotten fens, whose loves I prize
> As the dead carcasses of unburied men
> That do corrupt my air—I banish you.
>
> (III.iii.122–25)

But if Coriolanus's vision is granted its validity, the physical world of the trade and working class offers a system of checks more profound than the hero understands. Negatively, the people represent the imperfection in society that will prevent realization of Coriolanus's immutable Rome. Positively, they spot the flaw in Coriolanus's heroic effort to be absolutely heroic. In their mutual rejection, each side in this conflict of extremities ironically accentuates the value of the other. We cannot equate the worth of the people with "the dead carcasses of unburied men." What distinguishes them is in fact that very breath with which they reject Coriolanus. The maintenance of Coriolanus's absolute would require him to cut off that breath:

> Would the nobility lay aside their ruth
> And let me use my sword, I'd make a quarry
> With thousands of these quarter'd slaves, as high
> As I could pick my lance.

> (I.i.195–98)

Sicinius is shrewdly accurate when he charges that Coriolanus, in order to achieve his ideal, would have to "depopulate the city and / Be every man himself" (III.i.264–65). The political conflict, already hopelessly ambivalent, becomes impassable when the question of the political value of breath finally begs the value of life itself.

What Shakespeare achieves can be defined by contrast with the account in his source, for he conflates the two civil insurrections in Plutarch and focuses them ambiguously on the most fundamental need of life, the food necessary to maintain breath. In Plutarch there is nothing to perplex our moral bearings. Plutarch justifies the motivation for the first civil disturbance because the people are suffering from indisputably unjust laws favoring usurers, a complaint that Shakespeare parenthetically obscures (I.i.80). Plutarch's Coriolanus blithely ignores this injustice when arguing in the Senate against any "lenitie" that would oblige insurrection. After the people have retreated in protest to the holy hill, they respond to the morality of Menenius's fable on the condition that they are given Tribunes "whose office should be to defend the poore people from violence and oppresion" (p. 238).

Although Plutarch approves of the tribunal office to defend the people, he is contemptuous of Brutus and Sicinius. The second insurrection clarifies his contempt, and Plutarch is this time unsympathetic with the people: "The flatterers of the people

began to sturre vp sedition againe, without any new occasion,
or iust matter offered of complaint. . . . Now those busie prat-
lers that sought the peoples good will, by such flattering words,
perceiuing great scarsitie of corne to be within the citie, and
though there had bene plenty enough, yet the common people
had no money to buie it: they spread abroad false tales and
rumors against the Nobilitie, that they in reuenge of the people,
had practised and procured the extreame dearth among them"
(p. 241). Once more the rights and the wrongs of the situation
are without ambivalence: the seditious Tribunes use an unfortunate dearth to provoke the gullible people.

Out of these two disturbances Shakespeare creates a confrontation with unsettling ambiguities, suggesting the complexity of
confrontation by a refusal to clarify certain details. The absence
of clear cause allows our dramatic interest to become involved
in a moral conflict greater than the particularities could generate.
The confusion is calculated to allow sympathy for the rights
of both sides.

Plutarch authorially supports Menenius's denial of the Senate's responsibility for the people's hunger:

> For the dearth,
> The gods, not the patricians, make it, and
> Your knees to them, not arms, must help.
>
> (I.i.70–72)

Evidence for support is lacking in Shakespeare. We learn later
that free corn has been distributed, but there is no emphasis
or clarification as to where it came from. (In Plutarch, Rome
receives a supply of grain from Italy and Sicily, at which point
Coriolanus urges the Senate against a "frank donation.") If we
are inclined to accept Menenius's explanation for the dearth,
Coriolanus upsets this disposition when he scorns the people
merely for the vulgarity of their needs:

> They said they were an-hungry; sigh'd forth proverbs—
> That hunger broke stone walls, that dogs must eat,
> That meat was made for mouths, that the gods sent not
> Corn for the rich men only.
>
> (I.i.203–6)

The hunger, we note, is somehow "answered," but Shakespeare
obscures the matter with Coriolanus's concern over the Tribunes.

As Shakespeare's strategy becomes clear, so does his purpose.
The dilemma emblematizes in the body politic the inescapable
limitations of man's physical nature perennially at war with what

lifts man above the clay. The Citizen's proverb may be trite, but it is epigraphic: hunger can indeed tear down the walls of the Earthly City. Even with a conservative Elizabethan's horror of rebellion, Richard Hooker insists that the problem of what we shall eat and what we shall drink is antecedent to any ordered society because these needs are fundamental to life: "The Apostle, in exhorting men to contentment although they have in this world no more than very bare food and raiment, giveth us thereby to understand that those are even the lowest of things necessary; that if we should be stripped of all those things without which we might possibly be, yet these must be left; that destitution in these is such an impediment, as till it be removed suffereth not the mind of man to admit any other care."[34] Of course one scarcely need document the belief that dogs must eat; but it should be clear that from any Elizabethan point of view Shakespeare initiates a morally ambivalent confrontation generated by incompatible commonplaces, the most vulgar and the most idealistic. The ideal—that rebellion is never justifiable—cannot answer a quite unendurable reality.

The initial encounter ends, however, with a sly questioning of this unendurable reality, the people's hunger. The Romans are now preparing for war:

> The Volsces have much corn; take these rats thither
> To gnaw their garners.
>
> (I.i.247–48)

Unlike the citizens in Plutarch, who gladly fought after the redress to show their good will, these people, according to the stage direction, cowardly "*steal away*." How hungry are they? If Shakespeare does not absolve the Senate of responsibility, he also refuses to give us an undisturbed image of pitiful, starving humanity. One effect of Shakespeare's ambiguous treatment of the material, therefore, is to indicate the mutual guilt of both patricians and plebeians. But the ironic confusion also suggests that the ultimate cause of such disturbances extends beyond the responsibility of individuals or factions and simply confirms the inevitable imperfection of the Earthly City.

Surely the play substantiates Coriolanus's conviction that giving the corn not as a recompense but as a compromise born of necessity has sown "the cockle of rebellion, insolence, sedition" (III.i.70). Subsequent Roman history will bear out his

[34] *The Works of Richard Hooker*, ed. John Keble (Oxford: Clarendon, 1865), I, 240. (*Of the Laws of Ecclesiastical Polity* I.x.)

point of view, and it is understandable that Plutarch reveals no
sympathy for the people's demand. In "The Life of Julius
Caesar," Plutarch describes two instances in which corn is given
under just the circumstances that Coriolanus predicts: "*Cato
then fearing the insurrection of the poore needie persons, which
were they that put all their hope in Caesar, and did also moue
the people to sturre: did perswade the Senate to make a franke
distribution of corne vnto them, for a moneth*" (p. 762). During
Caesar's first consulship, the prime destroyer of the Republic
is quick to use this lever of influence, not in fear but in the desire
for more power: "*Now when he was entred into his office, he
beganne to put foorth lawes meeter for a seditious Tribune
of the people, then for a Consull: because by them he preferred
the diuision of landes, and distributing of corne to euery citizen,
Gratis, to please them withall*" (p. 764). These acts only pro-
moted the degeneracy of the Republic in Caesar's time.

The point that Shakespeare allows is that power, even if given
in the name of humanity, is power nevertheless and contains
the seed of its own corruption and destruction. Shakespeare
recognizes the right of the people to a voice as symptomatic
of a tragic necessity. The mob and its materialistic needs clarify
the impossible nature of Coriolanus's demand—that Rome, like
Julius Caesar, be as constant as the northern star. Like Brutus
in the earlier play, Coriolanus localizes the evil preventing perfection and would employ "a dangerous physic," literally destroy the opposing force: he would "at once pluck out / The
multitudinous tongue" (III.i.155–56). Although political parti-
sans find Brutus and Coriolanus at opposite poles, in the tragic
world of Rome they are brothers. They have a vision of a perfect city, and they are blind to what will prevent the realization
of that perfection.

IV

The Tribune tells Coriolanus:

> You speak o' th' people
> As if you were a god to punish; not
> A man of their infirmity.
>
> (III.i.80–82)

Whereas Brutus in *Julius Caesar* is blind to the infirmity of mankind, Coriolanus cannot see the godliness. The blindness of the

two heroes can provoke similar tragic effects because both lack the knowledge that man, as a godly quintessence of dust, is a paradox. Furthermore, he is a paradox constantly subjected to paradox. That subjection is in fact the most pronounced symptom of man's wearisome liability: he is born to one world, to another due. As far as Rome is concerned, the other world is among "those mysteries which heaven / Will not have earth to know" (IV.ii.35–36). In the absence of such revelation, Coriolanus has heroically committed himself to an ideal beyond the physical world of a small village. Absolutely loyal to that commitment, he has "affected the fine strains of honour, / To imitate the graces of the gods" (V.iii.149–50). This religious imitation, sanctioned by a communal spirit, accounts for his hatred of the common people with their irreligious and destructive opinion. Supporting Coriolanus in his attitude is the judgment of good men from Plato, to Cicero, to Augustine.

Coriolanus is nevertheless trapped by the paradox that such a moral attitude cannot be maintained absolutely, and it is the mob that clarifies the flaw in Coriolanus's attempt to do so. St. Augustine, at the same time that he condemns vainglory from Coriolanus's point of view, insists upon the paradox of such a condemnation from the people's point of view. One convicts himself of vainglory even in the act of condemning it:

The report of the people's mouths, and deeds known to men, carry along with them a most dangerous temptation from the love of praise: which, for the advancing of a certain private excellency of our own, collects men's votes as a beggar craves alms. It tempts, even when it is reproved by myself in myself: yea, even in that very particular, that it is reproved. And with a greater vanity does a man glory oftentimes of his contemning of vain-glory; for which reason he cannot now be said to glory in his contempt of vain-glory: for he does not truly contemn it, who glories at it.[35]

Coriolanus thus becomes guilty of self-love, a sin proceeding from "the same kind of temptation" as vainglory:

Such people puff themselves up, as please themselves in themselves, however they please not or displease others or care not to please. These may please themselves, but thee do they displease highly: not only for pleasing themselves in things not good, as if they were good, but also for so doing in thy good things as if they were their own.[36]

[35] *St. Augustine's Confessions*, II, 193 (X.xxxviii).
[36] *Ibid.*, pp. 193–95 (X.xxxix).

In the pagan context of *Coriolanus,* however, distinctions must be made; for pride and self-love, as I have insisted, will not account for the tragic experience in any simplistic way. First, Coriolanus is assuredly not indifferent to the "good report" of the Senate, ambivalent though he may be about its public expression. Second, if the good that he dedicates himself to is not an absolute good, it is the only one Rome knows. Coriolanus has not, in a fit of singularity, created another.

The Augustinian rigor, then, is not without moral complication after all. Even for the Christian who focuses his vision on the Heavenly City, the Earthly City is a fact that demands acknowledgment if not reconciliation. The situation is exacerbated for the pagan Coriolanus in his relation to the people. He would of course prefer that there be no relation. "You must desire them / To think upon you," Menenius instructs him before the election:

> Think upon me? Hang 'em!
> I would they would forget me.
>
> (II.iii.54–56)

But while they may be spiritually barbarians, they are physically Romans, and Coriolanus must reconcile himself to that fact not only to avoid a paradoxical vainglory but also to maintain the civic decorum on which Roman honor and morality depend. Although they start from different premises, Augustine is in agreement with Cicero: "There must bee vsed therefore a certayne reuerence towarde men, both to euerie one of the best sort, and also to the rest of meaner degree. For it is not onely a signe of an arrogant body, but also of one altogether lawlesse, to bee retchlesse, what euery man thinketh of him."[37] Augustine's concern for the individual's spiritual integrity and Cicero's concern for Rome's civic integrity coincide as much as Christian and pagan concerns can. But for Augustine, of course, there can be no true virtue or reverence toward men without *caritas.*

The people, because they are Romans, cannot forget Coriolanus. Therefore, if they are to remember him in such a way as to reflect what he is, he cannot play the role of an actor who is contemptuous of both his role and his audience. If the people are to speak decorously, he must represent the man he is in terms of the part prescribed. Coriolanus's distrust of the custom is quite reasonable; there is a real potentiality for corruption. But, as Cicero observes, unless one like Socrates is granted

[37] Nicholas Grimald, sigs. F 3ᵛ–F 4 (I.xxviii). Cf. *The City of God* V.xix.

"heauenly gifts," the practices established by older and wiser men should not be questioned as to their decorum: "As for things, which are done after custome, and ciuill ordinaunces, there is no precept to bee giuen of them. For they bee precepts of them selues."[38] Instead of fitting himself to the custom as have his predecessors, taking his honor with the prescribed form (II.ii.140–42), Coriolanus prevents the possibility of decorum by performing indecorously. He speaks the words and wears the costume of humility, but the performance is a mockery. When he refuses to show his wounds, he leaves out "one jot of ceremony" (II.ii.139) and in so doing denies the mouth through which the people can decorously speak.

Coriolanus's refusal to show his wounds completes the typological parody of the reverence and love behind Christ's stigmata and open hands. The situation begs "the possible other case" of which Rome is ignorant. Without anachronistically making the Christian relevance explicit, Shakespeare implies through the operative irony the Christian charity that Rome has not incorporated in its definition of virtue, and this failure has placed man and his city at odds with each other, with nature, and with life itself. Left entirely to Rome's direction and to his own fallen condition, Coriolanus paradoxically demonstrates the excellence beyond the clay that is natural to man and, at the same time, a spiritual perversion. He violates those natural laws that both guide and restrict mankind. The pervasive influence of Cicero's *De officiis* again seems unmistakable in defining the failure of Coriolanus in his relationship to mankind:

There must bee in all menne one entent: that a lyke may bee the profit of euery free man, and of all vniuersally. Which profit if each man plucke vnto himselfe, all mans fellowship shall bee dissolued. And if nature dooth also appoynt this, that man would haue men prouided for, whatsoeuer hee bee, yet euen for the same respect, beecause hee is a man, it must needes followe, that according to the same nature, the profit of all bee in common. Which if it bee so, wee all bee contayned in one, and the like law of nature. And if the same bee so, doubtlesse by the law of nature, wee are forbidden one to wrong another.

Now, the antecedent is true, therefore true also is the consequent. For that verely is reasonlesse, that some say, from their parent or brother, they wyll take nothing away, for cause of theyr owne profit, but of other Citizens, that there is another respect to bee had. These be in opinion, that they haue no law nor fellowshyppe

[38] *Ibid.*, sig. I (I.xli).

to keepe wyth Citizens, for a common profits sake, which opinion doth rip a sunder all the societie of a Citie.[39]

Coriolanus is finally both lawless and unnatural. His literal attempt to destroy Rome proceeds with fierce logic from an initial attitude that would demolish the structure of civil society:

> The rabble should have first unroof'd the city
> Ere so prevail'd with me.
>
> (I.i.216–17)

Coriolanus and the mob are at one in their willingness to destroy rather than to swerve from their own flawed natures. As long as the idea of Rome can be identified with Rome itself, Coriolanus is the city's servant. But Sicinius correctly urges "his singularity" (I.i.276) in that Coriolanus is committed not to the reality but to the ideal. The end—Coriolanus as enemy of Rome—is therefore in the beginning: "There is differency between a grub and a butterfly; yet your butterfly was a grub. This Marcius is grown from man to dragon; he has wings, he's more than a creeping thing" (V.iv.11ff.). In rising above the level of creeping things, Coriolanus becomes both godlike and monstrous, and the greatness of the character is therefore ambiguous in its moral worth.[40] Neither as god nor as monster would Coriolanus consider obligations in civil society to be based merely upon nature, upon the interests of fellow men in their common infirmity. When Coriolanus asks the people "the price of the consulship," the Citizen's disarming answer really only urges Coriolanus to consider himself one of their kind. But for Coriolanus the mob is bestial and therefore monstrous: to consider himself one of their kind is too great a price to pay. Ironically Coriolanus becomes what he most abhors. In denying the mob's humanity it is he who becomes the monster.

In his concern for value, in refusing to pay the price of asking kindly, Coriolanus insists on the fiscal imagery to such an extent

[39] *Ibid.*, sigs. Q 3–Q 4 (III.vi). The conception of the brotherhood of man had a commanding place in the thought of later Stoics. From the Christian point of view, however, brotherhood would have to be based upon more than an intelligent sense of self-preservation.

[40] See F. N. Lees, "*Coriolanus*, Aristotle, and Bacon," *RES*, 1 n.s. (1950), 114–25: "Because of the contrast of this variously intended conjunction of Coriolanus and divinity with the constant strain of animality . . . the phrase from the *Politics* 'He that is incapable of living in a society is a god or a beast' has long seemed to me a fitting brief comment on the play" (p. 117).

that it taints him spiritually as much as trade taints the mob. Just before the sentence of exile is pronounced, he brings the imagery of monetary transaction to a cruel climax:

> I would not buy
> Their mercy at the price of one fair word,
> Nor check my courage for what they can give,
> To have't with saying "Good morrow."
>
> (III.iii.91–94)

Incivility can go no further: Coriolanus would neither pay nor give the people a civil word. Shakespeare is certainly no sentimental libertarian regarding the people's humanity. He does not deny their political threat or their worthlessness in the positive evaluation of Roman nobility. The complex comprehensiveness of Shakespeare's attitude is suggested by Menenius when Volumnia urges her son to ask the people for "their good loves":

> This but done
> Even as she speaks, why, their hearts were yours;
> For they have pardons, being ask'd, as free
> As words to little purpose.
>
> (III.ii.86–89)

The worthlessness of the people's breath is ironically complemented by their ability to pardon freely, an attribute of genuine magnanimity. But Coriolanus perverts this potentially free exchange by insisting upon the fiscal metaphor, that his asking is a price. Furthermore, he blindly equates what is free with what is worthless. He cannot see that the pardon of the people, like their affirmative voice in the election, has a value—the value of human life in all its infirmity. Such value, however, is not incorporated into the idea of Rome, and Coriolanus cannot recognize it.[41]

Coriolanus's strict view of civic relationships as based upon some acknowledged coin of the realm, not on the value of life itself, allies the pagan with Shylock's legalistic justice and ma-

---

[41] Cf. L. C. Knights, "Shakespeare's Politics: with Some Reflections on the Nature of Tradition," *Proc. of the British Acad.*, 43 (1957), 115–32: "There is no suggestion that the social distinctions between patricians and plebeians ought not to exist: it *is* suggested that the diversified social group, the body politic, is in danger of corruption to the extent that *what lies behind diversity* is lost sight of. 'What lies behind' is of course simple humanity" (p. 122). Knights cites Boethius regarding the love that should hold society together. The failure exemplified in Menenius's fable can best be explained by reference to St. Paul's use of the same image (I Corinthians xii: 12–27).

terialistic values. Coriolanus loves the people "as they weigh," not as they are. In terms of Rome's contractual honor, they do not weigh at all, and Coriolanus would cut them off. Such a system of value, pressed absolutely, is as cruel as that represented by Shylock's scale and knife. Not surprisingly, Coriolanus becomes as consumed by the passion of revenge as the ignoble Jew; and, in the case of both Jew and Roman, Shakespeare makes it thematically clear that such a passion has developed because there is no access to the Christian ethos of love.

The evidence that *Coriolanus* is informed by the perspective and presentiments of Christian historiography is not entirely inferential. Although Shakespeare scrupulously maintains the pagan setting of the play, one does not have to rely upon negative evidence to affirm the operative irony that historically implies "the something better (better than the obnoxious, the provoking object) that blessedly, as is assumed, *might* be." Shakespeare's vision of the Roman ethos and political liabilities is clearly derived from the Christian critique of the moral and temporal limitations of the last and greatest world empire. The most immediate source for this critique and for the Christian view of universal history is to be found not in Augustine's *City of God* or Orosius's *Seven Books of Histories Against the Pagans*, but at the hand of every literate Elizabethan, in the Book of Daniel with its mystical history of the four monarchies. In the interpretive marginalia of the Geneva Version, the fourth monarchy is identified with Rome, this final world empire to be replaced only by the eternal kingdom of Christ.[42]

The first thing to note in examining this source of Christian historiography is that the providential view of history is not, as some critics would have it, undramatically simplistic. As in his treatment of English history, Shakespeare can discover dramatic causes in the actions of men because the ways of God are just and justifiable. As the commentary on the Book of Daniel insists, the seed of Rome's destruction lay within the fourth empire itself, distinguishing its fall from the more direct terminations of the previous three. Therefore that fantastic "great image" in the second chapter of Daniel, the legs of which represent Rome, has feet partly of iron and partly of clay in order to suggest a paradoxical weakness in strength. Rome has an inher-

---

[42] See my introductory chapter, pp. 7–13. In the following discussion I amplify the Calvinistic marginalia of the Geneva Version with reference to John Calvin, *Commentaries on the Book of the Prophet Daniel*, 2 vols., trans. Thomas Myers (Edinburgh: Calvin Translation Society, 1852–53).

ent inability to be at one with itself. As John Calvin explicates the emblem in his biblical commentary, "The Prophet furnishes us with a vivid picture of the Roman empire, by saying *that it was like iron,* and also *mingled with clay,* or mud, as they destroyed themselves by intestine discord after arriving at the highest pitch of fortune" (I, 177). The two materials are "a sign of disunion" and therefore "without any external force" at the coming of Christ will "[fall] to pieces by itself" (I, 165). The Romans will destroy all previous kingdoms "as yron breaketh in pieces, & subdueth all things"; but, the Geneva Version glosses cogently, "they shal haue ciuil warres and continual discordes among them selues."

If, in *Coriolanus,* premonitions of Rome's inevitable civic discord represent the incompatible clay, Coriolanus suggests all the strength and cruelty of that iron associated with the Roman ethos. The metal refers, according to Calvin, both to Rome's martial strength and to "the depraved nature of mankind" (I, 165). Of the four visionary beasts in the seventh chapter that symbolize the four monarchies, the Roman beast with its teeth of iron and nails of brass is truly "a monster," as the Geneva Version notes, "& colde not be compared to anie beast, because the nature of none was able to expresse it." Likewise, Shakespeare's images of Coriolanus, "a lonely dragon" (IV.i.30), combine metallic and mechanic properties to suggest something beyond simile—"a thing / Made by some other deity than Nature" (IV.vi.91–92)—not quite beast, man, or god, but shifting figuratively and morally among those possibilities:

He no more remembers his mother now than an eight-year-old horse. The tartness of his face sours ripe grapes; when he walks, he moves like an engine and the ground shrinks before his treading. He is able to pierce a corslet with his eye, talks like a knell, and his hum is a battery. He sits in his state as a thing made for Alexander. What he bids be done is finish'd with his bidding. He wants nothing of a god but eternity, and a heaven to throne in.

(V.iv.16ff.)

He is a mechanical robot, a "mailed" and grim reaper, a "thing" like the fourth beast who "devoured, and brake in pieces, and stamped the residue under his feete":

> from face to foot
> He was a thing of blood, whose every motion
> Was tim'd with dying cries.

(II.ii.106–8)

His bloody brow
With his mail'd hand then wiping, forth he goes,
Like to a harvest-man.
(I.iii.34–36)

Death, that dark spirit, in's nervy arm doth lie,
Which, being advanc'd, declines, and then men die.
(II.i.151–52)

with thy grim looks and
The thunder-like percussion of thy sounds
Thou mad'st thine enemies shake, as if the world
Were feverous and did tremble.
(I.iv.59–62)

As Calvin explains, "Neither a name nor representation could be found for it" (II, 53).[43]

In the eleventh chapter of Daniel, a detail from the angel's apocalyptic tracing of universal history symbolically captures the unnatural, inhuman quality of the Roman ethos. The king who represents the monarchy and history of Rome "shal regarde [neither] the God of his fathers, nor the desires of women, nor care for any God: for he shal magnifie him self aboue all." Religious deprivation is inextricably connected with Rome's secular failure. That women's desires shall be unregarded signifies, according to the Geneva marginalia, "that they shulde be without all humanitie: for the loue of women is taken for singular or great loue." In developing this idea, Calvin brings all the wealth of Neoplatonism to enrich the passage:

I interpret the phrase, *the desire of women*, as denoting by that figure of speech which puts a part for the whole, the barbarity of their manners. The love of women is a scriptural phrase for very peculiar affection; and God has instilled this mutual affection into the sexes to cause them to remain united together as long as they retain any spark of humanity. . . . As therefore God has appointed this very stringent bond of affection between the sexes as a natural bond of union throughout the human race, it is not surprising if all the duties of humanity are comprehended under this word by a figure of speech. It is just as if the angel had said; this king of whom he prophesies should be impious and sacrilegious, in thus daring to despise all deities; then he should be so evil, as to be utterly devoid of every feeling of charity. We observe then how completely the Romans were without natural affection, loving neither their wives nor the female sex. . . . This king, then, should cultivate neither piety nor humanity. (II, 349–50)

[43] For an excellent discussion of this martial imagery, see Traversi, *An Approach to Shakespeare*, pp. 222–31.

In these same figurative and moral terms Shakespeare exposes the failure on the natural level that is symptomatic of Rome's spiritual plight. The synecdoche for this complex of tacit moral commentary is Coriolanus's wife Virgilia who, as John Middleton Murry pointed out, has a significant role in the very fact of her subordination to the Roman matriarch Volumnia.[44] Virgilia's desires are essentially and dramatically unregarded in Rome. What this "gracious silence" (II.i.166) offers in terms of love cannot be realized in a world where the contrarieties of peace and war, of procreation and destruction, of love and hate, of good and evil, turn into morally chaotic paradoxes.

Throughout the play the warm exhilaration of human fellowship is either the prelude or the postlude to war. The peaceful hiatus then destroys all civility. Perhaps no scene in the play contains more friendly cordiality than the brief encounter between the Roman traitor and the Volscian spy who joyfully anticipate the outbreak of hostilities. The political drama almost parodies the commonplace of the therapeutic war:[45]

Let me have war, say I; it exceeds peace as far as day does night; it's sprightly, waking, audible, and full of vent. Peace is a very apoplexy, lethargy; mull'd, deaf, sleepy, insensible; a getter of more bastard children than war's a destroyer of men.

(IV.v.221ff.)

If peace "makes men hate one another," war evokes the language of love, as when Coriolanus greets Cominius on the battlefield:

> O! let me clip ye
> In arms as sound as when I woo'd, in heart
> As merry as when our nuptial day was done,
> And tapers burn'd to bedward.

(I.vi.29–32)

Aufidius echoes this sexual image when he and Coriolanus form their alliance:

> Know thou first,
> I lov'd the maid I married; never man
> Sigh'd truer breath; but that I see thee here,
> Thou noble thing, more dances my rapt heart
> Than when I first my wedded mistress saw
> Bestride my threshold.

(IV.v.113–18)

[44] "A Neglected Heroine of Shakespeare," in *Countries of the Mind* (New York: Dutton, 1922), pp. 31–50.

[45] See Kenneth Muir, "The Background of *Coriolanus*," *SQ*, 10 (1959), 137–45.

A servingman confirms that Aufidius "makes a mistress of him, sanctifies himself with's hand, and turns up the white o' th' eye to his discourse" (IV.v.196ff.).

The overtones of homosexuality indicate, as in the pathology of Chaucer's Pardoner, a spiritual perversion. In lifting man above the clay, the Roman ethos has also separated him from nature. In so far as nature is deficient and must be corrected by art, the ethos is civilizing and ennobling; but in so far as nature is the life-giving instrument of God, the ethos is destructive, perverse, and inhuman. Shakespeare's moral view of nature in *Coriolanus* lies somewhere between the complexity of *King Lear* and the simplicity of *Macbeth*. In her first scene Volumnia employs Lady Macbeth's imagery to place in grotesque opposition emblems of natural procreation and heroic aspiration:

> The breasts of Hecuba,
> When she did suckle Hector, look'd not lovelier
> Than Hector's forehead when it spit forth blood
> At Grecian sword, contemning.
>
> (I.iii.40–43)

The morality of *Macbeth*, in its dramatic environment of Christian absolutes, aligns Lady Macbeth's unnatural attitude toward love and procreation with satanic evil; the pagan environment of *Coriolanus* aligns Volumnia's pejorative comparison on the side of Roman virtue. The matriarch's very first words betray what is shown to be a hopeless conflict between the act of love and the act of honor:

I pray you, daughter, sing, or express yourself in a more comfortable sort. If my son were my husband, I should freelier rejoice in that absence wherein he won honour than in the embracements of his bed where he would show most love.

> (I.iii.1ff.)

With the concept of honor Shakespeare completes the Christian perspective of *Coriolanus*, for the complex treatment of that concept reveals at every turn, as I have tried to show, the Augustinian critique of pagan Rome's one elevating grace. That grace, however, is not a saving one; it leads to the dead end of Coriolanus alone, morally in as idiotic a relation to humanity as Macbeth. The morality of Roman honor is as paradoxical as the activity of war in which one wins that honor.[46] While

---

[46] See Paul A. Jorgensen, "Theoretical Views of War in Elizabethan England," *JHI*, 13 (1952), 469–81; and "Shakespeare's Use of War and Peace," *HLQ*, 16 (1953), 319–52.

Coriolanus represents Shakespeare's last glorification of the royal occupation, futility and death lie at the heart of that glory. We would certainly not expect Shakespeare to exclude the moral ambivalence of war from a play dealing with the descendants of Cain, not when his Henry V encountered the same moral tension even on the splendid eve of Agincourt:

I am afeard there are few die well that die in a battle; for how can they charitably dispose of anything when blood is their argument?

(IV.i.140ff.)

When Coriolanus, in the closing moments of the play, insists on the fame that should be registered of his lonely victory, the hollow glory echoes the vanity that Petrarch describes concerning "titles of warres, warfare, and Cheifteinship":

Ioy. Beying a Captayne in the warres, I am become famous with victories. *Reason.* Howe muche better were it, that beying a gouernour in peace, thou becamest famous in vertues. *Ioy.* I haue susteyned many warres. *Reason.* Thou hast bereeued thyselfe and many others of rest and quietnesse, a woorthye woorke. *Ioy.* I am famous for victories and triumphes. *Reason.* Many tymes euyll is more knowne then good, and a darke tempest more spoken of then a fayre Sunshyne day. To conclude, thou has priuided titles for thy Tumbe, talke for the people, and nothyng for thy selfe.[47]

Coriolanus is left with nothing, not even a name that can be voiced without irony. As Aufidius's mockery implies, "Coriolanus in Corioli" is an absurdity. He dies "a kind of nothing, titleless," having failed to become Rome.

In becoming the hero of revenge, Coriolanus reveals his feet of clay in terms of earlier imagery that had argued his absolute integrity. He was reluctant to appear before the Romans in the deceptive gown of humility; yet he allows his disguise in Antium to give "a false report of him" (IV.v.150)—"Lest that thy wives with spits and boys with stones, / In puny battle slay me" (IV.iv.5–6). He refused to pay the people for their good report or for their mercy, but his return to Rome intends the precise completion of a fiscal transaction based upon hate:

as many coxcombs
As you threw caps up will he tumble down,
And pay you for your voices.

(IV.vi.135–37)

---

[47] *Phisicke against Fortune*, sig. R 3.

Hate and revenge can bend the absolute Coriolanus and reconcile him to reality, but love and justice cannot. Coriolanus and
Aufidius "can no more atone / Than violent'st contrariety"
(IV.vi.73–74), says Menenius in disbelief. But enemies in war
easily atone in the spirit of hate and revenge, whereas Coriolanus, the aristocracy, and the mob fail in their Ciceronian obli-
gation "to loue, maintain, & preserue ye common attonment &
fellowship of all mankinde."[48] Coriolanus, when faced with his
mother, wife, and child, cannot break "all bond and privilege
of nature" (V.iii.25); but he cannot preserve them either. For
Calvin and St. Augustine it is impossible without true piety to
maintain "a natural bond of union throughout the human race."
And Shakespeare's Coriolanus, who according to his best lights
has "imitate[d] the graces of the gods," is as much a victim of
history as of his own infirmity.

[48] Nicholas Grimald, sig. I^v (I.xli).

Julius Caesar

Our Roman Actors

SHAKESPEARE'S Roman tragedies, as MacCallum stressed in 1910, represent an extension of themes and conflicts developed in the English history plays. For MacCallum as for Bradley, this historical aspect of the later plays was a liability working against some ideal of "free" tragedy.[1] If we reject this negative attitude, however, we can see, positively, that Shakespeare discovered in writing the English history plays a kind of moral conflict that would generate tragedy in the world of Rome. The distinction between the two realms and periods is crucial: the Christian setting of the English histories is as determinative as the pagan setting of the Roman tragedies. The moral environment in the English plays has an absolute appeal that even in the most complex political circumstances gives a moral perspective to the conflict. This absolute is admittedly an ideal, but it is an ideal capable of realization through God's beneficent providence for England. When the ideal is not operative, it is still in the background as the normative, although violated, standard of judgment. Of course the ideal is usually *not* operative, for drama demands conflict and the ideal ends all conflict. Nevertheless, as Arthur Sewell observes, "even where disorder most threatens, we have a sure expectation that it will not triumph, and the order that will shortly be established always presides over our attitudes and hopes."[2] The progression of English history, unlike that of Roman history, is toward a realization of the ideal and is therefore, as Alfred Harbage points out, a comedy.[3]

The ideal requires a Christian magistrate who is king both by fact and by right. The fact of his wearing the crown is insufficient; his right to the crown must come from beyond the Earthly City with its flux of factions and individual men. This

[1] *Shakespeare's Roman Plays and Their Background* (London: Macmillan, 1910), p. 308, et passim.

[2] *Character and Society in Shakespeare* (Oxford: Clarendon, 1951), p. 74.

[3] *As They Liked It* (New York: Macmillan, 1947), pp. 158–59.

divine sanction, interrelating the Earthly and the Heavenly cities, is ordinarily conferred by those charters of time, hereditary rights, that impose stability and order upon the mutable world. When these charters are broken, a direct intervention may finally be necessary to restore the ideal, a providential intervention—which is also, significantly, a genealogical resolution—such as we see working behind Henry Tudor, Earl of Richmond and future Henry VII.

Shakespeare's history plays are not medieval chronicles of God's control over the affairs of England. The divine order and sanction must be supported by the free will of man; otherwise he loses his freedom and brings disorder upon England and himself.[4] Richard II, on the one hand, destroys himself in his failure to uphold the order upon which his legitimacy rests. Henry V, on the other hand, maintains the order and his position even though his own sanction, because not absolute, is limited and temporary. Nevertheless, even if Richard II is a very poor king and finally collaborates in his own destruction, the loss of the divine and natural order can be restored only by a new, intervening sanction, the one Shakespeare had shown at the conclusion of *Richard III*. And *Henry V*, while it epically treats the exploits of a heroic king, still must take place in a world that begs ironic questions: the most remarkable moment of the play, Henry's prayer on the eve of Agincourt, insists that the absolute has not been attained:

> Not to-day, O Lord,
> O, not to-day, think not upon the fault
> My father made in compassing the crown!
>
> (IV.i.288–90)

The moral world of *Henry V*, a provocative critical puzzle, simply does not allow for a realization of the ideal. The epilogue clarifies explicitly that Shakespeare has not forgotten the immediate and catastrophic continuation of historical events that he had dramatized a few years earlier. And throughout the play the heroic action meets a countercurrent of questioning irony. The justification of the war with France is qualified by the expediency of the clergy in distracting the king from their wealth, by the political necessity of busying giddy minds with foreign quarrels, and by Canterbury's elaborate genealogical recitation,

[4] See M. M. Reese, *The Cease of Majesty* (London: Arnold, 1961), p. viii, et passim.

which proves Henry's lineal right to France at the same time
that it recalls his disruptive claim to England. Glimpses of the
barbaric nature of war impressively but perplexingly intrude
upon the patriotic glories of Agincourt. Shakespeare, in fact,
may be close to questioning more than the conception of the
play will allow:

> O Ceremony, show me but thy worth!
> What is thy soul of adoration?
> Art thou aught else but place, degree, and form,
> Creating awe and fear in other men?
>
> (IV.i.240–43)

Shakespeare pulls Henry back rather factitiously from this preci-
pice of Elizabethan nihilism; the speech cannot fully confront
the issue of the king's moral responsibility or this challenge to the
very idea of heroics. Perhaps this is only to say that Shakespeare
is ready to write *Julius Caesar* and, like Hamlet, to face the
vanity as well as the heat of life in "that earth which kept the
world in awe" (V.i.209). But despite these hidden undercurrents
in *Henry V*, the irony is not that evasive kind that Wayne Booth
has diagnosed in the contemporary novel, irony which allows
the author to avoid committing himself to anything.[5] Rather,
the ironic vision includes the celebration of a very great king
and a very great victory with the mature awareness that this
England is not, with all her greatness, another Eden.

When Shakespeare developed in Richard II an ideal vision
of divine right that he fails to sustain and that the "new
world" of Bolingbroke refuses to respect, the playwright was
moving into a particular realm of tragedy, the realm of *Julius
Caesar*, but not, in spite of other relationships and progressions,
the realm of *Hamlet*. *Richard II*, at least in its latter half, anticipates the Roman tragedies—tragedies of aspiration in which the
noblest Romans attempt to translate the ideal into action. They
cannot succeed because of tragic limitations not only within
their world but also within themselves. Their tragedies are assured because they have an absolute commitment to their vision.
Without it, as in Richard's agony, they are nothing.

But the potential and ideal link between the eternal and the
temporal gives the English history plays, despite tragic and
ironic moments, an entirely different moral environment from

---

[5] *The Rhetoric of Fiction* (Chicago: Univ. of Chicago Press, 1961), p.
81.

that in the Roman plays.[6] What the Bastard recognizes at the sight of the dead Arthur—that "The life, the right, and truth of all this realm / Is fled to heaven" (*King John* IV.iii.144–45)—is the unrelieved condition of the Roman world. Because the unnatural severance of ideal and reality generates the dramatic conflict in the English plays, the nature of the resulting opposition is similar in kind to that in the Roman plays. But Rome is fallen with no hope of atonement. The ideals that the tragic heroes envision, representing a humanistic and heroic desire for perfection, cannot be requited within the confines of the Earthly City.

I

Sir Thomas North's translation of Plutarch's *Lives* gave Shakespeare not only the basis of characterization and event for *Julius Caesar;* it also furnished undigested evidence to confirm the moral values implicit in the perspective of Christian historiography. Shakespeare gives coherence and purpose to what must have appeared from his more encompassing point of view to be unresolved contradictions.[7] Plutarch's investigation of the assassination and its participants is far from simplistic; nevertheless, the biographer's ultimate approval of Brutus and his republican ideals finally brings about a political endorsement of his part in the conspiracy against Caesar. In the *Lives* proper (to postpone considering the dialectic involved in "The Comparison of Dion with Brutus"), that endorsement leads to two rudimentary, though apparently unrecognized, paradoxes in which Shakespeare saw potentialities for tragedy as well as irony: (1) Plutarch sympathetically isolates his Brutus from the cruelty and violence of the assassination and from the morally impure motives of his fellow conspirators; (2) Plutarch affirms Brutus's honor and wisdom even though the killing of Caesar has no effect, other than deleterious, on Rome's political need for the rule of one man.

After noting that Brutus framed his mode of life and action

---

[6] For a further development of my contention that the comic history of England and the tragic history of Rome are opposite sides of the same coin, see the Appendix, "The Moral Environment in Shakespeare's English History Plays."

[7] For a similar instance in which apparent incoherencies in the source result in coherent complexity in the play, see my discussion of *King John* in the Appendix.

"by the rules of vertue and study of Philosophy,"[8] a fact that accounts to a great extent for Plutarch's warm admiration, the biographer establishes the Roman's nobility by citing the approval given even by the supporters of Caesar: "So that his very enemies which wish him most hurt, because of his conspiracie against *Iulius Caesar:* if there were any noble attempt done in all this conspiracie, they referre it wholly vnto *Brutus,* and all the cruell and violent actes vnto *Cassius*" (p. 1053).

This isolation of Brutus from the central fact of violent murder on the basis of noble and unselfish motivation is almost totally complete in Plutarch. Shakespeare sees the irony of this impossible separation of ideal and reality, a separation revealed in Brutus's attempt to make the act a sacrificial rite transcending and thereby obscuring the reality.[9] Not only must the ideal distract from the reality; the motivating heart must feign innocence of the action:

> And let our hearts, as subtle masters do,
> Stir up their servants to an act of rage,
> And after seem to chide 'em.
>
> (II.i.175–77)

But just as the reality of murder cries out insistently after the deed, the ritual of blood accentuating rather than alleviating the fact of blood, so the act makes merely ironic the claim of a pitiful heart:

> Though now we must appear bloody and cruel,
> As by our hands and this our present act
> You see we do; yet see you but our hands,
> And this the bleeding business they have done.
> Our hearts you see not; they are pitiful.
>
> (III.i.166–70)

The moral schizophrenia that Brutus manifests when he translates the ideal into action seems to be derived from Plutarch's inchoate paradox.

Plutarch offers other hints that there is a moral and psychological dichotomy in Brutus's nature. The account of Caesar's ambivalence towards Brutus defines these opposing forces: "Now *Caesar* . . . did not trust [Brutus] ouermuch, nor was not without tales brought vnto him against him: howbeit he

---

[8] *Lives* (London, 1595), p. 1053.
[9] See Brents Stirling, " 'Or Else This Were a Savage Spectacle,' " *PMLA*, 66 (1951), 765–74. Included in a somewhat revised form in *Unity in Shakespearian Tragedy* (New York: Columbia Univ. Press, 1956).

feared his great minde, authority, & friends. Yet on the other side also, he trusted his good nature, & fayre conditions" (p. 1056). Perhaps the major difference between Shakespeare's and Plutarch's attitudes toward Brutus lies in their estimations of Brutus's "great minde." Plutarch seems to have unqualified admiration. Shakespeare recognizes potential irony in a "great minde" conflicting so violently with a "good nature."

Though this developing irony is gradual and sympathetic, Shakespeare's final comment, when Brutus and Cassius exchange views on suicide, is unmistakably critical. In the source for this passage, North mistranslated Amyot and in the process no doubt influenced Shakespeare's conception.[10] When Brutus retracts his earlier condemnation of Cato's suicide, North accounts for the philosophical inconsistency by authorially observing that Brutus was "yet but a young man, and not ouer greatly experienced in the world" (p. 1071). Plutarch (and Amyot) intended this detail as a part of Brutus's direct reply: in other words, Brutus answers that he had objected to suicide when he was young and inexperienced but that he has changed his mind, "being now in the middest of the danger." Shakespeare dramatically accentuates the error: the retraction must indeed have appeared to him symptomatic of a man whose idealism has tended to be at odds with experience. At any rate, Shakespeare emphasizes the philosophical inconsistency by not allowing a blind Brutus to acknowledge or even to recognize his own contradiction. The playwright chooses this moment of moral incoherence to echo North's laudatory phrase "great minde":

> *Cas.* If we do lose this battle, then is this
> The very last time we shall speak together.
> What are you then determined to do?
> *Bru.* Even by the rule of that philosophy
> By which I did blame Cato for the death
> Which he did give himself—I know not how,
> But I do find it cowardly and vile,
> For fear of what might fall, so to prevent
> The time of life—arming myself with patience
> To stay the providence of some high powers
> That govern us below.
> *Cas.*   Then, if we lose this battle,
> You are contented to be led in triumph
> Thorough the streets of Rome?

[10] For an account of North's error and Plutarch's real intent, see MacCallum, pp. 184–86.

> *Bru.* No, Cassius, no. Think not, thou noble Roman,
> That ever Brutus will go bound to Rome;
> He bears too great a mind.
>
> (V.i.97–112)

If Caesar was right to fear Brutus's "great minde"—though the reason for its danger is not the same in Plutarch as in Shakespeare—there was justification for trust in his "good nature, & fayre conditions." Indeed, Shakespeare's basic dramatic problem in the material for his play must have been, rights and wrongs aside, how so gentle and good-natured a man could take part in so bloody an act. The answer for Plutarch is all to Brutus's credit: *"Brutus* preferr[ed] the respect of his country and common wealth, before priuate affection" (p. 1054). For a large segment of critical opinion, this statement encompasses Brutus's tragedy. Certainly the material lends itself to a conflict between public and private affections; and Shakespeare makes use of that conflict. But for the core of *Julius Caesar* to lie here, the friendship between Brutus and Caesar would be central; and that friendship is not, in the Jamesian sense, dramatically rendered. To be sure, Shakespeare refers to the friendship and even assumes it; but he does not develop the tragedy of a man who for the welfare of his country kills his best friend. That is another, unwritten play. Shakespeare questions Plutarch's approval not because of the preference given to public over private virtues (though admittedly after *Henry V* Shakespeare was ready for such questioning); his ironic doubt is rather directed toward Plutarch's assumption that Brutus acted with wisdom in "respect of his country and common wealth."

Creating disturbing moral ambiguities, Plutarch's second unexamined paradox reinforces Shakespeare's skepticism. Plutarch approves of Brutus despite a recognition that Rome of necessity must have an absolute ruler. Plutarch first indicates this inevitability when he comes to the civil war between Caesar and Pompey:

The citie remain[ed] all that time without gouernement of Magistrate, like a ship left without a Pilote. Insomuch, as men of deepe iudgement & discretion seeing such furie and madnesse of the people, thought themselues happy if the common wealth were no worse troubled, then with the absolute state of a Monarchy & soueraign Lord to gouerne them. Furthermore, there were many that were not affrayed to speake it openly, that there was no other helpe to remedy the troubles of the common wealth, but by the authority of one man only, that should command them all. (p. 772)

After the overthrow of Pompey's sons in Spain, Rome reluctantly makes Caesar a perpetual dictator, but for a reason quite appealing to Tudor sensibilities:

The Romaines inclining to *Caesars* prosperitie, and taking the bit in the mouth, supposing that to be ruled by one man alone, it would be a good meane for them to take breath a little, after so many troubles and miseries as they had abidden in these ciuill warres: they chose him perpetuall Dictator. This was a plaine tyranny: for to this absolute power of Dictator, they added this, neuer to be affraide to be deposed. (p. 784)

Cicero and the republicans object, of course; but here is a political and practical consideration to which Plutarch responded. By the time of Philippi, Plutarch grants that more than practical forces and considerations are at work. Thus he accounts for the coincidence leading to Brutus's final defeat, his not hearing of the victory at sea:

Howbeit the state of Rome (in my opinion) being now brought to that passe, that it could no more abide to be gouerned by many Lords, but required one onely absolute Gouernor: God, to preuent *Brutus* that it should not come to his gouernment, kept this victorie from his knowledge, though in deede it came but a little too late. (p. 1075)

The question that Plutarch does not face is how to reconcile Brutus's wisdom with his evident blindness regarding the nature and condition of the state. If "men of deepe iudgement," not to mention God, see the necessity for an absolute ruler, on what grounds could a man whose life is directed by philosophy and whose main concern is for the good of Rome kill the obvious and even the de facto choice?

One can see in Shakespeare's source other considerations that, along with practical politics and providence, urge the necessity of one-man rule. Plutarch's exploration of the corrupt Roman Republic, where nearly everyone is ambitiously struggling for power or selfish gain, affords vivid evidence of a degeneracy that explains the need for a single authority. With the exception of Brutus, all the other participants in the event oppose Caesar not because of principle but because of envy. They want to be Caesar themselves:

All [were] perswaded that [Brutus's] intent was good. For they did not certainly beleeue, that if *Pompey* himself had ouercome *Caesar*, he would haue resigned his authoritie to the law: but rather they were of opinion, that he would still keepe the soueraigntie and absolute gouernment in his hands, taking onely, to please the people, the title of Consull or Dictator, or of some other more ciuill office. And as for *Cassius*, a hot, chollericke, & cruell man, that would oftentimes be caried away from iustice for gaine: it was certainly thought that he made warre, and put himselfe into sundry dangers, more to haue absolute power and authoritie, then to defend the libertie of his country. For, they that will also consider others, that were elder men then they, as *Cinna, Marius*, and *Carbo*: it is out of doubt that the end & hope of their victorie, was to be Lords of their country: and in manner they did all confesse that they fought for the tyranny, and to be Lords of the Empire of Rome. And in contrary manner, his enemies themselues did neuer reproue *Brutus*, for any such change or desire. (p. 1066)

It goes without saying that Antony and Octavius have the same desire "to be Lords of their country." There is either going to be perpetual civil war or someone is going to be Caesar, because the tendency and desire of everyone involved—except Brutus—is to rise to the top.

"*Cassius* euen from his cradle could not abide any maner of tyrants"; but in Plutarch only Brutus "could euill away with the tyranny" (p. 1056). "In manner," as Plutarch makes clear, the republicans are fighting for the tyranny, but on the condition that they be the tyrants. This world of commodity, which must have looked so familiar to Shakespeare, affects all levels of society. The common people sell their voices and give their support in exchange for theatrical entertainment. The soldiers at Philippi can scarcely fight, so strong is their desire for the spoils. Plutarch's Brutus, like Shakespeare's, is never fully aware of the baser motives of his fellow conspirators; but Plutarch's hero, unlike Shakespeare's, is certainly no idealist regarding humanity. Brutus's handling of his soldiers is realistic almost to the point of cynicism. For example, Plutarch judges that Brutus's "only fault" was in promising his soldiers two cities to sack as an incentive to fight (p. 1075).[11] At such a passage as this, one

---

[11] Plutarch's Brutus certainly recognized that a captain must appeal to what St. Augustine would call the soldiers' carnality: "For the most part of their armors were siluer & gilt, which *Brutus* had bountifully giuen them: although in all other things he taught his Captaines to liue in order without excesse. But for the brauery of armour, and weapon, which souldiers should cary in their hands, or otherwise weare vpon their backes: he thought that it was an encoragement vnto them that by nature are greedy of honor, and that it maketh them also fight like deuils that loue to get, and be affraied to lose: because they fight to keepe their armor and weapon, as also their goods and lands" (p. 1070).

can take full measure of Shakespeare's deviation. It is easy to offer such omissions as proof of Shakespeare's approval of Brutus; but while constructing a sympathetic hero, Shakespeare is primarily eliminating all evidence that jars with his conception of a Brutus who does not understand the quite fallen condition of humanity.

Another aspect of the nature of man that Shakespeare's world view could incorporate more easily than Plutarch's and that argued for the necessity of absolute rule stands in paradoxical opposition to carnal self-interest. In spite of all protests against submission, the people of Rome and even the conspirators look to a superior for a ruler. Plutarch sees it as "a wonderfull thing, that [the people of Rome] suffered all things subiects should doe by commaundement of their kings: and yet they could not abide the name of a king, detesting it as the vtter destruction of their liberty" (p. 974). This observation is taken from the "Life of Antonius," but Shakespeare follows the passage closely for Casca's report of Antony's offering Caesar the coronet. Shakespeare understands the ambivalence of the mob far better than Plutarch does, and in the play this irony flourishes. Whereas Plutarch shows the people to be incensed that Caesar returns triumphant after his victory in Spain, Shakespeare dramatizes a heroic welcome by these same former worshipers of Pompey. The mob has its reluctance to see Caesar pronounced king, but its instinct for hero-worship will not be denied. Ironically, Caesar's refusal of the symbolic crown merely increases the mob's adulation. When Shakespeare in the central scene of the play has that voice shout to Brutus, "Let him be Caesar" (III.ii.50), the implicit is acknowledged.

Shakespeare's Brutus does not know this tendency in man or at least cannot grapple with its implications. He is, however, unwittingly the beneficiary of it, not only during his oration but within the conspiracy itself. In Plutarch the secret letters from the people are sent to Brutus by those "that desired chaunge, and wished *Brutus* onely their Prince and Gouernour aboue all other " (p. 787). In having Cassius forge these letters, Shakespeare makes a meaningful change to show Cassius's duplicity and Brutus's gullibility and to avoid suggesting the people's dissatisfaction with Caesar. Nevertheless, the play follows Plutarch in the conspirators' demand that Brutus be their leader: "Now when *Cassius* felt his friendes, and did stirre them vp against *Caesar:* they all agreed and promised to take part with him, so *Brutus* were the chiefe of their conspiracie" (p. 1057). The suggestion that Brutus, to the consternation of Cassius, becomes a Caesar within the conspiracy would have startled Plutarch. Shakespeare develops the irony mercilessly, for the law of nature—not to mention that of God and of practicality—is not to be denied, whatever man's pretentions.

As a matter of fact, Plutarch must have seen this irony, if only momentarily as "a wonderfull thing." When Brutus and Cassius meet in Sardis, "there, both their armies being armed, they called them both Emperors" (p. 1068). The translation is exact, though throughout the Middle Ages and the Renaissance there was frequently a semantic confusion between the military title *imperator* and its subsequent meaning, after Augustus adopted it, of absolute ruler. Plutarch continues immediately with the material that Shakespeare would focus into the crucial quarrel between Cassius and Brutus, the dissension that Plutarch recognized "commonly hapneth in great affaires betweene two persons, both of them hauing many friends"—between two "Emperors," in this case. Although the quarrel has no moral import for Plutarch, he does show another manifestation of this Caesar principle (if I may so designate it) when, before the battle, "*Brutus* praied *Cassius* he might haue the leading of the right wing" (p. 1072). Significantly, Shakespeare transfers this detail to Antony and Octavius: since the quarrel scene states the theme sufficiently for the conspirators' side, Shakespeare now quickly hints that the principle is inevitably operating, in momentous anticipation of later history, within the other camp.

Two paradoxes, then, permeate the source material for *Julius Caesar*, but they are not developed or reconciled with Plutarch's fundamental approval of Brutus and disapproval of Caesar. The moral attitude is more complex, however, in "The Comparison of Dion with Brutus," when Plutarch compares Brutus's act of killing Caesar with Dion's overthrow of the tyrant Dionysius. Since the Greek episode is a relatively simplistic conflict of liberty versus tyranny, the contrasting ambiguities of the Roman event must be acknowledged if not resolved. "*Dion* of both deserueth chiefest praise," Plutarch declares. First, Brutus had Cassius for "cohelper," whereas Dion had to stand alone; in fact, Cassius must even be granted "the first beginning and originall of all the warre and enterprise." Though Plutarch never allows that Cassius and the others tainted the whole conspiracy, he grants that Brutus's ideal nature was not the primary force to action and that Cassius certainly "was not comparable vnto *Brutus*, for vertue and respect of honor" (p. 1078).

More important is Plutarch's awareness that the moral nature of Caesar cannot be compared with that of Dionysius:

For *Dionysius* denyed not, that he was not a tyrant, hauing filled Sicile with such misery and calamitie. Howbeit *Caesars* power and gouernment when it came to be established, did in deede much hurt at his first entry and beginning vnto those that did resist him: but afterwardes, vnto them that being ouercome had receiued his gouernment, it seemed he rather had the name and opinion onely of a tyrant, then otherwise that he was so in deede. For there neuer followed any tyrannicall nor cruell act, but contrarily, it seemed that he was a mercifull Phisition, whom God had ordeined of speciall grace to be Gouernor of the Empire of Rome, and to set all things againe at quiet stay, the which required the counsell & authoritie of an absolute Prince. And therefore the Romaines were maruellous sorie for *Caesar* after he was slaine, and afterwards would neuer pardon them that had slaine him. (p. 1079)

Here for the only time in Plutarch is the Caesar of medieval fame, one of the Nine Worthies. The juxtaposition of Caesar with an absolutely villainous figure forces this admission. Plutarch gave a contradictory, albeit more heartfelt, evaluation in the "Life" of the man: "So [Caesar] reaped no other fruite of all his raigne and dominion, which he had so vehemently desired all his life, and pursued with such extreame daunger: but a vaine name only, and a superficiall glory, that procured him the enuy and hatred of his countrey" (p. 790). But the biographer is too much the moralist not to admit that the evident goodness of Caesar, after his being declared dictator, must qualify the perfection of Brutus. Furthermore, there is the difficulty of reconciling Caesar's generosity to Brutus with his subsequent betrayal of his benefactor—"the greatest reproach they could obiect against *Brutus*" (p. 1079). Dion, Plutarch points out, rebelled only after Dionysius had wronged him. But, like the other paradoxes, "in this point, they were contrarie together": having a "priuate cause" puts Dion's motives on the level of commodity, whereas Brutus's action must apparently be based on principle splendidly isolated from personal considerations.

The paradoxes and moral ambiguities come through clearly in Plutarch, especially when he is attempting absolute justification. That the jarring elements are not meaningfully resolved is no discredit to him. For Plutarch, Brutus's ideal was a practicable one: it had worked in the best times for Rome and Greece, and it might work again. If God finally helped to create a monarchy, it was not the result of the condition of man or the laws of nature but the necessities of a specific period of unfortunate degeneration exacerbated by a few particular men like Julius Caesar. Brutus's attempt proved futile, but it was nevertheless honorable. Except for a few tactical errors, the blame for his failure must rest entirely on the age.

The evidence in Plutarch worked for an altogether different synthesis in Shakespeare. The material of the source—Brutus's sympathetic and ideal vision struggling against the need for a Caesar and the nature of man—was comprehensible and reconcilable in terms not available to Plutarch. Shakespeare did not have Plutarch's vantage point for a complete endorsement of Brutus. But the Christian humanism of a later age offered a perspective that helped Shakespeare to create a coherent tragic experience out of the confusion and confinement of the historical moment.[12]

II

It is a commonplace of criticism that Shakespeare reveals no genuine understanding of Roman republicanism.[13] Although this observation is accurate enough, it tends to obscure the more relevant point. Plutarch offers little evidence that a vital, practicable republicanism is at stake in the conflict. Shakespeare's understanding in this case is really not called for.[14] Caesar was made dictator "neuer to be affraide to be deposed" (p. 784); some "wished *Brutus* onely their Prince and Gouernor" (p. 787);

[12] See Robert Ornstein, "Seneca and the Political Drama of *Julius Caesar*," *JEGP*, 57 (1958), 51–56. Ornstein finds in a passage from Seneca's *De beneficiis* a resolution of some of these paradoxes similar to that in the political drama of the play. Ornstein admits (p. 55, n. 9) that "an extremely careful reading of Plutarch would furnish ideas very similar to Seneca's." I think that Shakespeare gave Plutarch such a reading. The complexities of *Julius Caesar* argue against Shakespeare's imposing "Seneca's succinct and coherent analysis" onto Plutarch's material; and that material, with its tantalizing moral ambiguities, is certainly more generative and inspiring.

[13] Coleridge's dismay over Brutus's soliloquy is well known. And see MacCallum, p. 205: "Of the political theory, however, which such an one [as Brutus] would have, Shakespeare had no knowledge or appreciation."

[14] The Augustinian tradition was that no true republic had ever existed, because there had never been true justice. True justice is found only in the Kingdom of Christ. See *The City of God* II.xxi and XIX.xxi.

Pompey, had he had the chance, would have taken "the title of Consull or Dictator, or of some other more ciuill office" (p. 1066): but by whatever name, the principle of absolute monarchy was already established, even though unofficially. It was therefore ironic, as Plutarch observes, that the word *king* frightened the Romans, because "they suffered all things subiects should doe by commaundement of their kings" (p. 974). Caesar's desire for that title, "the chiefest cause that made him mortally hated" (p. 786), is the ironic complement of the people's fear. Caesar's death almost becomes a tragedy of semantics.

The historical perspective of *Julius Caesar* incorporates the power of this semantic irony. In citing an example of Caesar's wit and mastery of words, Francis Bacon elaborately explicates the linguistic paradox of "what's in a name":

Caesar did extremely affect the name of king; and some were set on, as he passed by, in popular acclamation to salute him king; whereupon, finding the cry weak and poor, he put it off thus in a kind of jest, as if they had mistaken his surname; *Non Rex sum sed Caesar:* [I am not King, but Caesar:] a speech, that if it be searched, the life and fulness of it can scarce be expressed: for first it was a refusal of the name, but yet not serious: again it did signify an infinite confidence and magnanimity, as if he presumed Caesar was the greater title; as by his worthiness it is come to pass till this day: but chiefly it was a speech of great allurement towards his own purpose; as if the state did strive with him but for a name, whereof mean families were vested; for Rex was a surname with the Romans, as well as King is with us.[15]

The etymological history in store for Caesar's name did not escape the dramatists of the Senecan tradition begun by Muret (1544):

> Plus est vocari Caesarem; quisquis novos
> Aliunde titulos quaerit, is jam detrahit.[16]

The motif is in the University play *Caesar and Pompey, or Caesars Revenge:*

> *Caesar* I am, and wilbe *Caesar* still,
> No other title shall my Fortunes grace:
> Which I will make a name of higher state
> Then Monarch, King or worldes great Potentate.[17]

[15] *The Works of Francis Bacon*, ed. James Spedding (Boston: Taggard and Thompson, 1863), VI, 160. (*The Advancement of Learning*, Book I.)
[16] Quoted by MacCallum, p. 21, n. 1.
[17] *The Tragedy of Caesar's Revenge* (1607), Malone Society Reprints (1911), sig. F 2.

And in Sir William Alexander's *Julius Caesar:*

> But Greatness to be great, must have my name,
> To be a *Caesar* is above a King.[18]

In addition to the etymological irony that could be applied post facto, many members of an Elizabethan audience would no doubt have made the same mistake that Thomas Platter made in 1599 when he referred to the titular hero of the play as "the first Emperor."[19] As D. S. Brewer notes, "the tradition that [Caesar] was Emperor died hard. Even the learned John Stow (who regarded Caesar as 'the most ambitious and greatest traytour that ever was to the Romane State') says that he had 'raigned Emperour about three or foure yeares.' "[20] Throughout the English chronicles, Caesar had been designated emperor in a very misleading translation of his military title *imperator*.[21]

Although Shakespeare's Caesar, despite his thrasonical stance, never makes the explicit boast of the Senecan Caesars, the power of the name becomes thematically functional. R. A. Foakes has observed that the name Caesar is used 211 times in the course of this relatively short play.[22] Shakespeare could be sure of his audience's perspective when Cassius ironically appeals to Brutus:

> "Brutus" and "Caesar." What should be in that "Caesar"?
> Why should that name be sounded more than yours?
>
> (I.ii.142–43)

Cassius's attempt to bring the man down to the level of frail physical nature is reversed in Caesar's attempt to lift himself to an ideal concept of Caesar. Throughout the play, and nowhere more evidently than in Caesar's words and actions, the name rises beyond the individual, titlelike; in such a context the crowd can suggest that Brutus be the next Caesar; Antony can exclaim, "Here was a Caesar" (III.ii.253).

Given the evidence in Plutarch for the necessity of one-man rule and the irony that Caesar's own name was a title of greater

[18] II.i.21–22. Reprinted in *The Tragedie of Julius Caesar*, ed. H. H. Furness, Jr., New Variorum (Philadelphia: Lippincott, 1913), pp. 317–85.

[19] See Chapter I, p. 5.

[20] "Brutus' Crime: A Footnote to *Julius Caesar*," *RES*, 3 n.s. (1952), 53. The reference is to Stow's *The Chronicles of England* (1580).

[21] See Frederic Stanley Dunn, "Julius Caesar in the English Chronicles," *Classical Journal*, 14 (1919), 273–94.

[22] "An Approach to *Julius Caesar*," *SQ*, 5 (1954), 265–66. And see Maurice Charney, *Shakespeare's Roman Plays: The Function of Imagery in the Drama* (Cambridge, Mass.: Harvard Univ. Press, 1961), pp. 70–71.

potency than "king," Shakespeare's omission of a vital, practical republicanism is historically apt. The Senate is weak enough
in Plutarch. In transferring to Brutus its responsibility for Caesar's funeral, Shakespeare omits it as an administrative body altogether. As in Plutarch, it seems only to have the power to confer
the title "king" on Caesar; and that nomination is really of no
more practical significance than Antony's symbolic offering of
the coronet. Brutus's fear of the crown is, in John Palmer's
words, "a pedantic horror of kingship."[23]

But if Shakespeare allows dramatically that the principle of
absolute rule and the title of "Caesar" are realities, the irony
of a struggle against those realities does not preclude either sympathy or tragic grandeur for Brutus. If Shakespeare had considered the murder of Caesar sheer regicide,[24] like the killing
of a king in the framework of a Christian sanction, that sympathy and grandeur would have been inconceivable. Caesar, however, has risen to the top of a purely secular hierarchy within
the frame of natural politics; and though nature itself may be
the instrument of God, His sanction is not evoked. As a result,
the vision of Brutus can appeal to another Christian ideal existing
side by side with a glorification of hierarchy, an ideal far more
potent for the Elizabethan sensibility than Roman republicanism
could ever be.

Even the most ardent proponents of a hierarchical society
acknowledged that there had once been a time when a Caesar
would indeed have been an anomaly. The perfection of God's
original creation implied this Golden Age as a logical necessity.
A godly egalitarianism, though no doubt with patristic honors
for Adam, was aborted with the Fall; then man's degeneration
necessitated authoritarian institutions and restrictive laws.[25] The
fact that this lost ideal was associated with the radical enemies
of Elizabethan orthodoxy accounts in large part for the problematic tension of sympathies in the play. The ideal, sympathetically appealing in visionary isolation, becomes a deadly force
when transposed into the sphere of action.

Behind the Anabaptists' overthrow of Münster in the early

---

[23] *Political Characters of Shakespeare* (London: Macmillan, 1945), p. 7.

[24] For so affirmative a view of Caesar see especially Virgil Whitaker, *Shakespeare's Use of Learning* (San Marino, Calif.: Huntington Library, 1953),
pp. 224–50; *The Mirror up to Nature* (San Marino, Calif.: Huntington Library,
1965), pp. 123–32; and Sir Mark Hunter, "Politics and Character in Shakespeare's *Julius Caesar*," *Trans. Royal Soc. Lit.*, 10 (1931), 109–40.

[25] For an account of sin as the cause of servitude and the social hierarchy
see *The City of God* XIX.xv.

sixteenth century was the fanatical belief that, since a liberating Christ and the Apostolic Church had supposedly reinstated this egalitarian and communistic ideal, it was the Christian's duty to work toward the establishment of Christ's kingdom on earth: "Stand fast therefore in the libertie wherewith Christ hathe made vs fre, and be not intangled againe with the yoke of bondage." "Wolde to God they were euen cut of, which do disquiet you. For brethren, ye haue bene called vnto libertie" (Galatians v: 1, 12–13). With these Pauline admonitions and in the belief that Christ's kingdom was apocalyptically at hand, temporal governments and magistrates—not to mention the Roman anti-Christ—were considered opposing forces of the devil. In England, the spirit of social reform obscured theology in the populist rebellion centering around Robert Kett in 1549, but the connection was there. Underlying the rebels' petition of grievances was one essential principle: "We pray that all bondmen may be made free; for God made all free with his precious bloodshedding."[26]

Interestingly enough, Robert's grandson, Francis Kett, would be burned as a heretic in 1589 for similarly translating spiritual truth into physical reality. As Richard Bancroft diagnosed the heresy, in his sermon at Paul's Cross in 1588/89, "All the places in the prophets which did describe the spiritual kingdom of Christ, he applied to the materiall restauration of the earthly Jerusalem."[27] This famous ecclesiastical detective in the Marprelate investigation, the future Bishop of London and Archbishop of Canterbury, was attacking the Puritan reformers, most famously Martin Marprelate. At least for polemical purposes, these opponents of the ecclesiastical hierarchy and the supremacy of the crown in religious matters were associated with typical egalitarian anarchists. Thomas Cooper, citing the example of the Jack Straw rebellion in the reign of Richard II, observes that rebels not infrequently appeal to scriptural sanctions and to that complex of ideas related to the prelapsarian Golden Age:

At the beginning (say they) when God had first made the worlde, all men were alike, there was no principalitie, there was no bondage, or villenage: that grewe afterwardes by violence and crueltie. Therefore, why should we liue in this miserable slauerie vnder these proud Lords and craftie Lawyers? &c. Wherefore it behooueth all faithfull Christians and wise Gouernours, to beware of this false and craftie policie. If this Argument passe nowe, and be allowed

---

[26] See the entry under "Robert Kett" in the *Dictionary of National Biography*.

[27] *A Sermon Preached at Paules Crosse the 9. of Februarie* (London, 1588 [i.e., 1589]), p. 7.

as good at this time against the Ecclesiasticall state: it may be, you shall hereafter by other instruments, then yet are stirring, heare the same reason applied to other States also, which yet seeme not to be touched, and therefore can be content to winke at this dealing toward Bishops and Preachers.[28]

In the Elizabethan controversy with the Puritans, the most sensational topical matter during the years of Shakespeare's London debut, one can see anticipated, as Cooper warns, the conflict only half a century away—no bishops, no king.

Shakespeare was very familiar with this extreme idealism that could be used in an attempt to sanction subversion. From Kett's rebellion in 1549, recorded in Holinshed along with Sir John Cheke's admonitory "Hurt of Sedition," Shakespeare took details for the Jack Cade episode in *2 Henry VI;* and one must acknowledge the inspiration that makes these scenes perhaps the best in the play. The rebels are fighting for liberty. As Cade tells his wavering followers, "I thought ye would never have given out these arms till you had recovered your ancient freedom" (IV.viii.25). That time was, naturally, when "Adam was a gardener" (IV.ii.129). The revolution will restore the perfect concord of equality: "All shall eat and drink on my score, and I will apparel them all in one livery, that they may agree like brothers and worship me their lord" (IV.ii.70ff.).

Shakespeare makes the orthodox condemnation: envy is the basic motive; Cade wants to be king. But paradoxically involved in this political evil is a long tradition of Christian idealism that even orthodox fears did not deny. There is ample evidence that Shakespeare responded to that idealism. John F. Danby suggests that in King Lear's regeneration during the storm the charitable prayer for all poor, naked wretches implies the nonauthoritarian ideal of Christian equality—the good society necessary for the good man in a nontragic world.[29] In *The Tempest,* more explicitly, Gonzalo's ruminative proposal (II.i.137–62) to establish the ideal commonwealth on the island—"no name of magistrate," "No sovereignty," "I" excel the golden age"—is no mere gibe at Montaigne.[30] The orthodox answer now comes glibly from the wicked Sebastian and Antonio ("Yet he would be king on't"); and the ideal is not rejected, although profoundly tempered, within the play's thematic structure.

[28] *An Admonition to the People of England* (1589), ed. Edward Arber (Birmingham, 1882), pp. 118–19.
[29] *Shakespeare's Doctrine of Nature* (London: Faber, 1949), pp. 187–89.
[30] Frank Kermode, ed., *The Tempest,* Arden Shakespeare, 6th edition (London: Methuen, 1958), pp. xxxiv–xxxviii.

Neither is the pure strain of vision in Brutus obliterated by
the envy of Cassius. Nevertheless, the taint infecting the motivation to action reinforces orthodox confidence in the need for
inhibiting worldly authority. In his temptation of Brutus in the
second scene, Cassius betrays the flaws that the orthodox Spenser
found in active egalitarianism. The communistic Giant, in Book
Five of *The Faerie Queene,* is attempting to weigh all things
in nature

> to repaire,
> In sort as they were formed aunciently;
> And all things would reduce vnto equality.

He is clearly a demagogue, attracting "fooles, women, and boys"

> In hope by him great benefite to gaine,
> And vncontrolled freedome to obtaine.

Politically his main target is the same as Cassius's:

> Tyrants that make men subiect to their law,
> I will suppresse, that they no more may raine.

Artegall, the knight of Justice, tries to educate the Giant with
reference to God's will and ordinance in the disposition of kings
and subjects, in the hierarchical principle of nature and society.
Chiefly he refutes the Giant's scales and the materialism underlying this political dissension:

> For take thy ballaunce, if thou be so wise,
> And weigh the winde, that vnder heauen doth blow;
> Or weigh the light, that in the East doth rise;
> Or weigh the thought, that from mans mind doth flow.
> But if the weight of these thou canst not show,
> Weigh but one word which from thy lips doth fall.[31]

If not a source, this is an analogue for Cassius's petulant and
unwittingly ironic comparisons:

> "Brutus" and "Caesar." What should be in that "Caesar"?
> Why should that name be sounded more than yours?
> Write them together: yours is as fair a name.
> Sound them: it doth become the mouth as well.
> Weigh them: it is as heavy.

> (I.ii.142–46)

---

[31] I have cited the Variorum text in *The Works of Edmund Spenser,* ed.
Edwin Greenlaw et al. (Baltimore: Johns Hopkins Press, 1936), V
(V.ii.xxx–xliii). For the historical background of this episode see Frederick
M. Padelford, "Spenser's Arraignment of the Anabaptists," *JEGP,* 12 (1913),
434–48; and Merritt Y. Hughes, "Spenser and Utopia," *SP,* 17 (1920), 132–46.

Cassius, like the Giant, crudely applies physical and material values because he does not acknowledge any others.[32] Caesar is a mere man and physically a weak one. Cassius thinks it as absurd to be in awe of Caesar as to be in awe of himself: they were both created equal. Opposed to Cassius's materialism, Brutus idealistically stands up against "the spirit of Caesar." This basic difference between the two conspirators can be briefly indicated by their references to Antony's profit from the new order. Cassius speaks within the limits of the conspiracy:

> Your voice shall be as strong as any man's
> In the disposing of new dignities.
>
> (III.i.178–79)

Brutus speaks to the people:

> [Antony] shall receive the benefit of his dying, a place in the commonwealth, as which of you shall not?
>
> (III.ii.41ff.)

Brutus struggles to maintain a spiritual purity in the conspirators' action, to keep it unflawed by envious materialism. He has no plans for the state beyond Caesar's death; there will be no need to provide for "new dignities" or for parliamentary action. With the elimination of Caesar, the only evil Brutus recognizes, men can live together as brothers, with reason their only law. Brutus will restore the Golden Age.

So behind Brutus's part in the assassination of Caesar is an appeal that could evoke a far deeper response in the audience than any political ideology per se. But the ideal cannot ignore the reality of the condition of man: his depravity tragically necessitates coercive authority. Even Richard Hooker, as apologist for the glory of Elizabethan order, cannot escape the ancient cause: "Howbeit, the corruption of our nature being presupposed, we may not deny but that the Law of Nature doth now require of necessity some kind of regiment, so that to bring things unto the first course they were in, and utterly to take away all kind of public government in the world, were apparently to overturn the whole world."[33] For all his humanism, Hooker understands just what the establishment of a commonwealth must presuppose: "Laws politic, ordained for external order and regiment amongst men, are never framed as they

[32] See Derek Traversi, *Shakespeare: The Roman Plays* (London: Hollis & Carter, 1963), pp. 25–27.

[33] *The Works of Richard Hooker*, ed. John Keble (Oxford: Clarendon, 1865), I, 243. (*Of the Laws of Ecclesiastical Polity* I.x.)

should be, unless presuming the will of man to be inwardly obstinate, rebellious, and averse from all obedience unto the sacred laws of his nature; in a word, unless presuming man to be in regard of his depraved mind little better than a wild beast."[34]

The most influential voices demanding obedience—for example, in the official homilies of 1547 and 1571—went to the origin of government to find a justification in man's fallen nature and God's goodness in establishing the rehabilitating benefits of civilization. Disobedience and willful rebellion repeat Adam's original crime and are instigated by the promptings of the archrebel, Satan himself. It is interesting that the single use of a Christian reference in *Julius Caesar* comes in Cassius's temptation of Brutus, clearly an archetypal scene:

> O! you and I have heard our fathers say
> There was a Brutus once that would have brook'd
> Th' eternal devil to keep his state in Rome
> As easily as a king.
>
> (I.ii.158–61)

For the homilists, Cassius exactly states the alternatives, at least for England.

Still the distinction must be made that this is Rome. Although monarchy was definitely preferred, the Elizabethans were aware of other forms of government. The choice was not between monarchy and anarchy. Tyranny, moreover, was unquestionably the worst evil a state could suffer. Hooker, while acknowledging various possibilities of government, insists only that there be an agreement between the rulers and the ruled: "without which consent there were no reason that one man should take upon him to be lord or judge over another; because, although there be according to the opinion of some very great and judicious men a kind of natural right in the noble, wise, and virtuous, to govern them which are of servile disposition; nevertheless for manifestation of this their right, and men's more peaceable contentment on both sides, the assent of them who are to be governed seemeth necessary."[35] Like Brutus, Hooker sees that "to live by one man's will" can be "the cause of all men's misery."[36] Brutus has grounds for fear, and no citations of Tudor orthodoxy can dissolve them from the dramatic tensions of the play. At the same time, neither the dramatic nor the historical

---

[34] *Ibid.,* pp. 239–40. (*Laws* I.x.)
[35] *Ibid.,* p. 242. (*Laws* I.x.)
[36] *Ibid.,* p. 243. (*Laws* I.x.)

event (at least according to the evidence in North's Plutarch) suggests an operable alternative. The evil in Rome that destroys Caesar and brings on civil war confirms the impossibility of realizing Brutus's ideal. Furthermore, Brutus becomes a genuinely tragic hero only because, paradoxically, he himself is touched by the Caesarian spirit that refuses to accept the limitations of "flesh and blood." The play develops a conflict between the good of Caesar (political order, stability, and glory), flawed by his potential evil, and Brutus's ideal of a world in which no Caesar is necessary, flawed by the nature of man.

III

Shakespeare's enigmatic representation of Julius Caesar has been justified in many ways. For George Bernard Shaw, it was a simple matter of dramaturgy: Shakespeare wrote "Caesar down for the merely technical purpose of writing Brutus up."[37] More precisely, Granville-Barker perceived that Shakespeare was dramatically committed to rendering Caesar as a public figure in order not to obscure the private nature of Brutus.[38] These practical observations, while valid, nevertheless ignore the thematic and moral difficulties created by the characterization of the titular hero. Taken in isolation, the portrayal of Caesar lends support to both sides in this Roman conflict, as the familiar history of criticism of the play shows.[39] The critics who support Caesar argue that his greatness is assumed, that on the stage his magnificence comes through indisputably, that his physical weakness merely reinforces the grandeur of his spirit. The unattractive thrasonical characteristics permit us to give Brutus the necessary sympathy while we nevertheless see his terrible error. On the other side, Caesar's denigrators can make of the same evidence a case for Brutus's worst fears. Nonpartisans insist that the representation confirms Shakespeare's impartiality.

Ernest Schanzer was the first to recognize that Caesar's moral ambiguity is a "deliberate dramatic device" relative to the moral nature of Brutus's act. But Shakespeare does not leave us with only the perplexities of moral relativity; nor does he separate,

[37] *Shaw on Shakespeare*, ed. Edwin Wilson (London: Cassell, 1961), p. 206.

[38] *Prefaces to Shakespeare* (Princeton, N.J.: Princeton Univ. Press, 1947), II, 373–74.

[39] See Chapter I, pp. 3–6, for a summary of this critical history and a comment on Schanzer's thesis, mentioned below.

as Schanzer would have it, the interest of Brutus's private tragedy from the problem play of Caesar's potentiality. In the tragedy of *Julius Caesar* the two noblest Romans confront each
other, each attempting to realize an ideal in action. The fall of
Caesar thereby creates a diptych with the experience of Brutus.
Apparent opposites, the public and the private heroes complement each other. Although the focus remains upon Brutus, the
ambiguities in his tragedy are mirrored by the reverse image
of the enigmatic Caesar.

One can find in Plutarch a generative hint for Shakespeare's
method of portraying Caesar: "This humor of his was no other
but an emulation with himselfe as with an other man" (p. 785).
This "emulation with himselfe" becomes the motivating force
behind Caesar's histrionic nature. Casca, in describing Caesar's
off-stage performance, establishes in a verbal image what becomes perhaps the major presentational image of the play:[40]

If the tag-rag people did not clap him and hiss him, according
as he pleas'd and displeas'd them, as they use to do the players in
the theatre, I am no true man.

(I.ii.257ff.)

From this most prominent figure to the least significant, *Julius
Caesar* reminds us that all the world plays the actor. Whereas
Caesar nearly succeeds in his performance, Lepidus can be
quickly dismissed:

He must be taught, and train'd, and bid go forth;
A barren-spirited fellow; one that feeds
On abjects, orts, and imitations,
Which, out of use and stal'd by other men,
Begin his fashion. Do not talk of him
But as a property.

(IV.i.35–40)[41]

The style of the play is rhetorical, but it is not "rhetoric for
rhetoric's sake."[42] With an emphasis new in Shakespeare's devel-

[40] See Maurice Charney, pp. 7–8: "I use the word 'presentational' as a convenient term for the large body of images that is not part of the spoken
words of the text, but directly presented in the theater." Charney, in turn,
follows Susanne K. Langer, *Philosophy in a New Key* (Cambridge, Mass.:
Harvard Univ. Press, 1942). See her Chapter IV, "Discursive and Presentational
Forms."

[41] See the gloss in George Lyman Kittredge, ed., *Julius Caesar* (Boston:
Ginn, 1939), p. 164: "Lepidus is not fit to be an actor in the great drama
that is going on; he can simply be one of the lifeless things used by the
real actors (Antony and Octavius) in playing their parts."

[42] Granville-Barker, II, 350. See also R. A. Foakes, p. 264.

opment, the rhetoric of the Roman actor invites comparison
with the real nature of the man. The use of theatrical imagery
becomes a means of suggesting that the actor and the man are
not the same and that the world as stage invites and even demands a taking of parts. We can no longer trust what we hear.
Brutus tells the other conspirators:

> Let not our looks put on our purposes,
> But bear it as our Roman actors do.
>
> (II.i.225–26)

They need no such advice, however. Casca, in the opening pro-
cession, repeats Caesar's orders with sycophantic pomp. When
we next see him, he is disguised: as Cassius explains, "he puts
on this tardy form" (I.ii.298). In the next scene he has dropped
that disguise in terror of celestial foreboding. John Dover Wilson suggested that the inconsistency is a sign of revision; but
the same incoherence, as it were, is in Cassius.[43] He too has a
line, on his first appearance, that shows him obsequious to Caesar. After he tempts Brutus, he admits in soliloquy that the scene
has demanded a disguise. Although in this soliloquy he even
settles into the role of the stage Machiavel, the quarrel scene
will expose a man neither the audience nor Cassius himself has
seen before. Yet with this fragmentation Shakespeare achieves
the integration of character, and Cassius has admirers as warm
as Brutus's, in spite of avowed duplicity, envy, and ambition.[44]

Antony, when he first appears dressed *"for the course,"* has
little to say and seems almost outside the drama. His second
appearance is even less impressive:

> *Caes.* See! Antony, that revels long o' nights,
>   Is notwithstanding up. Good morrow, Antony.
> *Ant.*   So to most noble Caesar.
>
> (II.ii.116–18)

[43] *Julius Caesar* (Cambridge: Cambridge Univ. Press, 1949), p. 97. See Granville-Barker, II, 362: "Cassius is by no means all of a piece, and makes
the more lifelike a character for that." But about Casca he is doubtful: "It
is all very well to say with Dowden that Casca appears in the storm with
his 'superficial garb of cynicism dropt,' and that, while dramatic consistency
may be a virtue, Shakespeare here gives us an instance of 'a piece of higher
art, the dramatic inconsistency of his characters.' " But, he continues, "what
means is the actor given of showing that this is a dramatic inconsistency?"
(p. 376). Perhaps the actor can rely upon the context of inconsistencies
in the major characters to clarify and make meaningful his own.
[44] See, for example, Sir Mark Hunter, pp. 127–31.

Obviously he is unsteady from the night before. He says not another word before Trebonius steers him out of the way before the murder. When he returns, he at last has his part to play. In the theatricality of his shaking the bloody hands he becomes distracted in genuine grief; he misses his cue. But he covers the lapse, and by the time he is on the public stage, delivering the funeral oration, he is so brilliant that one must refer to Caesar's comment that he loves the theater. Then the cold calculator of the triumvirate presents another face: is it the real one?

Of course duplicity and role-playing are facts of life, but Shakespeare's exploitation of those facts in this play points not only to the difficulty of knowing the true man but to a means of knowing and, most important for the playwright, to a method of revealing. All of the parts must be reckoned with. Even in so private a character as Portia, her magnificent role as Cato's daughter and Brutus's wife collapses into "mere woman" when she is awaiting news from the Senate. As with Caesar and Brutus, her death is a commentary upon both her aspiration and her limitations.[45] Yet her failure, like that of the two noblest Romans, does not negate the appeal to greatness. The final revelation about Portia takes account of her earlier scenes as much as Antony's action in the triumvirate involves the seemingly harmless reveler and the impassioned revenger of a friend. The mode of representation is not confined simply to the use of a deceptive persona: there is self-delusion as well as the delusion of others; emulation of one's ideal self as well as simple hypocrisy.

The theatrical imagery with which Brutus adorns the murder parallels the method of characterization. Brutus's play-acting is not for the "tag-rag people." He is interested in drama as ritual, ritual that can subsequently be used as subject matter for drama. The act is to be the outward sign of an inward and spiritual liberation:

> *Bru.* Stoop, Romans, stoop,
> And let us bathe our hands in Caesar's blood

[45] This view of Portia's tragedy can be found in Plutarch. She does not trust herself to share Brutus's secret " 'vntill that now [with the "voluntary wound"] I haue found by experience, that no paine nor griefe whatsoeuer can ouercome me' " (p. 1059). But before the assassination she is "too weake to away with so great and inward griefe of minde" (p. 1060). Portia's naiveté regarding the difference between the physical and the spiritual and, at the same time, their inextricability parallels Caesar's and Brutus's lack of self-knowledge.

Up to the elbows, and besmear our swords.
Then walk we forth, even to the market-place,
And waving our red weapons o'er our heads,
Let's all cry "Peace, freedom, and liberty!"

Cas. Stoop then, and wash. How many ages hence
Shall this our lofty scene be acted over
In states unborn and accents yet unknown!

Bru. How many times shall Caesar bleed in sport,
That now on Pompey's basis lies along
No worthier than the dust!

(III.i.106–17)

Schanzer notes that the murder scene is almost "a play within a play," but the effect is hardly that of "distancing" the action "so that we feel towards it more as we do towards 'The Murder of Gonzago' than the murder of Duncan."[46] Playgoers perhaps are not "deeply moved"; they are rather overwhelmed by the violent clashing of the ritual with the bloody reality. Nevertheless, Brutus's noble attempt prevents us from completely endorsing Antony's simplistic view of the conspirators—"these butchers!"

We can scarcely be profoundly moved by Caesar's death since of all the Roman actors Caesar is by far the greatest. We get just enough glimpse of a man behind the role to know that it is a man struggling to play a part. "He would be crown'd" (II.i.12), there is no doubt of that;[47] and we miss the point of his words and actions if we do not apprehend that they are all calculated to impress Rome with his qualifications for the part of Caesar. The hint for this unique characterization was in Plutarch, as I have suggested, but the particular theatricality that Caesar's "emulation with himselfe" takes was available in the Senecan tradition of the thrasonical Caesar that Shakespeare knew and used.[48] The Senecan tradition, however, used rhetoric

[46] *The Problem Plays of Shakespeare* (London: Routledge & Kegan Paul, 1963), p. 66.

[47] So far as I know, only Norman Rabkin ("Structure, Convention, and Meaning in *Julius Caesar*," *JEGP*, 63 [1964], 252, n. 7) has questioned Caesar's desire: "If Shakespeare wanted to justify the assassination on the grounds that Caesar would be king, one might expect stronger indication that such [a desire] indeed is the case." The matter of justification is, of course, another question; but the conspirators' fear, Antony's offering of the coronet, and Caesar's deliberative behavior all insist upon this desire for the crown.

[48] Harry Morgan Ayres, "Shakespeare's *Julius Caesar* in the Light of Some Other Versions," *PMLA*, 25 (1910), 183–227. For Shakespeare's knowledge of the Senecan Caesar see *As You Like It* V.ii.32ff. And see Joan Rees, "*Julius*

for rhetoric's sake: words are taken at their face value. Shake-speare instead adopts the old-fashioned technique of presentation to hint at the ambiguity and the unknown in the man's nature. As Brutus recognizes, only time can reveal Caesar for what he really is.

There is much to be said for the part of Caesar. He differs from Coriolanus, for example, in more than the ability to act. Casca, in describing the off-stage episode, refers to the rabble-ment in language Coriolanus might use (I.ii.245ff.), but Caesar could scarcely think of the mob in such low terms. His vision of Rome encompasses the entire city: he knows and wants the power of the people, the consent of the governed that Hooker insisted was necessary. Caesar, again unlike Coriolanus, knows instinctively the regal combination of keeping his exalted image and at the same time humbling himself as a servant of the state.

Two currents work against Caesar's intent. One is represented by Cassius's envy:

> Such men as he be never at heart's ease
> Whiles they behold a greater than themselves.
>
> (I.ii.208–9)

With all his acting skill, Caesar cannot overcome this envious opposition: to be greater than any other individual is the *sine qua non* of a Caesar. Moreover, Cassius "loves no plays," and the public show of Caesar cannot affect him. Cassius "looks / Quite through the deeds of men," as if Caesar were indeed a mere actor, failing to convince him of the reality of a perfor-mance. Caesar's analysis of Cassius, balanced and fair, corrobo-rates what Cassius has revealed of himself in his temptation of Brutus. If Caesar's motivations are wicked, Cassius cannot be duped by the show. At the same time, in refusing to be swayed by a man's public performance, Cassius cuts off the main source of knowledge whereby one man is able to know another. He must judge everyone by reference to his own nature, and there-fore his simplistic judgment of Caesar condemns himself.

The other current working against Caesar is Brutus's theoreti-cal objection to the danger of one-man rule:

Caesar—an Earlier Play, and an Interpretation," *MLR*, 50 (1955), 135–41. The tradition that the historical Caesar relished genuine acting was a *topos* to dignify the profession. Thomas Heywood, in his *Apology for Actors* (1612), mentions Caesar's delight and excellence in playing *Hercules Furens* (Scholars' Facsimiles and Reprints [New York, 1941], sig. E 3).

Th' abuse of greatness is, when it disjoins
Remorse from power; and, to speak truth of Caesar,
I have not known when his affections sway'd
More than his reason.

(II.i.18–21)

The possibility of monarchy's degenerating into tyranny cannot
be ignored, a possibility recognized by most political theorists
in the Renaissance. The passage bears careful scrutiny not only
because it expresses the main threat as Brutus sees it but also
because it establishes the test that Caesar must pass in order
to prove himself no potential tyrant. Reason, not passion, must
rule the will, so that action proceeds from the deliberations of
the rational soul and not from a sensual lust for power.

Ironically, the test comes for Caesar in the scene of his assassination. The conspirators stage an action to provoke the fatal
"act of rage" (II.i.176). Metellus Cimber kneels in mock flattery
and presents his suit to Caesar for the repeal of his brother, an
action that prompts Caesar into the posture of heroic and exqui-
site arrogance. But the arrogance of Caesar's words ought not to
obscure meaning and motivation. Thinking that he is about to be
crowned, Caesar responds to the theoretical objections that Brutus has expressed and in the very terms of Elizabethan psychology that Brutus employed:

These couchings and these lowly courtesies
Might fire the blood of ordinary men,
And turn pre-ordinance and first decree
Into the law of children. Be not fond
To think that Caesar bears such rebel blood
That will be thaw'd from the true quality
With that which melteth fools—I mean, sweet words,
Low-crooked curtsies, and base spaniel-fawning.

(III.i.36–43)

Caesar insists that he hates flattery; it will get Cimber nowhere.
Publius Cimber was justifiably banished, and that sentence will
remain in effect until there is a cause for repeal. In Brutus's
terms, the affections are not swaying more than the reason. The
alternative, to show "remorse" or pity, would under the circumstances prove that Caesar is susceptible to the swaying of affections and flattery.

After the other conspirators have joined in this unreasonable
plea, Caesar continues his argument, but now on the cosmic
level. The speech is one of the great moments of tragedy in

the *de casibus* tradition. The Senecan rhetoric for the first time becomes poetry, and one can regret that for so many critics the irony of Caesar's blindness parodies rather than heightens a tragic effect. Rather than merely being the final justification for the murder, the metaphor of the northern star has its place both poetically and politically as the one relieving image in the midst of a chaotic state without a fixed point for guidance:

> I could be well mov'd, if I were as you;
> If I could pray to move, prayers would move me;
> But I am constant as the northern star,
> Of whose true-fix'd and resting quality
> There is no fellow in the firmament.
> The skies are painted with unnumb'red sparks,
> They are all fire, and every one doth shine;
> But there's but one in all doth hold his place.
> So in the world: 'tis furnish'd well with men,
> And men are flesh and blood, and apprehensive;
> Yet in the number I do know but one
> That unassailable holds on his rank,
> Unshak'd of motion; and that I am he,
> Let me a little show it, even in this.
>
> (III.i.58–71)

It is almost "a plea," writes Derek Traversi, "an appeal to the world to support him in this self-estimate."[49] If we turn back to Brutus's soliloquy—

> he would be crown'd.
> How that might change his nature, there's the question
>
> (II.i.12–13)

—we see that Caesar dies magnificently defending himself from ever being guilty of Brutus's one reason for murdering him: he cannot change; he could not if he wanted to.

Caesar has acted out the part of an immutable Caesar, a first mover unmoved. When everyone but Brutus is at his feet and Caesar asks, "Doth not Brutus bootless kneel?" it must appear to him his moment of triumph. He is demonstrating to the cautious republican that no amount of kneeling and flattery—all that could tempt kingship—can sway him from constancy. As in Plutarch, Caesar sought "all the waies he could to make euery man contented with his raigne" (p. 785). Caesar's justification for refusing Cimber's petition, however, is entirely Shakespeare's own, as is Brutus's objection to Caesar's being crowned. Both

[49] Traversi, p. 46.

justification and objection have an Elizabethan point of reference politically, psychologically, and morally. By denying that
he has "rebel blood," Caesar literally refuses to be affected by
Cimber's flattery; morally, he denies that "affections" and passion can govern his will; allegorically, he can never overthrow
the state; anagogically, he claims to be man in his original state
of perfection.

Needless to say, we cannot accept Caesar's public image in
toto. The role of Caesar is suspect not only because the man
shows through but also because it demands an impossible isolation from the common bond of humanity. "I could be well
mov'd, if I were as you," he says and proceeds to remove himself
metaphorically from the human sphere altogether. Man does
have "rebel blood," and the materialistic view of Cassius falls
into place in the overall picture. Cassius denies the spirit, but
Caesar denies the body. Man's physical nature does hold back
the soul's struggle for perfection, and reason can work only
with the "apprehensions" of the senses. Caesar's posture of immutability is ironic because absolute constancy demands indeed
the incorruptible essence of the northern star, and Caesar is
about to prove vividly that he is "flesh and blood." The Caesar
that he wants to be is ironically like the Caesar Brutus wants
to kill:

> We all stand up against the spirit of Caesar,
> And in the spirit of men there is no blood.
> O that we then could come by Caesar's spirit,
> And not dismember Caesar!
>
> (II.i.167–70)

Caesar's fall implies a personal tragedy, but Shakespeare develops the personal tragedy only in Brutus. The flaws in the two
men, however, are the same: they have ever but slenderly known
themselves. Brutus's tragic failure will be treated in the next
section, but the relation of Caesar's characterization to the moral
nature of Brutus's act can be anticipated. The potentiality for
evil in Caesar is very real, all the more since he so arrogantly
and unnaturally insists that no such potentiality exists. If that
potentiality had not existed in Brutus, the conspirators, and the
rest of the Roman state, the removal of Caesar would have been
as justifiable as Richmond's removal of Richard III. Instead, Brutus destroys the representative of one impossible ideal for the
sake of another. Caesar's ideal requires the perfection of one man;
Brutus's requires the perfection of all.

IV

The classical injunction *nosce teipsum* scarcely needed to be recalled to any educated man in 1599, but Shakespeare was evidently influenced in *Julius Caesar* by a reading of Sir John Davies's poem, which was registered on April 14 of that year. Recent editors have agreed with Malone that there is a verbal parallel between the following dramatic exchange and the lines of *Nosce Teipsum* quoted below:[50]

> *Cas.* Tell me, good Brutus, can you see your face?
> *Bru.* No, Cassius; for the eye sees not itself
> But by reflection, by some other things.
> *Cas.* 'Tis just;
> And it is very much lamented, Brutus,
> That you have no such mirrors as will turn
> Your hidden worthiness into your eye,
> That you might see your shadow.
> . . .
> Therefore, good Brutus, be prepar'd to hear;
> And since you know you cannot see yourself
> So well as by reflection, I, your glass,
> Will modestly discover to yourself
> That of yourself which you yet know not of.
> (I.ii.51–70)

The relationship between the poem and the play is paradoxically increased by the fact that the philosophical image as used in the two works creates diametrically opposed implications: Cassius wrenches the image from its proper context to further his secret intent. Even though the commonplaces in these passages scarcely need pointing out, their thematic centrality has never been fully appreciated.[51] In his first step toward enlisting Brutus in the conspiracy, Cassius perverts the traditional metaphor for the rational soul's means of attaining self-knowledge. The proper context for the metaphor is to be found in *Nosce Teipsum*, in

[50] See T. S. Dorsch, ed., *Julius Caesar*, Arden Shakespeare (London: Methuen, 1955), pp. x–xi. The stanzas of *Nosce Teipsum*, quoted below, are cited from the facsimile of the 1599 edition reproduced in *The Poems of Sir John Davies*, ed. Clare Howard (New York: Columbia Univ. Press, 1941), pp. 117, 121.
[51] That the commonplaces are in need of fresh examination is shown by Paul A. Jorgensen, *Lear's Self-Discovery* (Berkeley, Calif.: Univ. of California Press, 1967). His brief comments on *Julius Caesar* (pp. 56–59) corroborate my view of Brutus, though he deals with only a limited aspect of the play and does not mention the image I am discussing.

a passage that shows the incoherence of the image when pursued
too far on the literal level. The poet is puzzled by man's inor-
dinate desire to know the external world and his reluctance to
know himself:

> [Is it] because the minde is like the eye,
>   (Through which it gathers knowledge by degrees,)
> Whose rayes reflect not, but spread outwardly,
>   Not seeing it selfe, when other things it sees?
>
> No doubtlesse, for the minde can backward cast
>   Vpon her selfe, her vnderstanding light;
> But she is so corrupt, and so defac't,
>   As her owne image doth her selfe affright.

True knowledge can come only from an inner, spiritual vision:

> Mine *Eyes*, which [view] all obiects nigh and farre,
>   Looke not into this litle world of mine,
> Nor see my face, wherein they fixed are.
>
> Since *Nature* failes vs in no needfull thing,
>   Why want I meanes mine inward selfe to see?
> Which sight the knowledge of my selfe might bring,
>   Which to true wisedome is the first degree.
>
> That *Powre* which gaue me eyes the world to view,
>   To view my selfe enfus'd an inward light,
> Whereby my *Soule* as by a mirror true,
>   Of her owne forme may take a perfect sight.

Joseph Hall, in his "Character of the Wise Man," deserves quot-
ing, for he maintains the literal eye image and comes up with a
delightfully garbled metaphor: "Both his eyes are never at once
from home, but one keeps house while the other roves abroad
for intelligence."[52] Cross-eyed or not, Hall's wise man has
self-knowledge.

For the Christian, the humanistic command becomes a matter
of salvation. At the opposite extreme from the humanist's pride,
John Calvin cites the Socratic dictum as an overture to his attack
on the degeneration of man's reason and will in the second book
of the *Institutes of the Christian Religion*. The original pagan
injunction, insists Calvin, was given in order that man know
"his own dignity and excellence: nor do they wish him to con-
template in himself anything but what may swell him with vain
confidence, and inflate him with pride." If man truly looks
within himself, he sees "a view of our miserable poverty and

---

[52] *Heaven upon Earth and Characters of Vertues and Vices,* ed. Rudolf
Kirk (New Brunswick, N.J.: Rutgers Univ. Press, 1948), p. 147.

ignominy, which ought to overwhelm us with shame." Man,
however, loves to be flattered; he is happy to think he has found
self-knowledge in vanity, "the most pernicious ignorance."[53]
Calvin, of course, denied man's rational soul any dignity at all.
But even Christian humanists did not question man's fallen nature, and indeed argued that the first step in the right use of
reason was to recognize that fact. For Elyot, Hooker, Spenser,
Davies, and the whole train of optimistic faculty psychologists,
man could go far to reerect his reason by understanding the
treacherous intricacies of the vegetable, sensitive, and rational
powers. Man needed to be aware of the liabilities of the imagination, of those "apprehensions" that could incite passion without
the mediation of reason. He had to recognize that man's will,
inclining toward evil, tended to operate without the approba-
tion of judgment. If the condition of man did not warrant Calvin's pessimism, a knowledge of man's evil tendencies and of
his ultimate limitations was sufficient to avert pride.

Shakespeare was obviously impressed by the thematic and dramatic possibilities of the eye-mirror metaphor. In *Troilus and
Cressida* Ulysses uses the same argument to dupe Achilles as
Cassius uses with Brutus (III.iii.95–123). This wrenching of
orthodoxy parallels Ulysses' earlier appeal to traditional concepts
of order for merely politic purposes.[54] Like Cassius with Brutus,
Ulysses would convince Achilles that a man can know himself
only through the eyes of others; Ulysses goes a step further
and asserts that public evaluation indeed creates a man's worth.
The argument is central to both plays. Certainly it is the deciding
factor in Brutus's tragic development. Before Cassius's manipulation begins, Brutus explains his recent melancholy in terms of
the eyes:

> If I have veil'd my look,
> I turn the trouble of my countenance
> Merely upon myself.
>
> (I.ii.37–39)

And he interrupts Cassius's strategy with a seeming irrelevancy:

> Into what dangers would you lead me, Cassius,
> That you would have me seek into myself
> For that which is not in me?
>
> (I.ii.63–65)

[53] *Institutes of the Christian Religion*, trans. John Allen, 7th edition (Philadelphia: Westminster Press, 1936), I, 265–67.
[54] See the discussion of *Troilus and Cressida* in L. C. Knights, *Some Shakespearean Themes* (London: Chatto & Windus, 1959), pp. 66–74.

Although Brutus has been caught in a metaphorical maneuver, this humble response, which contrasts so drastically with the later Brutus, shows his awareness of where the search for self-knowledge must be made. But, as Calvin insisted, all men are soothed by flattery, and Cassius's protestation that he is not flattering (ll. 71–78) clinches the point. The letters that Cassius forges continue his policy with the same perversion of *nosce teipsum:* " 'Brutus, thou sleep'st. Awake, and see thyself.' " Brutus's followers, with their adulation and malleability, increase his ideal image of himself as much as the followers of Caesar increase his. In the tragic world of the play, both Brutus and Caesar suffer from the lack of self-knowledge that Shakespeare was contemporaneously concerned with in the comic world of *As You Like It*. With the same philosophical image and motif (but used correctly), Rosalind punctures the idealistic pretentions of Silvius and his scornful, proud Phebe:

> 'Tis not her glass, but you, that flatters her;
> And out of you she sees herself more proper
> Than any of her lineaments can show her.
> But, mistress, know yourself.
>
> (III.v.54–57)

As when Decius flatters Caesar, Cassius gives Brutus's "humour the true bent." Brutus knows what Cassius has in mind and has been "with himself at war" over the potential danger of Caesar. Killing him is obviously one means of aborting that potential. The temptation scene does not quiet Brutus's uncertainty, but it indicates what the outcome will be. An irrational influence has entered to resolve the internal conflict. I would deny that Brutus has made a definite decision before his famous soliloquy or even during it. The first line—"It must be by his death"—states not determination but a horrible philosophical premise. The soliloquy attempts to hover at the theoretical level; as the argument moves to the conclusion, the verbs are the calculating imperatives of an impersonal proposition:

> So Caesar may.
> Then, lest he may, prevent. And, since the quarrel
> Will bear no colour for the thing he is,
> Fashion it thus.
>
> (II.i.27–30)

When taken with what follows, the soliloquy suggests no firm commitment, though with Cassius we can see that "three parts of him" are resolved. Afterwards, Lucius brings in the forged petition with its request for Brutus to " 'Speak, strike, redress!' "

> Am I entreated
> To speak and strike? O Rome, I make thee promise,
> If the redress will follow, thou receivest
> Thy full petition at the hand of Brutus!
>
> (II.i.55–58)

Even here one must observe the tragic *if*. In a few moments, when he remonstrates against the conspirators' taking an oath, the conditional word will have disappeared without any new consideration:

> What need we any spur but our own cause
> To prick us to redress?
>
> (II.i.123–24)

Between these two passages and before the arrival of the conspirators, the internal war still rages. Then, with "the choice and master spirits of this age" around him, Cassius repeats the seduction motif:

> no man here
> But honours you; and every one doth wish
> You had but that opinion of yourself
> Which every noble Roman bears of you.
>
> (II.i.90–93)

Brutus then gives Cassius his firm commitment in an interchange of whispers, while the others reveal their ignorance of true direction and the sun, appealing profoundly to our poetic imaginations with inconsequential talk.[55]

Brutus is prevented from following his true philosophic bent and above all the command *nosce teipsum*. He thinks that he has found self-knowledge in vanity, as Calvin would say of him. Shakespeare, however, sees Brutus as tragic, not damned. He is left with the overwhelming sense of Caesar's potential evil, which in his insistence upon certainty of reason becomes *realized* evil. Having focused all of the evil in his world on this one figure, Brutus disassociates "the spirit of Caesar" from the bond of humanity as much and as falsely as Caesar does. In the flattering eye of Rome Brutus becomes perfect; he can therefore see neither his own nor the others' flawed nature. When Caesar is rooted out, so localized is the state's corruption that even Antony will either be regenerated or die.

---

[55] Pointed out by Harold C. Goddard, *The Meaning of Shakespeare* (Chicago: Univ. of Chicago Press, 1951), pp. 316–17.

But Brutus would be Plutarch's philosopher still, though his imagination (to cite Robert Burton), being "apprehensive, intent, and violent," has misinformed the heart. Assuming the virtue that he suspected in Caesar, "Brutus reasons his way through life, and prides himself upon suppressing his emotions."[56] To justify every move he urges the infallibility of his reasons. Even the magnanimous treatment of Antony after the murder is a result of Brutus's assuming in the reveler the same priority of reason over emotion that he assumes in himself, a priority that is indeed an unnatural dissociation of reason from emotion:

> Our reasons are so full of good regard
> That were you, Antony, the son of Caesar,
> You should be satisfied.
>
> (III.i.225–27)

He sees no danger in the Roman mob because it likewise must respond to this appeal; so he overrides Cassius's fears and permits Antony to speak:

> I will myself into the pulpit first,
> And show the reason of our Caesar's death.
>
> (III.i.237–38)

Not understanding the power and significance of passion, he even allows Antony to have the last word. He feels free to leave, so confident is he that the mob's reason can withstand all "idle wind."

Brutus intends in his oration to make a rational appeal. "Be patient till the last," he begins, cautioning against emotional outbursts of the kind Antony integrates so skillfully into his performance. He urges the people to alert their minds so that they "may the better judge," though actually they need be no more alert than to hear Brutus's *ipse dixit:* "Believe me for mine honour, and have respect to my honour, that you may believe." But his simplistic and general assertions undermine his argument. The absolute moral certainty, which he did not have in the soliloquy, becomes as unreasonable and emotional as the absolute certainty of any politician who cannot afford to question either his own right or his opponent's wrong: "Who is here so base that would be a bondman? If any, speak; for him have I offended. Who is here so rude that would not be a Roman? If any, speak; for him have I offended. Who is here so vile that will not love his country? If any, speak; for him have I

[56] Granville-Barker, II, 358.

offended. I pause for a reply" (III.ii.27ff.). The mob is as impressed by Brutus's profession of infallibility as it was by Caesar's; therefore Brutus can now be the Caesar.

Even though the mob's response is more to the man than to the argument, one cannot ignore the charge of Caesar's ambition. For the Renaissance, Caesar was the inevitable *exemplum* of that vice, and the dramatization of the character attempts no refutation. Antony's approach is therefore prepared: Caesar was not ambitious, he was magnanimous. Although Antony's oration is consciously directed to the emotions, he offers as much reason as Brutus, perhaps more. At least Antony cites specific actions and details for support, whereas Brutus's argument, like his vision, fails to reckon with facts.

It was a Renaissance commonplace derived from Cicero's *De officiis* that the vice of ambition corresponds to the virtue of magnanimity.[57] As in Shakespeare generally, the commonplace offers a source of dramatic tension, not a simple resolution. Antony admits that, if Caesar was ambitious, "it was a grievous fault"; then, by ignoring any possible discrepancy between motive and act, Antony creates an entirely magnanimous Caesar. All was done for Rome, not for Caesar. Under the circumstances, that seems as reasonable as to insist that all was for Caesar, not for Rome. Who can determine the point at which such a virtue becomes a vice? We have to accept Antony's word until he refers to an episode within the framework of the play, and then we see that his view is as falsely simplistic as Brutus's:

> You all did see that on the Lupercal
> I thrice presented him a kingly crown,
> Which he did thrice refuse. Was this ambition?
>
> (III.ii.95–97)

We know the episode from Casca's point of view, hardly unbiased; but still we could never accept the plebeian's assurance:

> Mark'd ye his words? He would not take the crown;
> Therefore 'tis certain he was not ambitious.
>
> (III.ii.112–13)

[57] See, for example, Sir Thomas Elyot, *The Boke Named the Governour* (1531), ed. Foster Watson (London: Dent, 1907), pp. 243–46 (III.xvi). It is interesting that Brutus seems to typify the other "familiar vice folowinge Magnanimitie": "Obstinacie is an affection immoueable, fixed to wille, abandonynge reason, whiche is ingendred of Pryde, that is to saye, whan a man estemeth so moche hym selfe aboue any other, that he reputeth his owne witte onely to be in perfection, and contemneth all other counsayle" (III.xv, p. 242).

The answer to Antony's question is both yes and no, with the relative weight of the answers an unknown factor. Antony obviously has taken at face value the role of Caesar; but that is as reasonable as to ignore all action with the blithe assurance that hidden motives are simple and knowable. Antony's first coup, therefore, is to overthrow the infallibility of Brutus's reason:

> O judgment, thou art fled to brutish beasts,
> And men have lost their reason!
>
> (III.ii.104–5)

The plebeian grants his point: "Methinks there is much reason in his sayings."

Neither Brutus's nor Antony's version is acceptable. Each claims absolute justification in a matter where absolutes fail. Antony, of course, is concerned only with his love for Caesar and himself. He forfeits his claim on our moral sympathies after instigating the civil strife he predicted. Reason and absolutes do not concern him. But Brutus is committed to the conviction that he is right, and it is the essence of his ideal that Antony and all men will be able to agree with him. Were he correct in this assessment, the "redress" would indeed be complete. The irony is that not passion alone overthrows the plan, for Antony appeals to reason as much (or as little) as Brutus does. Brutus's abstractions, generalizations, and assumptions crumble in the material fact of a piece of paper. Caesar's will speaks to the senses and the passions, but it is real.

When we next see Brutus, the inevitable disillusionment has begun. The failure of Rome to support him in his estimation has made his perfection and that of his fellow conspirators all the more crucial: Antony and Octavius must be the traitors, not they (V.i.56–57). But the exigencies of war scarcely afford an environment for moral perfection. Plutarch's Brutus supplied his army by making moderate levies on the citizens of captured towns and by receiving a share of Cassius's outrageous extortions: he is, in short, realistic. The demand for absolute moral purity is only in Shakespeare. With appropriate irony, the most practical consideration in all public action—money—leads Brutus for the first time to question Cassius's moral nature. Brutus is indignant, Cassius becomes angry, and they quarrel. The tensions of the thematic structure converge with the psychological tensions of the two men; and the scene, as Coleridge perceived, is an imaginative triumph.

The section before the entrance of the poet (IV.iii.1–122) is bipartite in the structure of its moral point of view. Over the matter of Lucius Pella's corruption, Brutus's indignation, morally unimpeachable, rises to a climax in lines 66–69:

> There is no terror, Cassius, in your threats;
> For I am arm'd so strong in honesty
> That they pass by me as the idle wind,
> Which I respect not.

The claim of perfection in this burst of Caesarian rhetoric is preceded by the charge that Cassius is no better than Caesar. The angry Cassius, brushing aside Brutus's moral severity, claims a superiority in practical affairs that must be allowed to take precedence. Brutus cannot permit such an assertion. Indignation turns to anger, and his passion rises even while his argument is that Cassius's passion cannot disturb him. And he must challenge Cassius's claim:

> *Bru.* You say you are a better soldier.
>   . . .
> *Cas.* You wrong me every way; you wrong me, Brutus;
>   I said an elder soldier, not a better.
>   Did I say "better"?

With that last pathetic question, Cassius's world picture shatters. All men are not equal: the cause is both in his stars and in himself that he is an underling. As if to clarify this point, his present subjection is compared with his earlier subjection to Caesar:

> *Cas.* When Caesar liv'd, he durst not thus have mov'd me.
> *Bru.* Peace, peace! You durst not so have tempted him.
> *Cas.* I durst not?
> *Bru.* No.
> *Cas.* What, durst not tempt him?
> *Bru.*   For your life you durst not.

Cassius cannot let this accusation and its exposure of his delusion stand; his anger flickers in a threat. But he collapses before Brutus's posture of invulnerability.

Then, suddenly, at the very moment that Brutus's Caesarian claim of perfection is made, Shakespeare exposes the tragic blindness:

> I did send to you
> For certain sums of gold, which you denied me;
> For I can raise no money by vile means.

Still Cassius cannot reassert himself. He may know that "this
sober form . . . hides wrongs," but Brutus's presumption is too
powerful to be denied. Cassius is "check'd like a bondman"
(IV.iii.96). As several commentators have observed, the Caesarian principle of authority has been established within the
frame of the conspiracy.[58] Brutus's absolute rule was implied
from the beginning, but here for the first time he imperiously
overthrows a rival's assertion of superiority and even of equality.
It is not surprising that we hear echoes of Caesar:

> wrong I mine enemies?
> And, if not so, how should I wrong a brother?
>   (IV.ii.38–39)
>   Know, Caesar doth not wrong.
>   (III.i.47)

A distinction must be made, however. Brutus consciously plays
no role but rather acts in accord with his mistaken knowledge
of himself. The true self, which remains like a norm, will not
deny Cassius's appeal to love, and in the reconciliation Brutus
ignores moral absolutes. When the poet enters, Brutus cannot
tolerate the suggestion of flaws in the leadership, and the unattractive imperiousness rises again; but the Brutus of immeasur-
able worth returns in his admission, to Cassius, of grief for the
death of Portia. Shakespeare perhaps stumbled in juxtaposing
this poignance with Brutus's response to Messala's news of her
death, but I think it clear that Shakespeare wanted to extend
these meaningful alternations in Brutus's manner. On the private
level of love, Brutus has indeed an ideal nature. In his love of
Portia, Lucius, and Cassius he manifests that sense of equality
through charity that might well transform the age of iron back
into gold.[59] When he translates himself to the public stage, however, he must stoically suppress love, pity, and all other emotions. This is not to accept G. Wilson Knight's uncritical glorification of love as the absolute in the play, an absolute manifested

[58] Sir Mark Hunter, p. 132; Goddard, pp. 312, 324. See especially Gordon
Ross Smith, "Brutus, Virtue, and Will," *SQ* 10 (1959), 367–79; and Norman
Rabkin, pp. 240–54. MacCallum refers to Brutus as "the spiritual dictator"
(p. 266).
[59] Compare Casca's hope that Brutus can act as the alchemist to remove
all impurities in the conspiracy: "And that which would appear offence
in us / His countenance, like richest alchemy, / Will change to virtue and
to worthiness" (I.iii.158–60).

by Cassius and Antony.⁶⁰ Cassius, for example, tends to be merely sentimental:

> *Cas.* You love me not.
> *Bru.*   I do not like your faults.
> *Cas.* A friendly eye could never see such faults.
> *Bru.* A flatterer's would not.
>
> (IV.iii.88–90)

Love such as Cassius intends does obscure the rational soul and can be no more satisfactory a moral guide than Antony's love of Caesar was for him. Brutus and Caesar, however, fail at the opposite extreme. By demanding the constancy of reason, they make the Stoic's mistake of refusing to acknowledge the proper function of passion and feelings. The Christian tradition rejected such a conception of reason as "the Stoic's pride."⁶¹ Brutus, in the name of reason, must ignore his pity for Caesar, as he must ignore his love for Cassius and even Portia when public duty calls for his perfection. The moral incoherence grows until, at Messala's revelation of Portia's death, Brutus is for the first time as impenetrably an actor as Caesar.⁶² After playing the Stoic's part and thus belying those true feelings he has revealed to Cassius, the man of reason is once more in stride. "Good reasons

⁶⁰ *The Imperial Theme* (London: Oxford Univ. Press, 1931), pp. 32–95.

⁶¹ For St. Augustine's important critique of the limitations of Stoicism, see *The City of God* IX.iv–v and XIV.viii–ix. From the Christian point of view, the "affections" arising from charity, especially compassion and mercy, are good, and the Stoic's overweening trust in human reason is insidious. Christians are not to be Stoics any more than Epicureans, for St. Paul had disputed with both (Acts xvii). For a good discussion of the revival of Stoicism in the sixteenth century, see Rudolph Kirk's introduction to his edition of Justus Lipsius, *Two Bookes of Constancie*, trans. John Stradling (New Brunswick, N.J.: Rutgers Univ. Press, 1939), pp. 3–56. But see Henry W. Sams, "Anti-Stoicism in Seventeenth- and Early Eighteenth-Century England," *SP*, 41 (1944), 65–78.

⁶² Lacking bibliographical evidence, editors have generally assumed that the revelation in the scene with Messala was, after revision, imperfectly deleted in the printer's copy. See W. W. Greg, *The Shakespeare First Folio* (Oxford: Clarendon, 1955), 289–90; C. J. Sisson, *New Readings in Shakespeare* (Cambridge: Cambridge Univ. Press, 1956), II, 189–90. Brents Stirling, however, has offered persuasive bibliographical evidence of revision and, ironically, argues that the "new evidence for addition actually makes deletion less plausible than before" (p. 194). See his "*Julius Caesar* in Revision," *SQ*, 13 (1962), 187–205. For attempts to show that the Folio reading is appropriate to Brutus's character, see MacCallum, p. 242; John Palmer, pp. 55–56; Warren D. Smith, "The Duplicate Revelation of Portia's Death," *SQ*, 4 (1953), 153–61; and Brents Stirling, "Brutus and the Death of Portia," *SQ*, 10 (1959), 211–17.

must, of force, give place to better" (IV.iii.201), he declares, sending them to Philippi.

MacCallum observed that "the idea of Caesarism" dominates the latter half of the play; but that idea is more inclusive than he allowed, more than "the rule of the single master-mind," which Shakespeare sees as "the only admissible solution for the problem of the time" and against which Brutus imposes "mistaken and futile opposition."[63] The idea is more of a principle operating to some degree in all men, and it has several aspects. In its most glorious manifestation, it is the heroic aspiration that refuses to accept the limitations of human nature and strives for a perfection that cannot in reality exist. In this attempt the hero is like Sir Philip Sidney's poet who shows "the force of a divine breath" when "he bringeth things foorth surpassing [Nature's] doings: with no small arguments to the incredulous of that first accursed fall of *Adam*, since our erected wit maketh us know what perfection is, and yet our infected wil keepeth us from reaching unto it."[64] Caesar and Brutus, however, refuse the limitation of the will and insist upon translating vision into action. That translation then leads to the ignoble aspect of Caesarism: since the aspirer cannot in reality attain the ideal, he must either accept himself as less or, because that is incompatible with his nature, finally pose as the ideal. His true nature, left as it were unguarded, is then susceptible to all the ruling passions; his refusal to know himself leaves him tragically vulnerable.

On a lower level of man, the principle operates as a desire to be free from the restraint of any superior, for the liberty that, as for Spenser's Giant, is really licentiousness and must be checked. Cassius with his liberty merely attempts to gather the "dignities" and spoils. Such a rebellious and envious nature demands restraint. Significantly, the words that Antony relays to the conspirators account for his own apparent harmlessness before Caesar's death:

> Say I love Brutus, and I honour him;
> Say I fear'd Caesar, honour'd him, and lov'd him.
> (III.i.129–30)

The element of "fear"—of reverence and awe—is necessary for such as Antony and Cassius, and one must acknowledge that

---

[63] MacCallum, p. 214.
[64] "The Defence of Poesie," *The Complete Works of Sir Philip Sidney,* ed. Albert Feuillerat (Cambridge: Cambridge Univ. Press, 1923), III, 8–9.

only in their charitable subjection to Caesar and to Brutus, respectively, do they seem to realize their best natures.

There is no moment of recognition for Brutus. The confusion grows and with it his disillusionment, but that disillusionment is with the world, not with his ideal. He is determined to die rather than to accept less, certainly not the image of supreme bondage that Cassius evokes—their returning manacled to Rome. With no self-awareness, philosophical constancy and moral absolutes evaporate at this emotional affront to his vision of perfect freedom for himself and his city (V.i.97–112). The play does make a strange pause at the appearance of Caesar's ghost, as though Shakespeare sensed that the character of Brutus might develop in another way by recognizing his fallen nature. When the ghost identifies itself as "thy evil spirit," Brutus replies: "Ill spirit, I would hold more talk with thee" (IV.iii.286). Shakespeare, with no authority in Plutarch, identifies the spirit of Caesar, the spirit that Brutus wanted to destroy, with Brutus himself. Those qualities in Caesar that had caused Brutus to kill him—the attempted isolation from humanity, the presumptuousness, the potentiality for evil—are in Brutus. His full recognition of this spirit, however, would remove us from Shakespeare's pagan world. Like Coriolanus, Brutus must continue to behold himself only in the eyes of Rome.

Shakespeare chose, instead of having Brutus see the enemy within, to have the man refuse, indeed to be incapable of, recognition. If the tragedy is about a man who out of mistaken motives murders his best friend, Brutus's end is not morally satisfactory.[65] Nor is it satisfactory if the tragedy is about a man who, out of mistaken motives, murders a good and great king. Virgil Whitaker, who subscribes to this view of Caesar, insists that "the most serious weakness of the play from the point of view of moral exposition is undoubtedly Brutus's own failure to recognize the enormity of his mistake."[66] Sir Mark Hunter, who shared Whitaker's opinion of Caesar, went so far as to say that the play has no tragic hero.[67] But these two critics have imposed upon the play a conflict that the pagan setting does not support. The full impact of the tragedy comes only if we, like Brutus at the beginning of the play, see the potentiality for evil in the spirit of Caesar. But Brutus cannot stop that spirit because he is infused with it himself in all of its paradoxical glory. "The

[65] So Granville-Barker concludes (II, 359–60).
[66] *The Mirror up to Nature*, p. 132.
[67] Sir Mark Hunter, pp. 114–15.

enormity of his mistake" springs from an aspiration to transcend the realities of man's imperfections, from a desire to live in a world where no potentiality for evil exists. To demand a moral recognition is, in Shakespearean terms, to ask for a tragedy with a Christian setting. Brutus and Caesar with true self-knowledge could not remain themselves. It was their aspiration that made them the noblest Romans and earned their place in Shakespeare's House of Fame.

Brutus was wrong to murder Caesar because, whatever Caesar's inherent danger, Antony, Cassius, Casca, and all down to the last plebeian need him. He is the Caesar that Christ insisted must have his due, the Caesar that St. Paul demanded his followers to obey, even as a punishment for man's sins. Brutus cannot accept that, for he cannot accept man's fallen nature. And, indeed, Brutus's virtue and his aspiration are so appealing that at times we can share his vision of a nonauthoritarian Golden Age. The imaginative possibility of Brutus's commonwealth seems very real, since "our erected wit maketh us know what perfection is." Our tragic sense is stirred by the awe and terror of having to accept, and of admiring someone who refused to accept, "our infected wil."

Antony and Cleopatra

New Heaven, New Earth

HE CRITICAL EQUILIBRIUM that must be maintained between words and action is very difficult to
achieve in *Antony and Cleopatra*. "Kneel down, and
wonder!" has been the injunction since Coleridge's happy remarks on the play's captivating poetry, and few have resisted.
As a result, no play in the canon has been more vulnerable to
the danger of poetic analysis unqualified by dramatic actualities.
The danger has been compounded in that the dramatic structure
of *Antony and Cleopatra*, while ably defended under the inspiration of Granville-Barker, is more often viewed as a pattern
of poetry or even music rather than as something resembling a
plot.[1] And in poetry as in music it is easy to accentuate the most
romantically appealing themes. Drama, grounded by what happens, insists finally upon what men do even more than upon
what they say. The plot, as Aristotle affirmed, is the soul of
the drama; it reveals the characters in action.

The poetry is enough to upset the procedures of even the best
critics: "To do justice to Shakespeare [in *Antony and Cleopatra*], we must radically alter our critical approach, and begin
—and end—with the poetry itself."[2] This assertion, like all partial truths, is a dangerous one. To take an example of this poetry
with which we must begin and end:

> Let Rome in Tiber melt, and the wide arch
> Of the rang'd empire fall! Here is my space.
> Kingdoms are clay; our dungy earth alike
> Feeds beast as man. The nobleness of life
> Is to do thus, when such a mutual pair
> And such a twain can do't, in which I bind,
> On pain of punishment, the world to weet
> We stand up peerless.
>
> (I.i.33–40)

[1] *Prefaces to Shakespeare* (Princeton, N.J.: Princeton Univ. Press, 1946),
I, 367–407. But see Sylvan Barnet, "Recognition and Reversal in *Antony
and Cleopatra*," *SQ*, 8 (1957), 331–34.

[2] S. L. Bethell, *Shakespeare and the Popular Dramatic Tradition* (Durham,
N.C.: Duke Univ. Press, 1944), p. 144.

To embrace Antony's vision concerning the nobleness of life, on the theory that great poetry morally implies an authorial sanction, is as questionable as to look quite through it. Of the former approach, G. Wilson Knight is the influential example: "That is our final vision here: man is transfigured by love's orient fire. Without it he is, as the beasts, mere product of 'dungy earth.' Love here translineates man to divine likeness—it is the only 'nobleness of life.' "[3]

The distortion of the antiromanticist, however, may in reaction be more pernicious: "Freud would have characterized [Antony's] desire as indulgence in the pleasure principle to escape from reality."[4] Ever since T. S. Eliot punctured the poetry of the noble Othello as that of a man trying to cheer himself up, there has been a tendency to undercut heroic verse with an absurdly mundane reference to reality. Some critics have treated Othello, for example, as unresponsively as the aristocratic audience in *Love's Labour's Lost* treated Pompey the Great and Alexander. In *Antony and Cleopatra* it is critically insufficient to evaluate some of the grandest poetry ever written as "daydream" or "escape into a world of fantasy."[5] The moral judgment may not be as Victorian as that of Chambers in 1925, but a concentration on the action without an imaginative response to the poetry will result in a similar *exemplum*, altering Shakespeare's achievement beyond recognition:

In an evil day Antony crosses the path of the amorous Cleopatra, and is entangled in the strong toils of a passion which for him at least, whatever the dreams of the sentimentalists, makes no contribution towards a strenuous life. His captain's heart reneges all temper, and alliances and empires slip away while he becomes the bellows and the fan to cool a gipsy's lust. There is a struggle, of course. The instinct of domination and the instinct of sex are at odds in him; and if he chooses the worser course, it is not without clear consciousness on his part of the issues at stake.[6]

While the account is accurate on one level, questions are begged when this prudential moralism is superimposed upon the framework of the play. The tension between words and action—be-

---

[3] *The Imperial Theme* (London: Oxford Univ. Press, 1931), p. 217.
[4] William Rosen, *Shakespeare and the Craft of Tragedy* (Cambridge, Mass.: Harvard Univ. Press, 1960), p. 109.
[5] Derek Traversi, *Shakespeare: The Roman Plays* (London: Hollis & Carter, 1963), pp. 186, 170.
[6] E. K. Chambers, *Shakespeare: A Survey* (London: Sidgwick & Jackson, 1925), p. 251.

tween the poetry and the plot—creates a total effect, not just a style, of *feliciter audax.*

I

Like *Julius Caesar, Antony and Cleopatra* evokes ideals that on the level of imperfect, unredeemed nature are incapable of realization but that ennoble man even as they lead to his destruction. The ideal strives with the nature of man as, dramatically, poetry strives with action. The romantic dream of certain readers, following Swinburne and then Knight, is that the lovers transcend good and evil. More accurately, they never reach those absolutes. Certainly one can agree with MacCallum that in the world of *Antony and Cleopatra* "all ties of customary morality are loosed."[7] Perhaps R. A. Foakes describes the environment more helpfully when he observes that the play "does not invite us to judge its characters by absolute standards."[8] But in granting that the moral environment of the play challenges our moral perspective, one feels all the more that Shakespeare is controlling our point of view from some quite settled, albeit exalted, coign of vantage. Clearly Shakespeare is creating a tragedy (*pace* Bradley) the experience of which depends upon the exercise of our moral and ethical judgment.[9] The play begins and ends with Romans pointing fingers of moral exemplification at the tragic lovers; in between, the events are rendered in a complex structure of evaluative criticism.[10] Antony and Cleopatra are a moral chal-

[7] *Shakespeare's Roman Plays and Their Background* (London: Macmillan, 1910), p. 439.
[8] "Vision and Reality in *Antony and Cleopatra,*" *Durham University Journal,* 56 (1964), 66.
[9] *Shakespearean Tragedy* (London: Macmillan, 1904), p. 33. According to Bradley we do not apply our moral judgment to tragedy: "While we are in its world we watch what is, seeing that so it happened and must have happened, feeling that it is piteous, dreadful, awful, mysterious, but neither passing sentence on the agents, nor asking whether the behaviour of the ultimate power towards them is just. And, therefore, the use of such language in attempts to render our imaginative experience in terms of the understanding is, to say the least, full of danger." The critical stance nowadays would oppose this attitude. But Bradley himself made a footnoted exception of *Julius Caesar:* here, he admits, perhaps the question is asked, "Is the hero doing right or wrong?" But all of the Roman plays (and probably the other tragedies as well) must be excepted.
[10] Although one applauds William Rosen's critical concern with "how the point of view of an audience is established toward the protagonist" (p. ix),

lenge not only to Rome and to Egypt but to themselves. Indeed, in that challenge lies the drama.

In attempting to discover Shakespeare's frame of moral vision, moralistic and Christian interpretations have not fared very well. A member of Shakespeare's audience who rigorously expected before, during, and after *Antony and Cleopatra* that the wages of sexual passion, regardless of any extenuations, are physical and spiritual death is unlikely to have responded to the play. For a contemporary example, Virgil Whitaker, while he recognizes that the tragedy does not lie simply in "the destruction of a great soldier by sensual love," negatively concludes that any other issue is hopelessly confused.[11] The debate between Christian and non-Christian interpreters of Shakespeare is not likely to reach a settlement, but an exchange in *Shakespeare Quarterly* concerning this play suggests that a compromise could be reached that would at least permit communication. Dolora G. Cunningham sees as tragically significant "the complete confusion of sensual love with religious terms in the language." Antony and Cleopatra's "love amounts in itself to an easily recognizable parody of the Christian life." In the final act, according to Mrs. Cunningham, Cleopatra "struggles to transfer her allegiance from the authority of the senses to the values of a permanent order and so to prepare herself for eternity." She fails in her repentance to resolve the confusion, but "the sensuality is nevertheless refined by the attempt to die nobly."[12]

In response, Elizabeth Story Donno exposes the weakness of the evidence that Mrs. Cunningham brings to her argument; but in her moral sympathy for the lovers Mrs. Donno ironically underestimates the precision with which the poetry defines their religious apprehension of value.[13] To cite one controverted example:

> Eternity was in our lips and eyes,
> Bliss in our brows' bent.
>
> (I.iii.35–36)

"Any schoolboy," writes Mrs. Cunningham, would know that "eternity was no such place." Mrs. Donno, however, insists that

I think he errs in assuming the Roman introduction to Antony as authorial or normative. To be sure, Shakespeare brings us to one point of view, but one which merely begins our dramatic experience of moral stimulation.

[11] *The Mirror up to Nature* (San Marino, Calif.: Huntington Library, 1965), pp. 276–96.

[12] "The Characterization of Shakespeare's Cleopatra," *SQ*, 6 (1955), 9–17.

[13] "Cleopatra Again," *SQ*, 7 (1956), 227–33.

such passages "give cosmic dimension to the love which Cleopatra is describing." The critical dilemma thus drawn is, I believe, fallacious. While the religious imagery in the lovers' aspiration does not beg the response of a priggish schoolboy, the "cosmic dimension" is more precisely indicative than Mrs. Donno allows.

Shakespeare establishes the cosmic dimension immediately upon the first appearance of the lovers:

> *Cleo.* If it be love indeed, tell me how much.
> *Ant.* There's beggary in the love that can be reckon'd.
> *Cleo.* I'll set a bourn how far to be belov'd.
> *Ant.* Then must thou needs find out new heaven, new earth.
>
> (I.ii.14–17)

Antony's assertion is only one facet in this opening scene; but the echo of St. John's Revelation forcefully initiates Antony's heroic quest for the abolute—a quest for "new heaven, new earth" indeed bounded by the enigmatic potentialities of Cleopatra.[14] The quest is also bounded by history. Antony's aspiration establishes a frame of reference by alluding to a revelation that historically cannot be made until Antony's defeat. That defeat, with the death of Cleopatra, will historically be the *coup de grâce* for the Third Empire; then, with the obliteration of the Ptolemies and the enfeebled Macedonian line, the Fourth Empire, approaching its zenith, will unite the world under the Pax Romana. Octavius historically places the momentous events of the play:

> The time of universal peace is near.
> Prove this a prosp'rous day, the three-nook'd world
> Shall bear the olive freely.
>
> (IV.vi.5–7)

As Capell noted long ago, Shakespeare did not get this historical point of view from Plutarch.[15] The perspective is that of Christian historiography; it is Augustinian, ecclesiastical, and biblical.

In this climactic historical moment the religious imagery establishes for the lovers, with cosmic irony, both their standard and their tragic plight. This standard, because it implies their tragedy, has very complex ramifications. It certainly does not exclusively invite negative, dogmatic, and anachronistic moraliz-

---

[14] See my Introduction, pp. 12–13.
[15] *The Tragedie of Anthonie, and Cleopatra*, ed. H. H. Furness, New Variorum (Philadelphia: Lippincott, 1907), p. 274.

ing. The moral failure of the lovers is patently obvious, but to condemn the aspiration that must involve that failure is to condemn not only the heroic but the divine urge. In the moral environment of *Antony and Cleopatra,* an environment determined by the historical moment, no other means are available to rise above the kingdoms of clay. The only distinction between beast and man that this world knows is man's possession of reason; and human reason, even when not debased by pride and a lust for power, cannot reveal to itself new heaven, new earth.

The Renaissance concept of human love, however, generated exactly this paradox of ennobling idealism at odds both with the susceptibilities of man's physical nature and with the rational and ethical values of humanism. As an epigraph for this concept (and, incidentally, to relate the paradoxical ideal of love with an ideal explored in *Julius Caesar*) one can cite Leonard Marrande's *Judgment of Humane Actions,* Englished in 1629: "We may say of love, that which the Romanes said of an Emperour, that they knew not whether they received more good or evill of him."[16] According to the classical values of Right Reason and the Christian distrust of man's physical nature, sexual passion clouds the rational soul and draws man away from *caritas,* the love of God. But these ascetic and ethical traditions were opposed by the medieval glorification of romantic love and the philosophic justification of love as man's response to manifestations of heavenly beauty.

As a tragedy of heroical love, *Antony and Cleopatra* has its place, perhaps a unique one, in the traditions of Petrarchanism and Neoplatonism. The tensions of the play are to be directly charged to the complexities of those traditions with their conflicting ambiguities. To be sure, it was no very difficult matter for the theologian, the philosopher, or the faculty psychologist to distinguish, with *exempla,* between *amor intellectualis dei* and *amor vulgaris,* making simple moral evaluations accordingly. The latter form overthrew the reason, weakened the body, and corrupted the soul. "To the Elizabethan," writes Lawrence Babb, "a conflict between reason and love would necessarily be a conflict between virtue and vice."[17] The danger in literary criticism of relying upon these undeniable but simplistic ethics is evidenced in Franklin M. Dickey's *Not Wisely but Too Well,*

[16] Cited in Franklin M. Dickey, *Not Wisely but Too Well: Shakespeare's Love Tragedies* (San Marino, Calif.: Huntington Library, 1957), p. 20.
[17] *The Elizabethan Malady* (East Lansing, Mich.: Michigan State College Press, 1951), p. 150.

one of several recent attempts to reverse the critical glorification
of love in *Antony and Cleopatra*.[18] Although Dickey grounds
his study with an excellent chapter on "The Divided Nature
of Love: Elizabethan Ideals," he mistakenly imposes the relative
simplicity of the philosophers and moralists onto the complexities
of the play; and that relative simplicity is itself, as Dickey admits, "a jungle of paradoxes."[19]

The problem of isolating the higher from the lower love is
compounded, in England, by the skeptical rejection of strict
Platonism and by Protestant sympathy for married love, the
via media that became more of the ideal than Ficino or even
St. Paul would allow. In spite of the epic glorification of Elizabeth in *The Faerie Queene*, Spenser evinces some difficulty in
persuading us (if indeed he is trying to do so) of Belphoebe's
ideal nature in her virginal tolerance of the worshipful Timias.
Her actions and characterization are not quite free from the
cold sterility seen in Shakespeare's imagery when Theseus, in
A Midsummer Night's Dream, cautions the disobedient Hermia
with the punishment of remaining unwed:

> To live a barren sister all your life,
> Chanting faint hymns to the cold fruitless moon.
> Thrice-blessed they that master so their blood
> To undergo such maiden pilgrimage;
> But earthlier happy is the rose distill'd
> Than that which withering on the virgin thorn
> Grows, lives, and dies, in single blessedness.
>
> (I.i.72–78)

For Spenser, Britomart is the titular ideal of chasity, and her
"lover's malady," after she sees the reflection of Artegall, is in
its immediate manifestation indistinguishable from *amor vulgaris*,
although the future marriage is sanctioned by no less than God's
providence for England. Her nurse, alarmed at Britomart's
symptoms, even suspects the horror of an incestuous passion.
In such circumstances, the moral opposition between love and
reason must be waived, perhaps eventually to be transcended.
"No reason can find remedy," Britomart laments; but her nurse,
in spite of that character's traditional limitations, looks beyond
reason:

[18] See also Daniel Stempel, "The Transmigration of the Crocodile," *SQ*, 7
(1956), 59–72; and J. Leeds Barroll, "Antony and Pleasure," *JEGP*, 57 (1958),
708–20.
[19] Dickey, p. 19.

> though no reason may apply
> Salue to your sore, yet loue can higher stye,
> Then reasons reach, and oft hath wonders donne.[20]

The married state toward which Britomart's love progresses is idealized not only as the providential destination of the Arthurian-Tudor myth but as the glorification of chastity. As in Spenser's allegory, the progression of the lover's experience is a quest, and in that quest, as Mark Rose has observed, genuine love "stands so near to lust that only time . . . can finally distinguish one from the other."[21]

A Midsummer Night's Dream, like several of Shakespeare's romantic comedies, is structured upon the same progression, in which the madness of love, with its irrational and illusory nature, yields at the last to the ritual of marriage. In the passion of love clash the spiritual and the bestial, a moral paradox emblematized by Titania and the "translated" Bottom. "Reason and love," Bottom wisely points out, "keep little company together" (III.i.132). Love brings into play both man-the-god and man-the-beast, a duality that is, both comically and tragically, the wearisome condition of humanity. To love is to be at the same time both more and less than human. Passionate love is therefore morally ambiguous, but it is a necessary stage in a movement that takes man away from the daylight world of Athens, the world of experience and reason mythically represented by Theseus, and loses him in the dark green world of illusion and transformation that can as easily accommodate a Comus as an Oberon. The mythic and moral psychology dramatized in the green worlds of Milton and Shakespeare is essentially the same. The evil is romantically comic in Shakespeare, but as in Milton it works to overwhelm reason with fantastic irrationality and magical illusion. The experience, even with its potential of tragedy, is nevertheless a necessary adventure in the progression of the Athenian youths and Lady Alice to spiritual and physical maturity.

Marriage effects the reconciliation of spirit and flesh, of the public and private worlds. It is, comically, the ideal resolution because it is the ideal human state. In *Much Ado About Nothing*, the rational Benedick and Beatrice, superior in their ex-

[20] *The Works of Edmund Spenser*, ed. Edwin Greenlaw et al. (Baltimore: Johns Hopkins Press, 1934), III (III.ii.xxxvi).

[21] *Heroic Love: Studies in Sidney and Spenser* (Cambridge, Mass.: Harvard Univ. Press, 1968), p. 116. And see his Chapter One, "The Morality of Love," pp. 7–34.

quisite and independent selfhood, must participate in the divine principle of love if they are not to develop the perverse "singularity" of Richard III and Iago. With hilarious appropriateness the two lovers respond when the tricksters observe this propensity in them, and Shakespeare's ideal couple fall prey to illusion, to "nothing," as easily as Claudio and Hero. In this case, however, illusion leads to truth—although it can also lead to tragedy—and to the harmony of the marriage dance. To harmonize and even celebrate the duality of man's "giddy" nature, Shakespeare vivifies the tiresome jest of the cuckold's horns. The "sensible Benedick" must become "the savage bull" just as Jove was forced to "play the noble beast in love" (V.iv.47). But despite the potential loss of human dignity in the vulnerability of love, "there is," concludes Benedick, urging the Duke to marry, "no staff more reverend than one tipp'd with horn."

This reverend human love, the *via media*, must necessarily conjoin man's physical and spiritual nature because, as Donne insists in "The Ecstasie," body and soul are interdependent. Although Ficino had allowed for the *via media*, his strict Platonic dualism of body and soul could not but lead to a denigration, at best a toleration, of the former. On that well-known ladder of love, in order to ascend to spiritual levels, a discarding of the physical baggage was necessary. But in later syncretic developments of love's metaphysics, Neoplatonic severity was qualified by Aristotelian humanism. As A. J. Smith has shown in connection with Donne's great apologia, "the perfect love of souls actually [was seen to be] inseparable from, or dependent upon, the love of bodies."[22] If the *via media* did not become the *via sola*, it lost its mean position on the scale of value.

Obviously this morally approved love, in drama and real life if not in lyric poetry, must be sanctioned by the temporal and divine laws of marriage, and it may be objected at once that these attitudes toward love cannot pertain to Antony and Cleopatra: technically, because they are not to be married, their love must be *amor vulgaris*, and their affair, moralistically treated as an *exemplum*, must be condemned. But once again the plight of Rome creates a special and qualifying moral environment. In Shakespeare's pagan world there are no divine laws of marriage; and, temporally, Rome has depersonalized and degraded the institution into little more than political strategy. The affirmative point to be observed is that the relationship of Antony and

[22] "The Metaphysic of Love," *RES*, 9 n.s. (1958), 369.

Cleopatra, in its kind, cannot be precluded automatically from having the potentiality of spiritual value. In literature, because no doubt in life, paradoxes arise that entangle further those of the moralists. "In some literary works," writes Babb, "the courtly love tradition [and, I should add, the syncretic Neoplatonism which Babb ignores] is clearly the dominant influence. . . . In other works, notably in plays dealing with the love-reason conflict, the scientific and ethical tradition is dominant." But even if one grants the simplicity of alternatives, Babb concludes that "it is not always easy to define an author's attitude, for these two antithetical views are strangely interwoven in the thought and literature of Elizabethan and early Stuart England."[23]

In a conflict between love and reason such as in Sidney's *Astrophil and Stella* we see the strangeness of this inextricable weaving. Reason, in that sonnet sequence, has behind it all the force and idealism of Renaissance Christian humanism. The poet's responsibilities to his birth, learning, country, and God suffer because of his love for Stella, and the conflict generates a drama of self-reproach. At the same time, the love, even though adulterous and even though Stella's worth is dubious, can inspire virtue and its own ennobling vision. It is decidedly not merely the sort "which reachest but to dust," though Grosart in his nineteenth-century edition so ended the sequence, thereby avoiding the lack of moral finality in the actual conclusion. As Sidney ends the work, the poet can only beg impotently that Stella "dismisse from thee my wit, / Till it have wrought what thy owne will attends" (107)—presumably his becoming the ideal Courtier.

The moralist can easily diagnose, and Sidney recognizes, that what has weakened the poet's reason is *amor vulgaris*, which he cannot temper. But the dramatic experience defies moral categories in showing a man tragically possessed by desires at once ennobling and destructive, at once his "joy" and "only annoy" (108). The fact of his love takes its place among other incontrovertible although conflicting truths:

> It is most true, that eyes are form'd to serve
> The inward light: and that the heavenly part
> Ought to be king, from whose rules who do swerve,
> Rebels to Nature, strive for their owne smart.
> It is most true, what we call *Cupid's* dart,

---

[23] Babb, pp. 154–55.

An image is, which for our selves we carve;
And, fooles, adore in temple of our hart,
Till that good God make Church and Churchman starve.
True, that true Beautie Vertue is indeed,
Whereof this Beautie can be but a shade,
Which elements with mortall mixture breed:
True, that on earth we are but pilgrims made,
And should in soule up to our countrey move:
True, and yet true that I must *Stella* love. (5)[24]

Nowhere is a rejection of Stella suggested as either a real possibility or a satisfactory moral resolution. The situation thus has a tragic complexity not found in a moralitylike opposition of vice and virtue.

If *Astrophil and Stella* challenges the sufficiency of our moral point of view, the antagonism between reason and love increases when reason loses its humanistic and Christian relevance. Donne's "The Canonization" effectively dramatizes the voice of reason as absurdly limited, and the lovers—even by means of its moral rebukes—are poetically exalted to sainthood. Reversing his practice of puncturing the idealization of love with witty realism,[25] Donne characterizes a workaday, spiritless world—the world of clay—which the quite sexual lovers reject justifiably; in so doing, they achieve new heaven, new earth. We can employ Mrs. Cunningham's critical language and call Donne's poem a "parody of the Christian life" only if we see, with Cleanth Brooks, "that Donne takes both love and religion seriously" and uses the Christian imagery to assert the spiritual potentialities of the relationship.[26]

The conflict in *Antony and Cleopatra* is similar, though much more complex. By undermining the Christian and humanistic ground that establishes reason as an absolute virtue, Shakespeare counters the undeniable dangers of passionate love with the dangers of a lust for worldly power. The defects of Rome disturb any clear morality pattern; reason becomes all but indistinguishable from the cool temperance required for successful policy. Even so, Antony never finally rejects the values and ideals pro-

[24] *The Poems of Sir Philip Sidney,* ed. William A. Ringler, Jr. (Oxford: Clarendon, 1962), p. 167.
[25] See Donald L. Guss, *John Donne, Petrarchist: Italianate Conceits and Love Theory in "The Songs and Sonets"* (Detroit: Wayne State Univ. Press, 1966), pp. 137-38.
[26] *The Well Wrought Urn* (New York: Reynal & Hitchcock, 1947), p. 11.

fessed by Rome. Although it has been customary, since Granville-Barker defended the structure of *Antony and Cleopatra*, to
emphasize the polarities of Rome and Egypt, the tragedy is not
one of moral choice, with Antony embracing Egypt instead of
Rome. It is certainly not, like "The Canonization," a simple
alternative of public or private fulfillment. Like the other
Roman tragedies, *Antony and Cleopatra* is concerned, in Lord
David Cecil's words, "not so much with man's private inner
life, as with his life in the theatre of public affairs. . . . The
private life is, as it were, a consequence of the public life."[27]
    The love story never isolates itself from the contest for em-
pire, as the following schematization would have it: "Octavius
is pure empire, Cleopatra 'the finest part of pure love,' and in
neither character is there a tragic conflict. The struggle that
shakes the world is merely the outward result of the interior
conflict in Antony's mind. Power establishes its empire in the
Roman world, while love sets up its triumphant kingdom in
the hearts of two lovers."[28] Although it is difficult to spy into
her enigmatic nature, the critic errs drastically in judging Cleopatra as concerned only with a kingdom of the heart. Cleopatra's lover follows the distinguished line of Julius Caesar and
Pompey. He decidedly cannot be someone "unregist'red in
vulgar fame." The glory of empire is in fact necessary as the
setting for their love. The last message Antony sends Cleopatra
on his departure from Egypt reveals exactly what trappings their
love requires:

> "I will piece
> Her opulent throne with kingdoms. All the East,
> Say thou, shall call her mistress."
>
> (I.v.45–47)

The act that Octavius uses as justification for his move against
Antony is the establishment of this proper ambience for heroic
love:

> I' th' market-place, on a tribunal silver'd,
> Cleopatra and himself in chairs of gold
> Were publicly enthron'd; at the feet sat
> Caesarion, whom they call my father's son,
> And all the unlawful issue that their lust

[27] *"Antony and Cleopatra,"* in *Poets and Story-Tellers* (London: Constable,
1949), p. 9.
[28] Donald A. Stauffer, *Shakespeare's World of Images* (New York: Norton,
1949), p. 233.

> Since then hath made between them. Unto her
> He gave the stablishment of Egypt; made her
> Of lower Syria, Cyprus, Lydia,
> Absolute queen.
> . . .
> His sons he there proclaim'd the kings of kings:
> Great Media, Parthia, and Armenia
> He gave to Alexander; to Ptolemy he assign'd
> Syria, Cilicia, and Phoenicia. She
> In th' habiliments of the goddess Isis
> That day appear'd; and oft before gave audience,
> As 'tis reported, so.
>
> (III.vi.3–19)

Antony must be, in order to realize Cleopatra's idealization, "an Emperor Antony" (V.ii.76).

In a geographical sense the resulting conflict pits Egypt against Rome, East against West; but private love becomes an integral part of the struggle for world power and the historical emergence of one empire under one emperor. Antony, even more crucially than Octavius, needs to be absolute ruler. Ironically, Antony's claim of independence and absoluteness gives Octavius the pretext to eliminate his rival and to assume that status himself. The historical and political inevitability of monarchy is thus a central force in the play. As Octavius says in response to Antony's death:

> I must perforce
> Have shown to thee such a declining day
> Or look on thine; we could not stall together
> In the whole world.
>
> (V.i.37–40)

Octavius would attribute this inevitability to their "stars, / Unreconciliable"; but as usual Shakespeare reveals how the causes of destiny are to be found in man as well as in his stars. James E. Phillips excises the political element from the love story for the purpose of treating Shakespeare's idea of the state,[29] but in the play there is no separation. If Octavius's actions toward becoming lord of the world proceed from an ambition so cold as to be almost impersonal, Antony's proceed from a desire to be for himself and for Cleopatra the "man of men" (I.v.72).

---

[29] *The State in Shakespeare's Greek and Roman Plays* (New York: Columbia Univ. Press, 1940), pp. 188–205.

If, then, we can see with Richard Harrier that Antony is a
"heavenly mingle" and his position "a godlike spanning of two
cultures and worlds,"[30] if we see that Cleopatra most admires
the very virtues of Antony that she "is impelled by the nature
of her passion to undermine,"[31] schematizations of Rome and
Egypt, of public and private empires, of love and honor break
down.

The Roman virtue that Antony cannot reject is easily exposed
as false and Machiavellian;[32] but its moral value, while admittedly limited, counterpoises the paradoxical value of love.
Critics sometimes permit Cleopatra to be the final judge of
Roman honor, as when she sarcastically greets Antony's decision
to return to Rome:

> Good now, play one scene
> Of excellent dissembling, and let it look
> Like perfect honour.
>
> (I.iii.78–80)

To be sure, Roman honor—as we saw in relation to *Coriolanus*—is primarily a public virtue and as such is determined
by external evaluation. Therefore, as Ulysses cynically assures Achilles, it need not reflect substantial, inherent value.
But the dichotomy in Rome between the appearance and the
reality of honor is the moral equivalent of the dichotomy in
Egypt between the professions and the realization of love. On
the one hand there is the potentiality for political villainy that
can never be unmasked because of a public ideal of honor; on
the other there is the potentiality for bestial sloth that can never
finally degrade because of the ideal of ennobling love. As the
ideal of love jars with sensual nature, so that of honor conflicts
with political realities. For Pompey and Antony this conception
of honor obviously works against expediency. And Octavius—in
spite of Stauffer's assertion that he is "pure empire" and so devoid of any conflict—must fulfill his destiny within the confines
imposed by honorable appearances.

The degree of Octavius's culpability, like his uncle's in *Julius
Caesar*, is an unknown factor. In his first scene he protests his
innocence:

[30] "Cleopatra's End," *SQ*, 13 (1962), 63–64.
[31] Traversi, p. 97.
[32] See, for example, Michael Lloyd, "The Roman Tongue," *SQ*, 10 (1959),
461–68; and Thomas McFarland, "Antony and Octavius," *Yale Review*, 48
(1959), 204–28.

> You may see, Lepidus, and henceforth know,
> It is not Caesar's natural vice to hate
> Our great competitor.
>
> (I.iv.1–3)

And after Antony's death his protestation is the same:

> Go with me to my tent, where you shall see
> How hardly I was drawn into this war,
> How calm and gentle I proceeded still
> In all my writings. Go with me, and see
> What I can show in this.
>
> (V.i.73–77)

But Shakespeare deliberately makes the moral nature of Octavius's honor ambiguous. For example, Lepidus had "grown too cruel" (III.vi.32), Octavius explains, justifying to Antony the triumvir's liquidation. It is a masterly stroke: historical fact supports Octavius's explanation, but Shakespeare's dramatic representation does not. The audience, if it is sufficiently aware, is left to wonder whether Shakespeare intends Lepidus or Octavius to reveal the discrepancy between appearance and reality. The moral ambiguity of Octavius lies in his ability to use his honor to justify and support his rise. Unlike Pompey and Antony, Octavius never permits his sense of honor to conflict with opportunity and political exigencies. By adroitly turning the weaknesses of others against themselves, he can create with "perfect honour" the very opportunities he seizes, not unlike the equally ambivalent and enigmatic Bolingbroke in *Richard II*. Octavius's honor is not entirely pretense, but it is indistinguishable from his profit. Perhaps the final scenes best clarify Octavius's conception of honor as a public virtue: while he is culpable in trying to dupe Cleopatra with appeals to his honorable nature, that private dishonor would serve the public honor of his triumphant return to Rome. The virtue of Octavius is therefore completely relative; its failure as an absolute criterion is that it leaves the man a moral question mark, if not a cipher. But the emperor of the Augustan Age, "the time of universal peace," appeals to honor in the sordidness of *Realpolitik* in much the same way that Antony and Cleopatra appeal to love in the sordidness of lust.

In Shakespeare's pagan world the ideals of love and honor can only grow out of man's carnal nature. So if Antony is, as Octavius describes him, "A man who is the abstract of all faults / That all men follow" (I.iv.9–10), there is moral aptness for

Lepidus's paradoxical simile, that those "faults, in him, seem as the spots of heaven."[33] They can "become" him since they inextricably involve his greatness. In a Christian world this perfectly paradoxical nobility would be, I think, impossible. Here, however, man's highest vision has nothing divinely and dramatically sanctioned to focus on, and yet in this world, with the first words from his mouth, Antony is seeking revelation. It will be a "bungling quest" because all the means are flawed. Antony's every movement will meet the conflict between moral exclusiveness and the inclusiveness he seeks. The ideals of love and honor do not conflict. But lust, as it conflicts with love, and political power, as it conflicts with honor, prove quite incompatible. Antony's tragedy grows out of his heroic insistence on achieving both ideals, on maintaining the honor that is the necessary condition for love's integrity and fulfillment. His destruction results from the limitations and the exclusiveness that the imperfect realities impose.

II

Plutarch furnished the raw evidence for Shakespeare's moral synthesis in *Julius Caesar*. The debt of *Antony and Cleopatra* to Plutarch's "Life of Antonius," as far as the play's moral environment is concerned, is not as marked, although ironically Shakespeare follows the historical details very closely and makes magnificent use of North's own language. Perhaps this apparent contradiction is what provoked Coleridge's observation: "There is not one [play] in which he has followed history so minutely, and yet there are few in which he impresses the notion of angelic strength so much—perhaps none in which he impresses it more strongly."[34]

Plutarch's Antony, after a lifetime tenuously poised between his vices and virtues, is completely unbalanced and overthrown by the affair with Cleopatra: "The last and extreamest mischiefe of all other (to wit, the loue of *Cleopatra*) lighted on him, who

[33] See John F. Danby, *Poets on Fortune's Hill* (London: Faber, 1952), p. 147: "Here the ambiguities of the play's moral universe get their completest expression: faults shine like stars, the heaven is black, the stars are spots. Ambivalence need go no further." See also Willard Farnham's chapter on the play in *Shakespeare's Tragic Frontier* (Berkeley: Univ. of California Press, 1950), a study of the "paradoxical nobility" in the heroes of the late tragedies; and Benjamin T. Spencer, "*Antony and Cleopatra* and the Paradoxical Metaphor," *SQ*, 9 (1958), 373–78.

[34] *Lectures and Notes on Shakespeare* (London, 1883), p. 316.

did waken and stirre vp many vices yet hidden in him, and were neuer seene to any: and if any sparke of goodnesse or hope of rising were left him, *Cleopatra* quenched it straight, and made it worse then before."[35] No evidence in Plutarch's account justifies a modification of this severe judgment. "Plutarch has no eyes for the glory of Antony's madness," MacCallum notes succinctly.[36] Even more than the glory of madness, we miss in the source the paradox that Antony's virtues are inextricably a part of his vices. Willard Farnham has argued that Shakespeare found "the paradox of Antony . . . in a well-developed form that he was willing to accept with minor changes."[37] But for Plutarch, rather simply, Antony's noble virtues as a soldier are overwhelmed by his dissolute life; the man loses the battle in a clearly defined psychomachia. To be sure, Plutarch's Roman has an exuberant heartiness which, as in the play, accounts for the love and loyalty he inspires in his followers. But although it is a common paradox that a great capacity for life can be self-destructive, Shakespeare develops the moral implications of this paradox in Antony's love for Cleopatra, and Plutarch decidedly does not. For him, Antony's excellence as a Roman soldier is one thing—even though a drinking, swaggering, and whoring Roman soldier; the "lascivious wassails" in Egypt, however, are something else. In "The Comparison of Demetrius with Antonius," Plutarch grants Demetrius moral superiority for "onely [giving] himselfe indeed to pleasure, when he had nothing else to do" (p. 1010). This moral pragmatism is reflected in Octavius: "Let's grant it is not / Amiss to tumble on the bed of Ptolemy" (I.iv.16–17). Yet the paradox of Shakespeare's hero is that, while dissolution is making him "confound" the time (Plutarch's and Octavius's single view), Antony's love for Cleopatra has a positive value far greater than that of a tumble—though tumble they certainly do.

One can grant, with Geoffrey Bullough, that Plutarch's narrative "set up a poetic ferment in Shakespeare's mind"; but only in a very limited way did Plutarch offer "the means and incentive to combine moral judgement with a glowing sympathy which perceived grandeur in the most deplorable sins of passion and the inevitable dooms they brought."[38] That sympathy and gran-

[35] *Lives* (London, 1595), p. 979.
[36] MacCallum, p. 340.
[37] Farnham, p. 139.
[38] *Narrative and Dramatic Sources of Shakespeare* (London: Routledge & Kegan Paul, 1964), V, 252.

deur arise in Shakespeare from an appreciation of love not found in his primary source.

In Plutarch's treatment of Cleopatra, love is not really an issue. His Cleopatra has no paradoxical nature. She may be more queenly than in Shakespeare, if we mean that Shakespeare does not render her intellectual accomplishments or "sweet conuersation." But Plutarch makes it clear that Cleopatra sees Antony first and last as a key to power. Antony may satisfy her sexually, but political lust motivates her. Only when he is dying does she indicate generous feelings, "forgetting her owne miserie and calamity, for the pitie and compassion she tooke of him" (p. 1005). At her death she expresses further grief. Farnham comments: "It was ironic, then, though Plutarch does not underline the irony, that this designing queen who had traded herself to one Roman after another, apparently with thoughts only for her position in the world that Rome ruled, should have developed what appeared to be love for Antony after Antony had lost all power in that world."[39] But there is really no meaningful irony, because neither morally nor practically is there a dichotomy of love and empire. Cleopatra laments the loss of both, her realms of love and empire being mutually dependent. Plutarch could discover no sudden moral complication when his Cleopatra reveals that some genuine feelings were involved in a basically selfish affair. She is not, after all, monstrous. Plutarch is not hamstrung by having to see her as all this or all that.

Nor is there a conflict between love and honor, as Farnham insists when he charges that Cleopatra's reasons for dying are not quite clear: "It is possible to gain the impression that Cleopatra brooded over the possibility of being shamefully led in triumph through the streets of Rome. She did not resolve to kill herself until she was sure that she was to be taken away from Alexandria. Was a desire to avoid personal disgrace at Rome the primary reason, perhaps even the whole reason, for her decision to die, despite whatever she said and did that indicated profound grief for the loss of Antony? If so, why does Plutarch not say something definite about such a desire?"[40] This either-or dilemma, it seems to me, is not inherent in the material. Plutarch's Cleopatra kills herself when she is defeated, and she is not totally defeated until she is certain of losing her throne and her personal dignity. This motivation, however, contradicts neither her grief for Antony nor her desire to be buried with

[39] Farnham, p. 147.
[40] *Ibid.*, p. 145.

him in Egypt rather than, disgraced, ultimately in Italy. The nature of Cleopatra's love for Antony is of no real importance in Plutarch's account, only the nobility of her death. Plutarch approves of Cleopatra at the last because in the humiliation of abject defeat, as Cleopatra knows, honor demands suicide.

"Shakespeare did not contradict Plutarch's characterization," observes Benjamin T. Spencer, "but he added a paradoxical dimension to it which helped transform Plutarch's didactic account into the more complex stuff of tragedy."[41] Harold S. Wilson agrees: "We see causes and consequences of which Plutarch never dreamed."[42] The Renaissance ideal of love and its reflection in the literature and drama of the time may offer a sufficient source for this new dimension, but further evidence suggests that Shakespeare was influenced in his view of the material by the Senecan dramatists, especially Samuel Daniel, who introduced the story of Antony and Cleopatra into English dramatic literature.[43] Daniel's *The Tragedie of Cleopatra* (1594), as the poet acknowledges, was written under the influence and inspiration of the Countess of Pembroke's *Antonius* (1592), a translation of Robert Garnier's play and a practical part of this noble lady's effort to turn back the tide of "Grosse Barbarisme" on the English stage. *Antonius* seems to have influenced Shakespeare not at all, at least not directly. The evidence in the case of Daniel is sufficient, in the opinion of most scholars, to argue a direct relationship. The two Senecan plays discover a dramatic and moral issue that did not concern Plutarch but that for Shakespeare became central.

The Cleopatra of the Countess of Pembroke's *Antonius* is a sentimentalization of the figure in Plutarch. Upon her first appearance in act 2, with Antony defeated and suspecting her of duplicity with Caesar, she protests to her attendants with un-

[41] *"Antony and Cleopatra* and the Paradoxical Metaphor," p. 375.
[42] *On the Design of Shakespearian Tragedy* (Toronto: Univ. of Toronto Press, 1957), p. 163.
[43] See R. H. Case's introduction to the old Arden Shakespeare (1906), reprinted in M. R. Ridley, ed., *Antony and Cleopatra*, Arden Shakespeare, 9th edition (London: Methuen, 1954), pp. xxvi–xxx; Farnham, pp. 148–74; Ernest Schanzer, *"Antony and Cleopatra* and the Countess of Pembroke's *Antonius," N&Q,* 201 (1956), 152–54; Dickey, pp. 163–72; Arthur M. Z. Norman, "Daniel's *The Tragedie of Cleopatra* and *Antony and Cleopatra," SQ,* 9 (1958), 11–18; Bullough, V, 228–36. J. Leeds Barroll contends (in "Shakespeare and Roman History," *MLR,* 53 [1958], 341–43) that the interest of the Senecan dramatists in the subject matter and their "recently published writings may have directed Shakespeare's attention to the story."

qualified sincerity that she has always loved Antony and has always been faithful, though she passionately accepts all blame for his defeat. She is determined not to outlive him. Charmian with several arguments tries to persuade her against suicide; she insists that Cleopatra can "Honor his memory" even while she lives "In *Caesars* grace." Cleopatra answers:

> What shame were that! ah Gods! what infemie!
> With *Antony* in his good haps to share,
> And overlive him dead: deeming enough
> To shed some teares upon a widdow tombe!
> The after-livers justly might report
> That I him only for his Empire lov'd,
> And high estate: and that in hard estate
> I for another did him lewdly leave.
>
> (619–26)[44]

In desperation to "wrest out of [Antony's] conceit that harme-full doubt" of her love, she sends Diomede with the false news of her death—a sentimental motive ineptly imposed upon the historical act. Antony, already determined to end his life honor-ably, is urged on by her example. Cleopatra, whose death does not occur within the play, remains behind only to give him "due rites." Their relationship, then, has been one of passionate love that blinds reason and leads to dishonor and ruin. Antony, like Cleopatra, blames himself for the destructiveness of the passion, but their repentance is sufficient expiation and permits their con-tinuing to love as they face an honorable suicide.

Daniel seizes the moral significance of Cleopatra's death that *Antonius* merely touches in Cleopatra's exchange with Char-mian. Her death becomes the moral palliative for both love and honor; it justifies the lovers to history. Daniel's most important change is to bring us back to the historical realities of Plutarch. Pride, ambition, vanity, and lust have determined her feeling for Antony until they destroy each other. Then, in her misery, she discovers the truth of the belief that "onely the afflicted are religious": she reveals a new spiritual awareness and, for the first time, feels a true love for Antony. Consequently, instead of dying merely to share her lover's poor fortune and to join him in death, as in *Antonius*, Daniel's Cleopatra must die to pay a debt to Antony for not having loved him, to prove to him and to the world that now she does love him, and to perform

⁴⁴ For convenience of reference I have cited the texts of *Antonius* (1595 edition) and Daniel's *Cleopatra* (revised edition of 1599) reprinted in Bullough, V.

a rite that will be a marriage in death, thus consummating her own new "religious" feelings. She also has a horror of being a trophy in Octavius's Roman triumph, but that fear is a part of the same heightened sense of honor that demands her settling the account with Antony. Throughout the confrontation with Caesar she acts the part of one desiring to live in the hope that she can deceive him and, rather incidentally, save her children. To account for her delay, Daniel stresses her lack of means. She has "hands, and will," but an instrument is preferable:

> these weake fingers are not yron-poynted:
> They cannot pierce the flesh be'ing put unto it,
> And I of all meanes else am disappointed.
> But yet I must a way and meanes seeke, how
> To come unto thee, whatsoere I do.
>
> (1163–67)

Drama was never Daniel's forte and his Senecan models offered no assistance; but he does have a card up his sleeve for her death, undramatically reported by the Nuntius.[45] As Cleopatra is about to apply the asp, suddenly she experiences a conflict "twixt Life and Honor," a conflict made crucial because the moral necessity for her death has been well defined:

> Life bringing Legions of fresh hopes with her,
> Arm'd with the proofe of time, which yeeldes we say
> Comfort and helpe, to such as doe referre
> All unto him, and can admit delay.
> But Honour scorning Life, loe forth leades hee
> Bright Immortalitie in shining armour:
> Thorow the rayes of whose cleere glorie, she
> Might see *lifes basenesse*, how much it might harme her.
> Besides shee saw whole armies of Reproches,
> And *base* Disgraces, Furies feareful sad,
> Marching with Life, and Shame that still incroches
> Upon her face, in bloody colours clad.
> Which representments seeing, worse then death
> She deem'd to yeeld to Life, and therefore chose
> To render al to Honour, heart and breath;
> And that with speede, lest that her inward foes
> False flesh and bloud, joyning with life and hope,
> Should mutinie against her resolution.

[45] Among other alterations, in the 1607 revision Daniel dramatically represented the narrated action of Cleopatra's death, probably in an attempt to make his work theatrically viable. It is very doubtful that Daniel made this revision in response to Shakespeare's play. See Ernest Schanzer, "Daniel's Revision of His *Cleopatra*," *RES*, 8 n.s. (1957), 375–81.

And to the end she would not give them scope,
Shee presently proceedes to th' execution.
And sharpely blaming of her rebel powres,
False flesh (saith she) and what dost thou conspire
With Caesar too, as thou wert none of ours,
To worke my shame, and hinder my desire?
Wilt thou retaine in closure of thy vaines,
That enemy *Base life*, to let my good?
                          (1558–83, italics added)

I have quoted extensively (the passage goes on for over thirty
lines) to show how Shakespeare, since he has dramatized his
Cleopatra's waverings, magnificently transforms Daniel's alle-
gorical account:

I am fire and air; my other elements
I give to baser life.
                                        (V.ii.287–88)

I agree with recent authorities that the echo of Daniel's "lifes
basenesse" and "Base life," heard again in Cleopatra's "This
proves me base" (l. 298), argues a direct influence. The similari-
ties of dramatic and moral concern, however, are more persuasive as evidence. The triumph of Shakespeare's heroine—

Husband, I come.
Now to that name my courage prove my title!
                                        (V.ii.286–87)

—is the triumph of Daniel's:

These rites may serve a life-desiring wife,
Who doing them, t' have done enough doth deeme.
                                        (1156–57)[46]

Shakespeare takes over the crucial elements in Daniel's dramatic
and moral view of Cleopatra's suicide. Both plays dramatize a
new Cleopatra rising from Antony's ruin and both invest her
suicide with high moral significance that clarifies and illuminates
the tragic experience. Her fulfillment in death, through her attaining the means and the resolution, gives genuine dramatic
conflict to both versions.

Daniel's heroine is, and has been, more of Plutarch's queen
than Shakespeare's. Daniel's Cleopatra is not brought by

---

[46] I have not seen this parallel remarked; but most source studies note
that only Daniel, before Shakespeare, emphasizes Cleopatra's vision of a marriage in death. A hint is in Plutarch: "Then she dried vp his bloud that
had berayed his face, and called him her Lord, her husband, and Emperour"
(p. 1005).

Antony's death to appreciate a foreign ethos. She had honor and dignity at the top of fortune's wheel, and she must resolve to maintain them at the bottom. But, in good Senecan fashion, moral virtue is required now, whereas pride and ambition sufficed before. It is this new virtue, this genuine honor, brought about by suffering, that makes her capable of love for the first time. In this respect, Daniel is morally more responsible and realistic than the sentimentalists of the French play. By linking the capacity for love to a virtuous sense of honor and integrity, Daniel gives love a moral gauge, and therefore a value, totally missing in *Antonius*. There the lovers repent that their passion has destroyed them, but they continue to love: their relationship remains, morally, a "sencelesse" one, and Cleopatra's death will be only a confirmation of it. Daniel brings his lovers to the new relationship of husband and wife; her death

> tride the gold of her love, pure,
> And hath confirm'd her honour to be such,
> As must a wonder to all worlds endure.

(1195–97)

Daniel's heroine thus gives moral justification to her place, and to Antony's, in the House of Fame.

Arthur M. Z. Norman, in collecting and supplementing the evidence that *Cleopatra* is a source for Shakespeare's play, believes that Daniel's version served as a precedent for "Shakespeare's daring use of two climaxes."[47] I agree. Shakespeare, treating both protagonists, could see that the quality of Antony's tragedy is contingent upon Cleopatra's moral nature and integrity. Her enigma, then, becomes dramatically as crucial as that of Caesar in the earlier Roman play. In summarizing this crux, one can say that Antony's passionate, blinding love is the *donnée* of all versions, and Shakespeare accepts it. But he adds to it Antony's ennobling aspiration to find in that love immutable and absolute value. Cleopatra's response to Antony's love is the unknown factor in all versions, even when, as in the Garnier-Pembroke play, the author sentimentally answers the unknown by simply assuring us that Cleopatra has always been true. To the extent that she is merely a lustful gypsy, a vain woman, a designing queen, or some combination of these— someone who will betray and sell out to the current darling of fortune—to that extent Antony's desires are mere folly, and his downfall is a tragedy not of the Shakespearean but of the

[47] Norman, p. 11.

simplistic *de casibus* kind, in the direct tradition of *The Mirror for Magistrates:* the central tragic fact is the hero's fall from fortune's wheel as a result of lust. Philo and Demetrius prepare us for such a moralistic tragedy, Shakespeare wisely beginning his splendid manipulation with the most commonly accepted point of view. Cleopatra is a "strumpet" and, following the Neo-platonic theories that valued love according to the value of the object beloved,[48] they judge Antony a "fool." Cleopatra's first word, as McFarland and L. J. Mills observe, is not reassuring;[49] it is conditional, and Antony's reply little more than a Petrar-chan cliché:

> *Cleo.*   If it be love indeed, tell me how much.
> *Ant.*   There's beggary in the love that can be reckon'd.

The flash from Revelation, however, is of another poetic and moral world altogether; but Cleopatra has already restricted him in advance:

> *Cleo.*   I'll set a bourn how far to be belov'd.
> *Ant.*   Then must thou needs find out new heaven, new earth.

To the extent that her vision can complement his, affording at least the potentiality for realization, Antony's tragedy and hers transcend the *de casibus* tradition. The nature of Cleopatra and her capacity to find out new heaven, new earth, indeed "set a bourn" for our sympathy with Antony's aspiration and a scale for the relative weight of folly and affirmation in his fall.

Such a moral and dramatic contingency is not exactly new in Shakespeare. In *Troilus and Cressida* he had written a love tragedy in which the hero insists upon absolute and transcen-dental value in his passionate love for a woman. This love too is opposed to reason: as Cressida observes, "to be wise and love / Exceeds man's might; that dwells with gods above." Troilus nevertheless idealistically aspires to reconcile both values and willfully imposes upon Cressida the capacity to sustain the im-mutable ideal. The tragic word, as in *Antony and Cleopatra,* is *if:*

> O that I thought it could be in a woman—
> As, if it can, I will presume in you—
> To feed for aye her lamp and flames of love;
> To keep her constancy in plight and youth,

[48] See Guss, pp. 130, 149.
[49] McFarland, p. 205; L. J. Mills, "Cleopatra's Tragedy, *SQ,* 11 (1960), 148.

> Outliving beauty's outward, with a mind
> That doth renew swifter than blood decays!
> Or that persuasion could but thus convince me
> That my integrity and truth to you
> Might be affronted with the match and weight
> Of such a winnowed purity in love.
>
> (III.ii.154–63)

By her very name as a *topos* of faithless woman, Cressida prepares us at the outset for the tragic emphasis to be upon Troilus's blindness. Idealism is too hopelessly and historically at odds with reality. Cleopatra, however, is no Cressida, if only because Cleopatra is, dramatically, a tantalizing uncertainty. She is for us and for Antony an enigmatic paradox of potentialities. Antony, likewise, is no Troilus. When Antony is blind, he can see that he is blind. He does not, like Troilus, idealistically "presume" in Cleopatra. Antony is painfully and even skeptically aware that he has merely risked her integrity. If Shakespeare in *Troilus and Cressida* handles the conflict between love and reason negatively, even satirically, in *Antony and Cleopatra*, without any loss of moral realism, he at least poses the affirmative.

III

The source of Antony's integrity is honor; without it, as he tells Octavia, he loses his own identity (III.iv.22–23). Antony's sense of honor, like Coriolanus's, is morally superior to that ordinarily professed in Rome. For Antony, honor represents an acknowledgment of intrinsic worth; if he is recognized as the foremost man, it must be because he *is* the foremost man. Antony will not tolerate even the suspicion of a discrepancy between appearance and reality such as he justifiably senses in Octavius. On this moral basis Antony challenges his rival to personal combat:

> Tell him he wears the rose
> Of youth upon him; from which the world should note
> Something particular. His coin, ships, legions,
> May be a coward's, whose ministers would prevail
> Under the service of a child as soon
> As i' th' command of Caesar. I dare him therefore
> To lay his gay comparisons apart,
> And answer me declin'd, sword against sword,
> Ourselves alone.
>
> (III.xiii.20–28)

This challenge, although most readers can respond to the heroics, is usually taken as corroboration of Antony's growing infatuation, as in fact Enobarbus takes it:

> Yes, like enough high-battled Caesar will
> Unstate his happiness, and be stag'd to th' show
> Against a sworder! I see men's judgments are
> A parcel of their fortunes, and things outward
> Do draw the inward quality after them,
> To suffer all alike. That he should dream,
> Knowing all measures, the full Caesar will
> Answer his emptiness!
>
>   (III.xiii.29–36)

The moral tension of this confrontation between Antony and Octavius is not unlike that between Bolingbroke and Richard II. Richard and Antony, for all their differences, have an ideal vision that the harsh realities of power will not respect. For Antony, the superiority of his opponent lacks substance; Caesar's money, ships, and armies are merely decorative. But for Enobarbus, the "gay comparisons" are the substantial reality; a single combat between "the full Caesar" and Antony's "emptiness" would be only a staged "show." In our knowledge of Antony's heroic worth, Shakespeare asks us to appreciate both evaluations.

Certainly Enobarbus is incorrect when he considers Antony's challenge as a sign of blindness in defeat. Such rashness has characterized Antony's honor throughout, at his moments of greatest strength. In the negotiations between the triumvirate and Pompey, Antony precisely anticipates the behavior that will contribute to his defeat at Actium. Peace offers having been made, Pompey comes prepared to accept, his advantages at sea being far outweighed by his opponents' strength on land. But Pompey must first save face and menace lamely:

> And that is it
> Hath made me rig my navy, at whose burden
> The anger'd ocean foams; with which I meant
> To scourge th' ingratitude that despiteful Rome
> Cast on my noble father.
> Caes.   Take your time.
> Ant.   Thou canst not fear us, Pompey, with thy sails;
>   We'll speak with thee at sea; at land thou know'st
>   How much we do o'er-count thee.
>
>   (II.vi.19–25)

Although Antony had meant to thank Pompey first for kindnesses to his mother and "At heel of that, defy him" (II.ii.162), he cannot resist responding rashly with a challenge to Pompey's implied threat, and his challenge offers exactly the same conditions, with the same disadvantages, that he will accept from Octavius at Actium. Meanwhile Octavius, attuned to the realities of the situation, must patiently wait until honors are soothed and while Antony endangers the transaction. Octavius cannot be distracted. He can wait until the momentum of Pompey's force subsides and then destroy him. But Antony's superiority as a man of power must be absolute, not relative to policy. Before Antony's last battle, when the preparation against Octavius is both for land and for sea, he exclaims:

> I would they'd fight i' th' fire or i' th' air;
> We'd fight there too.
>
> (IV.x.3–4)

He sees the maintenance of his honor as an elemental conflict. His greatness must be genuinely essential and in no way dependent upon the opportunities that Octavius manipulates to defeat him.

There is never any question that Antony will choose honor over love or love over honor. Immediately, however, we face the paradox that, although *Antony and Cleopatra* is not strictly a tragedy of moral choice, its hero is a chronic chooser or, as Ernest Schanzer negatively phrases it, "a chronic deserter." But Schanzer wisely cautions us: "I feel sure it would be a gross falsification of Shakespeare's conception to see Antony in these changes as a conscious deceiver, hiding his true feelings and intentions from Caesar, Octavia, or Cleopatra. Rather should we see him as sincere in all his protestations, believing each to be true at the moment it is uttered, until he is suddenly drawn into a contrary allegiance."[50] These fluctuations are the result of Antony's particular moral dilemma:

> What our contempts doth often hurl from us
> We wish it ours again; the present pleasure,
> By revolution low'ring, does become
> The opposite of itself.
>
> (I.ii.120–23)

To get to the moral cause of his revolving attractions and revulsions is to recognize the special moral environment of the play. Antony, in his quest for absolute value, is denied a focus

[50] *The Problem Plays of Shakespeare* (London: Routledge & Kegan Paul, 1963), p. 145.

for total commitment because all the means are partial. Ideally the perfection of the circle encompasses Rome and Egypt, but the realities of sensual love and of political power are mutually exclusive. To succeed, Antony must bestride the ocean, his reared arm cresting the world. On the imaginative and poetic level, the true circle exists; in the realm of action, the circle becomes Antony's wheel of fire.

The opening scene of the play initiates Antony's chronic choosing. Philo's exhortation that Demetrius witness an *exemplum* of lust alerts us to Antony's action, and a choice would best demonstrate Philo's point. The opportunity comes when the Roman messenger intrudes upon Antony's apocalyptic assertion, puncturing eternity with time. Cleopatra's "wrangling" responses to this intrusion then provoke Antony's choice. Though of infinite variety in her passions, Cleopatra is never gratuitously variable. Because she fears that the news may cause Antony to depart, she taunts him for being subject to the commands of a woman and a boy "scarce-bearded," for not being in the position of absolute power to do as he likes. With a sarcastic parody of his responsibilities to Caesar and Fulvia, she ironically touches the honor that Philo and Demetrius assume is lost. Because Antony will not be an underling or anyone's fool, her taunt elicits from him the grandiose claim of love's independence from worldly kingdoms. But this, we must be quick to note, is not what the queen wants to hear: "Excellent falsehood! / . . . / I'll seem the fool I am not. Antony / Will be himself." After Cleopatra again insists that he hear the messenger—"wrangling" now because Antony will not hear him and should, whereas a moment earlier Antony would hear him and, from her perverse point of view, should not—they proceed in search of "some pleasure."

Philo and Demetrius agree that their view of the situation has been confirmed. But the scene has complex tensions beyond their perception. From the general Roman point of view, the conflict is between honor and lust. With Antony's profession of *contemptus mundi*, that view begins to dissolve into a conflict between worldly power and eternal love, the conflict of "The Canonization." But when Cleopatra in no way responds to Antony's appeal, his assertion becomes folly. Like the Roman soldiers, Cleopatra sees that Antony is not himself when he dismisses all concern for worldly kingdoms: in her wrangling she exhibits her awareness that Antony must maintain his honor as a soldier for them to "stand up peerless." Cleopatra has provoked an unsatisfying and temporary choice. In Rome, Antony will make another ephemeral choice similarly provoked by Caesar's suggestion that Antony is dominated by a woman:

> *Agr.*   Great Mark Antony
> Is now a widower.
> *Caes.*   Say not so, Agrippa.
> If Cleopatra heard you, your reproof
> Were well deserv'd of rashness.
> *Ant.*   I am not married, Caesar. Let me hear
> Agrippa further speak.
>
> (II.ii.123–28)

Caesar is no doubt pleased with the choice he has manipulated. In the opening scene, however, Cleopatra cannot be entirely satisfied: Antony's decision conflicts both with "the strong necessity of time" and with Cleopatra's own contradictory desires.

It is as difficult to make unequivocal assertions about Cleopatra as it is about Julius Caesar, but if we see her as pure love with no inner conflict we are not going to appreciate the drama of her infinite variety. When in the third scene she faces the inevitability of Antony's departure, her final words are a tribute to his Roman honor:

> Your honour calls you hence;
> Therefore be deaf to my unpitied folly,
> And all the gods go with you! Upon your sword
> Sit laurel victory, and smooth success
> Be strew'd before your feet!
>
> (I.iii.97–101)

According to Harold S. Wilson, "she taunts him and dismisses him with icy dignity"; L. J. Mills hears "hissing and sneering" in the consonants.[51] Nothing could be further from the spirit of the text or the concerns of Cleopatra. Even if her tribute can come only after her attempt to keep him proves futile, the tension of her contradictory desires breaks when she sees that the parting is inevitable. The rhapsodies of her love, we note, are never heard when they are together. Only when Antony is the Roman soldier who loves his Egypt does her praise of him rise to the level of the final scene. His departure returns him to that Roman sphere where he has earned and must maintain his rank as her "man of men."

---

[51] Wilson, p. 173; Mills, p. 149.

Between scenes 1 and 3, Antony chooses again, contradicting the first scene; but Antony's new choice will also prove untenable. Cleopatra prepares us for the alternation: "A Roman thought hath struck him" (I.ii.80). Antony hears the messengers, and the news now overflows, the timely events requiring his immediate return to Rome. Shakespeare has only obliquely indicated the inner conflict that provokes Antony's change. The search for "some pleasure" has not discovered new heaven and new earth; the scene with the prophetic soothsayer reveals the exclusively sensual nature of Egypt's expectations. The soothsayer's prediction for Charmain—"You shall be yet far fairer than you are" (I.ii.16)—will come true on a spiritual plane, but that will be only under the influence of "the Roman fashion." Charmian's reply—"He means in flesh"—shows that she insists, now, upon the physical level. This atmosphere is clearly incapable of supporting an aspiring mind. Antony reverses his decision and swings to the severe Roman point of view, echoing Philo's diagnosis in scene 1:

> These strong Egyptian fetters I must break,
> Or lose myself in dotage.
>
> (I.ii.113–14)

This point of view, already exposed as partial, is challenged this time not by an assertion of transcendental love but by a genial Roman tolerance. In a comedy Enobarbus, with his charitable skepticism, would be confirmed at the close. In *Antony and Cleopatra*, where a comic reconciliation is thwarted, the comic "plain man" himself has a distinctive tragic fall.[52] Nevertheless, Enobarbus comes close to being the moral center of vision. He is a part of the Roman world, but rises above its absurd pretensions in his awareness that there is little to distinguish his world from the world of pirates and thieves (II.vi.86ff.). He holds a superior moral position in the play not only because he sees the limitations of Rome but because he sees a proper place for Egypt in the soldier's life. He becomes, in fact, the greatest support for Antony's desire to maintain both worlds.

There is, of course, never any question of what choice should be made if a choice becomes necessary. As he tells Antony, when hearing of his master's determination to leave Egypt:

[52] For Enobarbus's comic role in the play, see Elkin C. Wilson, "Shakespeare's Enobarbus," in *Joseph Quincy Adams Memorial Studies* (Washington, D.C.: Folger Shakespeare Library, 1948), pp. 391–408.

Under a compelling occasion, let women die. It were pity to cast
them away for nothing, though between them and a great cause
they should be esteemed nothing.

(I.ii.134ff.)

Several readers have heard sexual overtones, as sounded in *Hamlet*, in the last *nothing*,[53] and the bawdy reference certainly
clarifies Enobarbus's attitude. When a soldier's activity is required, women are reduced, if not literally to nothing, to their
most naturalistic and unsentimental function. Since life is not
made up of an uninterrupted series of compelling occasions (unless, like Octavius, one is creating those occasions), Cleopatra
has her place as more than nothing, and Enobarbus appreciates
that place more than anyone with the exception of Antony:

> Age cannot wither her, nor custom stale
> Her infinite variety. Other women cloy
> The appetites they feed, but she makes hungry
> Where most she satisfies; for vilest things
> Become themselves in her, that the holy priests
> Bless her when she is riggish.

(II.ii.239–44)

The tribute is so impressive because, confining himself entirely
to the level of lust, Enobarbus can project Antony's transcen-
dentalism while reveling in the sensual. Even as only a courtesan
she defies the reality of lust ("Past reason hunted, and no sooner
had / Past reason hated"); as a whore she achieves a sainthood
of sorts. She quite miraculously allows man to overcome the
temporal and physical limitation Troilus characterizes as "the
monstruosity in love, . . . that the will is infinite, and the execution confin'd; that the desire is boundless and the act a slave
to limit." Such a woman is not, obviously, to be thrown over
lightly. Although he is Antony's severest critic when the occupation of lover threatens that of soldier, Enobarbus never evinces
concern over his certain knowledge that Antony will leave
Octavia and return to Egypt. Knowing the political reality, that
the "pair of chaps" are inevitably going to "grind the one the
other" (III.v.15), Enobarbus can point out no moral significance
in the mere fact of Antony's return to Cleopatra. There is no
reason why a soldier should not have his battle and his
woman—though he must not, as Antony does at Actium, have
them both at once.

[53] See, for example, Leo Kirschbaum, "Shakspere's Cleopatra," *Shakespeare
Assoc. Bulletin*, 19 (1944), 170, n. 13.

Thus in scene 2, although Enobarbus enthusiastically approves the departure, he cannot let Antony's new Roman continence reject Cleopatra entirely:

Ant. She is cunning past man's thought.
Eno. Alack, sir, no! Her passions are made of nothing but the finest part of pure love. We cannot call her winds and waters sighs and tears; they are greater storms and tempests than almanacs can report. This cannot be cunning in her; if it be, she makes a show'r of rain as well as Jove.
Ant. Would I had never seen her!
Eno. O sir, you had then left unseen a wonderful piece of work, which not to have been blest withal would have discredited your travel.

(I.ii.141ff.)

Some readers have detached Enobarbus's first sentence here as absolute approval of Cleopatra, but the diction, tone, and irony of the passage fairly bristle. The final attitude, however, is unmistakable, and it is confirmed by Enobarbus throughout the play: the wonders of Cleopatra are not to be missed, though as a tourist attraction she definitely is subordinated to the main purpose of Antony's "travel." As for her performance as a lover, Antony's puritanical judgment will not suffice. In his lively bantering with the old Petrarchan artifices, Enobarbus grants that Cleopatra's passions are less than genuine; but she uses them with cunning more in the sense of skill than of real deceit. Enobarbus, in short, has deduced the lover's strategy that Cleopatra describes to Charmian in the next scene.

Antony goes to the queen with his Roman resolve, but by the end of the scene he will, for the first time in the play, be himself. Cleopatra first uses the method of attack that she employed in the opening scene:

What says the married woman? You may go.
Would she had never given you leave to come!

(I.iii.20–21)

But Antony has a firm control on his honor now. He knows his obligations, and Cleopatra cannot successfully insinuate that those obligations imply dishonorable subservience. Next she accuses him of dishonorably betraying his commitment to her:

Why should I think you can be mine and true,
Though you in swearing shake the throned gods,
Who have been false to Fulvia?

(I.iii.27–29)

Cleopatra's concern for his Roman marriage ironically reverses the most conventional sexual morality and at the same time appeals to those standards of fidelity. But relationships can be made in the Roman world without any investment of feeling. "Why did he marry Fulvia, and not love her?" Cleopatra asks in the first scene, whether fully aware of the irony we cannot know. Antony's cold assurance to her that Fulvia is dead, however, is the very opposite of assurance, since now she can perversely predict "In Fulvia's death how mine receiv'd shall be."

Whatever the paradox of Cleopatra's position in this scene and in spite of her cunning, one must grant that her moral view of the integrity of human relationships is superior to Antony's. (There is a further ironic dimension in that Antony's reaction to Fulvia's death, though comically deflated by Enobarbus, had not been cold at all.) Cleopatra has a real moral basis for her new gibes at Antony's honor, wily though they are:

> *Ant.*　　　　My precious queen, forbear,
> And give true evidence to his love, which stands
> An honourable trial.
> *Cleo.*　　　　So Fulvia told me.
>
> 　　　　　　　　　　　　(I.iii.73–75)

Cleopatra almost goes too far in charging his "perfect honour" to be "excellent dissembling." For one moment Antony is clearly capable of rejecting her, of choosing honor over a love that will deny any moral value to that honor. And Antony is not betraying her. His mood of total rejection has been changed early in the confrontation by Cleopatra's appeal, for the first time in the play, to Antony's transcendental vision:

> Eternity was in our lips and eyes,
> Bliss in our brows' bent, none our parts so poor
> But was a race of heaven. They are so still,
> Or thou, the greatest soldier of the world,
> Art turn'd the greatest liar.
>
> 　　　　　　　　　　　　(I.iii.35–39)

Antony breaks the "Egyptian fetters," but the vision of love is the purer in that it acknowledges the demands of honor. He leaves as her soldier, "making peace or war / As thou affects." The reconciliation is perfect (but only because he is leaving); it is a valediction forbidding mourning:

> Our separation so abides and flies
> That thou, residing here, goes yet with me,
> And I, hence fleeting, here remain with thee.
>
> 　　　　　　　　　　　　(I.iii.102–4)

If any doubt remains that the single influence of Egypt is deadly to the Roman Antony, both Pompey and Octavius acknowledge that only Antony's presence will preserve the triumvirate. Therefore Antony and Octavius are easily reconciled, but with a seal that, at least for Antony, can only be temporary. This reconciliation is hopelessly incompatible with the reconciliation he has made with Cleopatra. Yet in his revulsion from the poison of Egypt, in his commitment to a reconciliation with Octavius, and in that precipitous response to Octavius's gibe, Antony accepts the impossible marriage to Octavia. But it is not really a choice. He might tell Cleopatra, as he has just told Octavius, that he has neglected, not denied, her. As Schanzer insists, we cannot see Antony as a "conscious deceiver." He has, to be sure, consciously rejected the Egyptian poison; but he has not rejected Cleopatra. In his promise to Octavia to keep his "square," however, he forgets for the moment that his ideal is not a straight line but a circle.[54]

Within the same scene of this promise, Antony chooses again. The appearance of the soothsayer, intruding upon the Roman tempo and atmosphere, must in any production be impressive. The soothsayer has been suspected, as Plutarch suspected him, of being Cleopatra's pawn, but his haunting prognostications in the second scene of the play establish for him a more mysterious alliance. Appropriately enough, his words are again mystifying, so much so that some editors[55] have attempted to remove the contradiction in his responses by emendation:

> *Ant.* Now, sirrah, you do wish yourself in Egypt?
> *Sooth.* Would I had never come from thence, nor you thither!
> *Ant.* If you can—your reason.
> *Sooth.* I see it in my motion, have it not in my tongue; but yet
> hie you to Egypt again.
>
> (II.iii.10ff.)

The reason for the contradiction, as the soothsayer implies, does not lend itself to exposition. Antony's attachment to Egypt will indeed prove fatal, but Egypt is only a secondary cause. Considering the inevitability of Octavius's victory, the soothsayer can only urge Antony to remain apart from his lucky rival. The

---

[54] I accept Ridley's reading of "I have not kept my square" (II.iii.6): "Not, I think, 'kept within due bounds,' as it is sometimes explained, but 'kept to the straight line.' The metaphor is from a carpenter's set square, by which a line can be ruled not only straight but in the right relation to another" (p. 67).

[55] See the note in Ridley, p. 67.

soothsayer knows only fortune; it is not in his line to be concerned with man's responsibility for his own fate. And once again
the mere hint of dishonorable subjection touches Antony to the
quick:

> I will to Egypt;
> And though I make this marriage for my peace,
> I' th' East my pleasure lies.
>
> (II.iii.39–41)

In his new choice Antony is fatuously blind to the consequences
of his marriage to Octavia. As revealed by the emphasis on
"pleasure," the poison is working again. He does not, nevertheless, act upon this decision. When he and Octavia are leaving
Rome, he is annoyed that Octavius should caution him regarding
his marital integrity:

> You shall not find,
> Though you be therein curious, the least cause
> For what you seem to fear.
>
> (III.ii.34–36)

After so many choices, none of which involves the totality
of his nature, it is appropriate that Shakespeare does not render
Antony's decisive move to return to Egypt. G. Wilson Knight
justifies this deliberate obfuscation: "We cannot analyse the exact responsibility for the breach [between Antony and Octavius]
when it occurs. Each blames the other: which refusal to allot
explicit blame is throughout a quality in this play. Such realism
is vital: life witnesses ever the same futility of surface 'causes,'
the same complexity of inimical loyalties and loves, the meaningless ineptitude of 'rights' and 'wrongs.' The deep things have
their way, and appearances are froth."[56] Yet some observations
on Shakespeare's realism need to be made. Generally, the technique and its moral function are the same as in the conflict between Bolingbroke and Richard II. In the ambiguities of the
situation, both rivals share the guilt. Clearly Antony succumbs
to the magnetic power of Egypt. In the realm of political causes,
however, Octavius seems unquestionably the aggressor. He re-
moves Lepidus and breaks faith with Pompey. Even before Octavia's return as emissary, her brother has become independent
of Antony and absolute in the Roman sphere, cause enough for
Antony's move. It is ironic, then, that Octavius can use Antony's
return to Egypt and his absolute behavior in the Eastern half

[56] Knight, p. 276.

of the world to justify the Western attack. Like the other choices, this one has, to a great extent, been forced upon Antony. But this time the forces creating his conflict are closing in. The disaster at Actium is the structural turning point. In his fatal and climactic decision to fight by sea, Antony attempts to force the perfection of the circle, prompted in his error by both love and honor.[57] For the first time, Enobarbus condemns his master's course of action, comically exposing the tragic folly:

> If we should serve with horse and mares together
> The horse were merely lost; the mares would bear
> A soldier and his horse.
>
> (III.vii.7–9)

Antony and Cleopatra view the situation differently. With Antony once more the Egyptian, Cleopatra strikes a Roman attitude. Her own honor has been touched:

> Is't not denounc'd against us? Why should not we
> Be there in person?
>   A charge we bear i' th' war,
> And, as the president of my kingdom, will
> Appear there for a man.
>
> (III.vii.5–6, 16–18)

All of her poison, it seems, has been purged. Whereas Antony condemned her idleness in the opening scenes, she comically reverses the situation, rebuking his:

> Celerity is never more admir'd
> Than by the negligent.
> *Ant.*   A good rebuke,
> Which might have well becom'd the best of men
> To taunt at slackness.
>
> (III.vii.25–28)

Shakespeare has drastically altered Plutarch's account of her motivation. In the source Cleopatra followed Antony in order to assure his not returning to Octavia; she insisted on the sea battle purely for her own safety. Instead, Shakespeare allows a glimpse of Antony's ideal reconciliation, with the qualification of its comic absurdity: an emperor and an empress, two public figures, will assure their absolute position in the world for their private love. To this change of the source, Shakespeare joins the determining factor of Antony's honor: if they are to be ab-

[57] It is usual to stress one or the other here; but see Harold S. Wilson, p. 168.

solute, he must fight Octavius at sea "For that he dares us to't." Again it is Enobarbus who very simply underscores the imperfect reality that Antony's idealism must ignore: "So hath my lord dar'd him to single fight." Antony's ideals of love and honor join in precipitating the fall. Honor is blind to reasonable strategy; nevertheless, Antony's side is slightly ahead (III.x.11–13) at the crucial moment in the battle. But Cleopatra is of course unable to sustain her role, one which would demand the exclusion of all sensual, feminine nature, of all that both generates poison and prevents her from being a Fulvia. She cannot be a man, and her flight prompts Antony's choice, in spite of both lovers, between lust and honor.

Thus he has, for the moment, lost both love and honor, and he is ready to give up:

> I am so lated in the world that I
> Have lost my way for ever.
>
> (III.xi.3–4)

He tries to resign from the conflict and to retire in Egypt or even to become "A private man in Athens" (III.xii.15). But the force of Caesar, unwittingly to be sure, will not permit this ignobility. Antony quickly reconciles himself to Cleopatra and, with a new profession of *contemptus mundi*, unfurls a tattered honor:

> Fall not a tear, I say; one of them rates
> All that is won and lost. Give me a kiss;
> Even this repays me.
>   . . .
> Love, I am full of lead. Some wine,
> Within there, and our viands! Fortune knows
> We scorn her most when most she offers blows.
>
> (III.xi.69–75)

The order for wine and food jars with the attempted Stoic elevation and recalls that the fortune he is scorning is of his own making. The heroic magnanimity of his love struggles against, but is hopelessly entangled in, the liabilities of physical passion.

Antony's more genuine sense of honor is not gone from him long. After the reconciliation with Cleopatra, he challenges Octavius to a trial by combat even as "the boy" rejects the earlier dishonorable capitulation, one made while Antony thought Cleopatra untrue. Because his own integrity is contingent upon the integrity of Cleopatra, her enigmatic nature during his decline and after his death becomes the central dramatic concern, a concern that I believe Shakespeare adopted from Daniel and the Senecan tradition.

Antony's desperate quarreling with Cleopatra parallels the quarreling of Brutus with Cassius. Both heroes have envisioned an ideal, refusing to accept a flawed reality. At corresponding points in the two plays, both Romans have seen the collapse following immediately their putting these ideals into action—Brutus assassinating Caesar, Antony fighting for love and the world with a "chastened" Cleopatra. When they have to acknowledge a hostile world and a hostile fortune, the substance of their ideals is their last defense against chaos and total dissolution. Brutus's integrity demands that of his fellow conspirators; Antony's demands the integrity of Cleopatra. The anger of desperation is inevitable in both tragic experiences, given the inevitability of flawed characters and circumstances.

Criticism easily goes astray in trying to read Cleopatra's motives in the scene with Thidias.[58] Until the end of the play, the enigma of the Egyptian queen is functional and crucial dramaturgically. The complexity of Antony's tragic experience lies in her being unable to say, like the Garnier-Pembroke heroine, that she has been, is, and always will be faithful to Antony—though some critics have said it for her. Until his death, it is Antony's fate that concerns us, Cleopatra having done nothing to gain interest on a tragic level. She seems perfectly able to take care of herself regardless of what happens. The dramatic factor in her behavior, as in the scene with Thidias, is that it keeps the audience as well as Antony unsure of her. It is essential to the tragic tension that Cleopatra appear entirely capable of moving either way. One can contrast the situation with that in *Troilus and Cressida:* while we see the unsound basis for the blind Troilus's ideal, Antony is on a level with the audience in his uncertain vision of the uncertain Cleopatra. She might yet prove to be a Cressida; but she might prove something else. She is still dramatically and morally noncommittal.

When he discovers Thidias kissing Cleopatra's hand, the effect on Antony, as after the defeat at Actium, is complete dislocation. "I am Antony yet," he cries desperately in a Jacobean assertion of identity against the threat of dissolution, but without the confidence of the Duchess of Malfi. Antony's violence subsides in

[58] For some good words of caution regarding "Shakespeare's Dramatic Vagueness," see the essay of that title by Fredson Bowers, *Virginia Quarterly Review*, 39 (1963), 475–84. I maintain the Folio designation of the character as Thidias rather than Alexander's adoption, following Plutarch, of Thyreus.

pathetic awareness of Cleopatra's significance in determining his tragedy:

> Alack, our terrene moon
> Is now eclips'd, and it portends alone
> The fall of Antony.
>
> (III.xiii.153–55)

He accepts, simply and humbly, her protestations of innocence. Their identities are thus restored, those identities he must believe in, and he can once more trust in his honor: "I and my sword will earn our chronicle." As always, the love vision is ideal only when conjoined with his honor as a soldier. It is on the public stage that they must earn their place as lovers in the House of Fame.

The way to preserve both love and honor is clear, either victory or death in battle:

> I will live,
> Or bathe my dying honour in the blood
> Shall make it live again.
>
> (IV.ii.5–7)

Though the brief victory is clouded by the desertion of Enobarbus and "the god Hercules," the ideal is briefly operative in a moment of final suspense before the crushing defeat. Cleopatra has been reduced from a captain to an aide-de-camp, but her military subordination promises more than the arrangement at Actium. Admiringly, Cleopatra helps her Roman prepare for battle, Antony restricting himself to "a soldier's kiss." They seem effortlessly to have discovered the relationship they have struggled to achieve:

> O love,
> That thou couldst see my wars to-day, and knew'st
> The royal occupation! Thou shouldst see
> A workman in't.
>
> (IV.iv.15–18)

On his victorious return this perfection is captured with an extravagant image only Shakespeare could have dared:

> O thou day o' th' world,
> Chain mine arm'd neck. Leap thou, attire and all,
> Through proof of harness to my heart, and there
> Ride on the pants triumphing!
>
> (IV.viii.13–16)

The way to victory or to an honorable death in battle is cut

148 Shakespeare's Pagan WorldShakespeare's Pagan World

off by the "discandying" of the Egyptian fleet. The forces of dissolution, which Antony himself had set in motion at Actium, are too strong. Once again Antony suspects Cleopatra's duplicity; and although nothing in the play corroborates, and later events refute, her culpability, Antony is so convinced and Cleopatra is so noncommittal that we are impressed with her potentiality for guilt. Again Antony insists upon the inextricability of his two royal occupations:

> I made these wars for Egypt; and the Queen—
> Whose heart I thought I had, for she had mine,
> Which, whilst it was mine, had annex'd unto 't
> A million moe, now lost.
>
> (IV.xiv.15–18)

Since his return to Egypt, Antony's military success has indeed depended upon Cleopatra's integrity and upon his certainty of it. Enobarbus, merely one of those "annex'd" hearts, decides to desert only when he is convinced that Cleopatra has betrayed Antony. Antony too cannot separate in his mind the loss of military strength and the loss of Cleopatra. Again he gives up. He determines to kill Cleopatra and then himself. Love and honor are gone, and Antony loses his identity: "Here I am Antony; / Yet cannot hold this visible shape" (IV.xiv.13–14).

The false news of Cleopatra's death quickly restores love and a chance for honor. Instead of a mad suicide, "The courage of a woman" teaches him to tell Caesar " 'I am conqueror of myself.' " Cleopatra was faithful after all. The nobility of her death proves love and integrity. His death will unite them "Where souls do couch on flowers." He envisions their replacing Dido and Aeneas at the center of public attention, Shakespeare allowing Antony to forget that Aeneas had deserted Dido and gone about his Roman business.

The news that Cleopatra still lives arrives too late and Antony must alter his view of the situation. In committing suicide, he has at least partially regained his honor. As for love, he wearily and unquestioningly accepts it for what it has been, not for what it might be. The proof of her integrity has dissolved, and he is without transcendental visions. Instead of his ecstatic image of souls couching on flowers, he must face only "The miserable change," his defeat being tempered by a glorious past and a "valiant" death (IV.xv.51–58). He advises Cleopatra on her negotiations with Caesar, no doubt assuming that that is what she will do.

Antony's view of his tragedy thus reaches no very impressive height. If Philo or Octavius were on the stage, they might sympathetically make the same observations. Even these limited tragic sentiments are challenged, however, by the almost comic circumstances of Antony's agony—by Cleopatra's deception, by his ironic vision of a love-heaven, by his bungling with the sword, by his being lifted not to the Platonic spheres but, awkwardly, to the monument Cleopatra will not leave for fear of capture. Elizabethans were impressed by Roman suicide, but surely this one is both messy and absurd. The audience fortunately is not given much time to ponder, for immediately Cleopatra begins to speak—even comically interrupting Antony in his dying words. The nature of Antony's tragedy is still contingent upon her enigma. Even at his death Antony's view is only fragmentary; but Cleopatra will put all of the fragments of his great vision together.

IV

Antony and Cleopatra is in the anomalous position of being Shakespeare's delightful tragedy. Death for Cleopatra has lost its terror, if not its sting. The fear of something after or simply the horror of cessation is not a part of the effect, an effect all tragedy works with to some extent. Instead, the grave offers a victory:

> No grave upon the earth shall clip in it
> A pair so famous.
> (V.ii.356–57)

Throughout the play the love-death imagery has pointed to this embracing grave, to some "mettle in death" that only a saint, certainly no tragic personage, can envision. By being absolute for death, Cleopatra and her Antony become absolute in death and achieve the eternal embrace and the acme of worldly fame, their two motivating ideals. The sense of triumph in the final scene, with the corollary of Caesar's "defeat," is thus very strong, and some of the most enthusiastic pages of Shakespearean criticism have been written on its unique effect and its illumination of the entire play. But in this final scene, that conflict in the play between poetry and action continues, the conflict between love's idealistic aspiration for "new heaven, new earth," and the imperfect realities imposed by the "dungy earth." L. C.

Knights cautions us: Cleopatra "may speak of the baby at
her breast that sucks the nurse asleep; but it is not, after all,
a baby—new life; it is simply death."[59] The effect, however,
is not simplistic. We respond ambivalently because the tragic
merges with what is essentially the comic vision:[60] a clown appropriately brings on the means of death.

The full extent and function of comedy within the tragic
movement of the play have not been explored. A. C. Bradley
remarked on the comic tone, especially in the first half, as working against the tragic effect of the Great Four and as a symptom
of Shakespeare's trying "something different";[61] but Bradley's
view of tragedy did not critically accommodate this difference.
Certain aspects of comedy in the play have been treated, particularly critical comedy. Harold Goddard emphasizes the comic
exposure of worldly power, admitting that *satire* is not quite
the word.[62] Brents Stirling finds the entire play satirical in nature, and he treats it in a manner akin to O. J. Campbell's investigation of Shakespeare's "satirical tragedy."[63] But, since the play
cannot substantiate for Stirling a moral norm, it easily becomes
anyone's guess what is satirical and what is not. The world of
the satirist, as Alvin Kernan defines it, is "a battlefield between
a definite, clearly understood good . . . and an equally clear-
cut evil."[64] Since the world of *Antony and Cleopatra* is marked
by the absence of a "clearly understood good," the simple norm
for judgment must be extrapolated. Matthew N. Proser is much
more persuasive in treating the critical comedy "as a qualifying
point of view," but this facet of comedy needs to be placed
within a larger comic pattern and as a part of a comic vision,
beyond laughter, which Proser felicitously captures when he
dubs Cleopatra the "queen of comedy."[65]

---

[59] *Some Shakespearean Themes* (London: Chatto & Windus, 1959), p. 149.

[60] This suggestion was made, without elaboration, by Geoffrey Bush, *Shakespeare and the Natural Condition* (Cambridge, Mass.: Harvard Univ. Press,
1956), p. 130.

[61] "Shakespeare's *Antony and Cleopatra*," in *Oxford Lectures on Poetry*
(London: Macmillan, 1909), pp. 284–85.

[62] *The Meaning of Shakespeare* (Chicago: Univ. of Chicago Press, 1951),
pp. 573ff.

[63] *Unity in Shakespearian Tragedy* (New York: Columbia Univ. Press,
1956), pp. 157–92.

[64] *The Cankered Muse* (New Haven, Conn.: Yale Univ. Press, 1959), pp.
21–22.

[65] *The Heroic Image in Five Shakespearean Tragedies* (Princeton, N.J.:
Princeton Univ. Press, 1965), pp. 189ff.

The structure of the play follows a familiar pattern of Shake-spearean comedy. The worlds of Egypt and Rome are analogous to the tavern and court of *Henry IV*, Venice and Belmont in *The Merchant of Venice*, and the forest and court of *A Midsummer Night's Dream* and *As You Like It*—to what Northrop Frye calls the "green world of comedy" and the "red and white world of history."[66] In Egypt, as in Falstaff's tavern, the sanctions and restrictions of society have been overturned into one endless holiday spirit:

> There's not a minute of our lives should stretch
> Without some pleasure now.
>
> (I.i.46-47)

The "now" is the only reality, a constant present in which the considerations and responsibilities of past and future do not exist. Cleopatra is as little concerned with time as Falstaff, unless hours were to be measured by her means of pleasure. When her companion in the revels has departed, she might as well "sleep out this great gap of time" (I.v.5). She is more the queen of nonrule than of misrule:

> But that your royalty
> Holds idleness your subject, I should take you
> For idleness itself.
>
> (I.iii.91-93)

As in the Saturnalia, this idleness is an open defiance of the workaday world with its unquestionable business, its rigid conventions and values. By making no serious pretense of being other than it is, Egypt remains invulnerable to the normal world's moralistic attack, as after Antony's rebuke, just cited, Cleopatra can parry the thrust with a profession of true feeling:

> 'Tis sweating labour
> To bear such idleness so near the heart
> As Cleopatra this.
>
> (I.iii.93-95)

The public world of Rome, however, with its gap between moral appearance and moral reality, is wide open to comic exposure, especially since Rome makes no allowance for the pri-

[66] "The Argument of Comedy," *English Institute Essays 1948*, ed. D. A. Robertson, Jr. (New York: Columbia Univ. Press, 1949), p. 70. In the following paragraphs I am also generally indebted to C. L. Barber, *Shakespeare's Festive Comedy* (Princeton, N.J.: Princeton Univ. Press, 1959); and Geoffrey Bush, *Shakespeare and the Natural Condition*.

vate, natural man. Personal feelings and relations, along with all loyalties, are subsumed under public affairs and ambitions. The Roman world's comic flaw lies in its moral pretense and in its demand for a complete and exclusive commitment. It justifies this demand by professing the ideal of honor; but honor, as we see in Octavius, cannot survive untarnished by the realities of policy and imperfect man.

Egypt offers personal freedom for the life of the emotions, a life that is either denied by the rigidity of Rome or compartmented into degraded subordination. (For Octavius, a "tumble" with Cleopatra is "not amiss.") In the true holiday spirit of Egypt, humanity in all its infinite variety becomes of interest in and for itself, not just as a social body to be controlled:

> and all alone
> To-night we'll wander through the streets and note
> The qualities of people.
>
> (I.i.52–54)

The very activity, as Katherine Mansfield ecstatically observed, is "so *true* a pleasure of lovers."[67] And it is love, of course, that the green world fosters, "the triumph of life over the waste land,"[68] a holiday that releases the absurd along with the best of the individual spirit. Love also makes its demand for an absolute commitment and generates idealistic claims that comedy questions without rejecting in the dual spirit of Rosalind-Ganymede. In the usual progression of Shakespearean comedy, love leads to marriage, always "the plot of comedy," according to Geoffrey Bush; and "it is the women of comedy who by their own natural philosophy arrange the happy endings."[69] Thus a reconciliation between the two worlds is effected by this public act. The lovers return to a world that, after the comic purgation, acknowledges and grants a place for the individual spirit.

The pattern and thematic concerns of *Antony and Cleopatra* therefore support the many facets of Shakespearean comedy. The pure holiday spirit of Egypt encourages the radically comic, sometimes bordering on farce. The conflict of Egypt and Rome engenders critical comedy. In the Roman scenes Shakespeare even comes close to a comedy of manners, perhaps because for the only time in his career he is treating a historical subject in

[67] *Journal of Katherine Mansfield*, ed. J. Middleton Murry (New York: Knopf, 1927), p. 207.
[68] Frye, p. 67.
[69] Bush, pp. 24, 27.

which the welfare of the state has little relevance. Above all, the comedy of love is the basis of the protagonists' tragedy. Nowhere more than in the aspiration of love does the comic spirit emerge. The desire for a perfect realization of the emotional life creates the attraction of that green world where one can celebrate and even reestablish the Golden Age. The individual's desire must perforce be an indictment of the real world, which drives the comic lovers from its precincts. Frye characterizes the two worlds and their inevitable conflict: "We spend our lives partly in a waking world we call normal and partly in a dream world which we create out of our own desires. Shakespeare endows both worlds with equal imaginative power, brings them opposite one another, and makes each world seem unreal when seen by the light of the other."[70] This conflict is complicated further, as Hegel recognized, by the limitation not of the dream or of the real world but of the aspirer himself as the instrument for fulfilling the dream. "In such a case what substance there is only exists in the individual's imagination." The aspiration, though incapable of fulfillment, is nevertheless not denied its value. In the comic resolution the aspirer is reconciled to the limitations of himself and the world but "remains at bottom unbroken and in good heart to the end"; he rises above the contradictions involved in his aspiration even though suffering "the dissolution of its aims and realization."[71] There is potential for comedy as well as for tragedy in the discrepancy between the real and the ideal, a potential Sidney had tapped, before Shakespeare's romantic comedies, in the *Arcadia:* "Those trublesome effectes yow say [Love] breedes bee not the faultes of Love, but of him, that loves, as an unable vessell to beare suche a power."[72]

Hints of a connection between *Antony and Cleopatra* and *Henry IV* have not infrequently been made. W. J. Courthope described Antony as "a Henry V without his power of self-control."[73] Others have compared Cleopatra and Falstaff.[74] Ernest

[70] Frye, pp. 72–73.
[71] *The Philosophy of Fine Art*, trans. F. P. B. Osmaston (London: Bell, 1920), IV, 303–5.
[72] *The Complete Works of Sir Philip Sidney*, ed. Albert Feuillerat (Cambridge: Cambridge Univ. Press, 1923), IV, 19. See Neil L. Rudenstine, *Sidney's Poetic Development* (Cambridge, Mass.: Harvard Univ. Press, 1967), pp. 23–45, et passim.
[73] New Variorum, p. 489.
[74] See, for example, Bradley, "Shakespeare's *Antony and Cleopatra*," pp. 299–300; and Harold S. Wilson, pp. 172–73.

Schanzer was the first to see the earlier work as the closest analogue to the later "in its effect on the play's structure and on
the whole organization of its material."[75] He does not suggest
what is at the heart of their similarity, that the two worlds of
comedy have been transplanted into genuine history. The workaday world becomes the history of England and of Rome instead
of, say, Theseus's court.

There is, however, one essential difference between the comic
patterns in the two plays. In *Henry IV* there is no reconciliation
on the comic level. As C. L. Barber points out regarding the
famous rejection, "Hal's lines, redefining his holiday with Falstaff
as a dream, and then despising the dream, seek to invalidate that
holiday pole of life, instead of including it."[76] The green world
has served its function in reflecting two very limited moral en-
vironments and in allowing Hal to establish a third possibility.
But that third possibility is not a reconciliation, because it has
room for Bolingbroke and none for Falstaff. Whatever limitations this may mean for Hal (and *Henry V* strongly urges that
there are many), the fault lies primarily in Falstaff; it is he who
refuses reconciliation and insists on having both worlds on his
own terms. Moreover, the fact that this historical world is English establishes an absolute sanction in which personal considerations, even for this world's ideal king, are finally beside the
point. If our comic sense, then, is rather jarred by the rejection
of Falstaff, it is because the two strains in the play and the expectations they arouse are at the last moment yoked by violence
together, a violent yoking that enables Shakespeare to create
powerful drama out of an event foreshadowed and ordained
from the very first.

In *Antony and Cleopatra* our comic expectations are fulfilled
in the tragedy, but not by Antony. He, like Hal, stands between two worlds. In Egypt, before his return to Rome, Antony
could say with the Prince, "If all the year were playing holidays,
/ To sport would be as tedious as to work." The holiday wears
thin; the search for "some pleasure" masks and finally generates
boredom. But because there is no place at all in Rome for a
reconciliation with this spirit (the ludicrous scene on Pompey's
ship might be considered a vain attempt), Antony's tragedy is
assured. He insists upon a comic reconciliation that is shown to
be impossible. No total rejection of Cleopatra is called for: the
morality of Rome simply does not justify such a sacrifice,

[75] *The Problem Plays of Shakespeare*, pp. 162–67.
[76] Barber, p. 219.

neither does its destiny nor the welfare of its people. If the perfect freedom of the holiday is rejected, so is the opposite pole of denying all outlet for the expressive heart.

The comic dilemma becomes the tragic dilemma, as underlined by the fate of Enobarbus. This character from the comic world, as I suggested earlier, would have found a place very near the center of a comic reconciliation. In such a reconciling and purging of Antony's two imperfect worlds, Enobarbus's voice would have been the merriest. But Cleopatra, at Actium, "like a cow in June, / Hoists sails and flies"; and Antony chooses, willy-nilly, between a suddenly jaded world and the world of history. When the two worlds disastrously prove incompatible, Enobarbus deserts. He is forced by reason into a choice that in the comic world would have been unreasonable: he is made to deny the spiritual reality of the heart's affections. With perfect poetic justice, his heart breaks. Shakespeare has subtly prepared us for Enobarbus's mistake. In his undercutting of Roman honor, in his inability to see more than the sensual possibilities of Egypt, Enobarbus has shown his reason to be attuned primarily to the harshest reality. He has exposed the folly and absurdity, but he is clearly not prepared to give his life for the substance of aspiration behind that folly and absurdity. The comic "plain man" cannot survive in this tragic world. Instead of earning "a place i' th' story," and conquering "him that did his master conquer" (III.xiii.45–46), he must be ranked "A master-leaver and a fugitive" (IV.ix.22). Shakespeare, by allowing Enobarbus a tragic recognition of his mistake, has given fame to one who has little place in Plutarch's story; but true greatness belongs to those who refuse to make this impossible choice.

Antony refuses, finally, to choose, even though he makes many choices. Although he is defeated and even cheated by two worlds, in his death Antony embraces both what he was, the noblest Roman, and what he has, the Egyptian. The two cannot, however, be reconciled for him. But Schanzer incorrectly claims that the play suggests "no third moral order," as does *Henry IV*.[77] A reconciliation exists in what Geoffrey Bush calls "the perfect image" of comedy:

The vision of both the comedies and the histories belongs to the effort of the mind toward certainty and conclusion. The great plans of Bacon and Spenser, in this widest sense, belong to the same argu-

[77] *The Problem Plays of Shakespeare*, pp. 166–67.

ment of hope; their vision is the vision of comedy. The endeavor toward certainty is an attempt to reach a settlement with the world that is contained in a single and absolute commitment; it is an endeavor toward the perfect shape of truth, and toward the recovery of an original wholeness in which fact is gathered into an arrangement that transfigures it.[78]

In *Antony and Cleopatra* it is the heroine who does this manipulating of fact, thus finding the wholeness that has eluded Antony. She steps forward like the queen of comedy, arranging the happy ending of marriage and thereby winning the admiration and approval of the Roman world's highest moral sense. The comic purging and reconciliation take place to our delight while we are moved by the tragedy of its requiring the lovers' death. The only room allowed them in the world is a grave. But the world also grants them (and here is the tragic reconciliation) the height of fame.

Cleopatra's delay in effecting the conclusion has prompted almost as much wrong-headed criticism as Hamlet's. Certain observations need to be made. When Samuel Daniel began his *Cleopatra* with a heroine determined to die, he was faced with the dramatic problem of justifying her delay—actually, of inventing a plot. He solved the problem by emphasizing, to varying degrees, her lack of means, the need to throw Caesar off guard, and her attempt to arrange for her children's safety. In the report of her off-stage death, Daniel suggests a solution much more promising in its potential for revealing and developing character and for moral drama. He acknowledges that Cleopatra experienced a conflict "twixt Life and Honor": "She must shew that life desir'd delay."

Shakespeare faced the same problem, although only for the duration of one scene, and solved it perhaps with Daniel's aid. The scene begins with Cleopatra's proud resolution; then Proculeius, Dolabella, and Caesar enter successively for an interview. When all are gone she immediately sends for the countryman, her means of death since Proculeius has seized and disarmed her. Stated this way, the events tell of no delay: she obviously cannot apply an asp to her breast until all Romans are off stage. Fortunately, there is a question of delay, of what Richard Harrier has called her "double-mindedness."[79] For whatever reason, Cleopatra desires the confrontation with Caesar, holds back most of her fortune, seeks confirmation of what is to be her fate at

[78] Bush, p. 36.
[79] Harrier, p. 64.

Caesar's hands, and, finally, acknowledges the "woman" in her who would fight "resolution." To just what extent the woman has been struggling we have no way of knowing. But Shakespeare leaves that struggle and wavering as the dominant impression of her delay by making the other reasons either ambiguous (the tricking of Caesar in the Seleucus episode) or unemphatic (the fate of her children, her lack of means).

We ask many questions in this final scene, but one that should never have been asked is "Does she kill herself to be with Antony or to escape Caesar?"[80] No one asks the question of Antony when he pictures to Eros, even after the decision to join Cleopatra in death, the dishonorable alternative of being Caesar's trophy. The question assumes a factitious separation of love and honor that Antony's experience should not allow us to make. If the play has demonstrated anything, it is that there can be no integrity in love without honor, no heroical love at all. Putting the question another way—would Cleopatra have lived if she could have made her own terms with Caesar?—we are involved in the real dramatic suspense of the final act, the suspense on which hangs the tragic and comic reconciliation.

Cleopatra's inexhaustible desire for life, even at her moment of leaving it, distinguishes her tragedy from all other Shakespearean tragic deaths, certainly including Antony's. She may be weary of the world, but not of life. Shakespeare accepted this inescapable fact of her nature that Daniel could only treat allegorically in the Nuntius's description of her last fight between Life and Honor. But Shakespeare's triumph was in refusing to change the nature of his heroine merely to let history have its way. His Cleopatra unites her "double-mindedness"—Life and Honor—by envisioning death as the absolute fulfillment of life, as a triumphant reconciliation of the tragic contradictions. This comic victory ironically emerges while we fear that her desire for life will ruin everything. Instead, it glorifies everything.

It is not usually noted that Cleopatra's vision of rejoining Antony occurs only when the countryman is approaching with the basket of figs. Before this point the possibility is not even suggested. At the end of act 4, when she resolves to follow "the high Roman fashion," Antony is "wither'd," "fall'n," "cold." The world, which had equaled heaven while he lived, is now

[80] Mills, p. 159. See Eugene M. Waith, *The Herculean Hero* (London: Chatto & Windus, 1962), p. 214, n. 6: "Although devotion to Antony is not the sole reason for her suicide, fear of disgrace in Rome is not so much an alternative reason as a supporting one."

"No better than a sty." She speaks of her "resolution," but death is the poetically unappealing "secret house." In spite of her profession, this end is not for Cleopatra; undermining her words, her messenger in the following scene reveals her desire to know Caesar's "intents." Her strategy is too ambiguous for us to reject her determination totally. Her position will not change so much as add new dimensions. At this point, however, the vision of her tragedy is no higher than Antony's: it merely accepts the defeat, accepts the conflict that has caused it, and ushers the protagonists out with a modicum of face-saving and without a glimmer of understanding.

When next we see her, at the beginning of the final scene, her vision of death has enlarged:

> My desolation does begin to make
> A better life. 'Tis paltry to be Caesar:
> Not being Fortune, he's but Fortune's knave,
> A minister of her will; and it is great
> To do that thing that ends all other deeds,
> Which shackles accidents and bolts up change,
> Which sleeps, and never palates more the dung,
> The beggar's nurse and Caesar's.
>
> (V.ii.1–8)

It is the voice of the Senecan heroine, but Cleopatra is going to discover more than is dreamt of in this philosophy. She now speaks, however, of "A better life," already a thrust beyond "the secret house of death"; and the conditions of that life are those that from the first scene of the play Antony has shown to be the necessary conditions for their ideal love: deeds, accidents, change, and especially the dung have definitely caused their downfall. But her vision of death as sleep cannot appeal long to Cleopatra. She will never shed all of the dung in her nature; her love for Antony has its beginning in the flesh. Likewise, her attempt to echo Antony's "Kingdoms are clay" is no more genuine for her than it was for her momentarily blinded lover. Caesar himself may be paltry, but to be in his position is not. The glory of earthly power growing out of those kingdoms will be a part of her final vision as will the love growing out of the dung: Cleopatra will still be queen, her lover "an Emperor Antony." Her grandiose philosophy in this passage finally avoids all that is important in the play by rejecting both the good and the evil of life, by eliminating the significance of all human action in the name of fortune. Both love and world are well lost.

The final dimension will emerge when Cleopatra fills this sleep of death with the imaginative substance of a dream.

Cleopatra's great powers of imagination were established for us after Antony's departure for Rome. David Kaula sees her idleness as promoting "an incessant imaginative activity which carries her freely beyond the here and now."[81] Cleopatra, however, in a comic exchange with the eunuch Mardian, places the potency of the imagination elsewhere: " 'Tis well for thee / That, being unseminar'd, thy freer thoughts / May not fly forth of Egypt" (I.v.10–12). Her physical longing then creates a preview of the masterpiece in the final act: Antony is "The demi-Atlas of this earth, the arm / And burgonet of men."

In addition to physical longing, her capture by Proculeius adds a new urgency to her imaginative activity. In the desperation of the moment, she can evoke death in the most brutal of images, not "the secret house" or last sleep, but the death that takes babes, beggars, and dogs. With the receptive Dolabella, however, her freer thoughts begin to range once more, this time beyond the world of nature where there is nothing left remarkable. Physical longing rises to spiritual longing, as her vision is of an Antony standing like Colossus on the earth but rising into the spheres. Bestriding the ocean, Antony unites Egypt and Rome into one world. Soldier and lover are fused, as Proser points out;[82] Antony is absolute Emperor. As a purely natural force, he is perfected. The properties of spring and autumn merge, evoking the generative perfection of the Golden Age or the prelapsarian garden:

> For his bounty,
> There was no winter in't; an autumn 'twas
> That grew the more by reaping.
>
> (V.ii.86–88)

Like Spenser's Adonis in the Garden of Venus, Antony triumphs, on the purely natural level, over the liabilities of winter and death.[83] This is not the Antony of the play, as Knights astringently observes; nor is this the world of the play. But it is the Antony and the world of the lovers' aspiration.

---

[81] "The Time Sense of *Antony and Cleopatra*," *SQ*, 15 (1964), 221.

[82] Proser, p. 183.

[83] Cf. Spenser's *FQ* III.vi.42: "There is continuall spring, and haruest there / Continuall, both meeting at one tyme"; Milton's *PL* V.394–95: "*Spring* and *Autumn* here / Danc'd hand in hand"; Shakespeare's *Tempest* IV.i.114–15: "Spring come to you at the farthest / In the very end of harvest!"

If the drama invites us to evaluate her vision, the charge of "something self-deceiving and unreal" misses the mark.[84] Cleopatra is not deluded; the vision, as she prefaces it, is from a dream of what Antony was:

> I dreamt there was an Emperor Antony—
> O, such another sleep, that I might see
> But such another man!
>
>   (V.ii.76–78)

Only after the poetic creation does she bring in the relevance and the criterion of actuality. She asks the conditionally realistic Dolabella:

> Think you there was or might be such a man
> As this I dreamt of?
> *Dol.*   Gentle madam, no.
> *Cleo.* You lie, up to the hearing of the gods.
> But if there be or ever were one such,
> It's past the size of dreaming. Nature wants stuff
> To vie strange forms with fancy; yet t' imagine
> An Antony were nature's piece 'gainst fancy,
> Condemning shadows quite.
>
>   (V.ii.93–100)

Cleopatra is consciously fighting all the grim actualities in the world. She must protect her vision from the two charges of the skeptics that would make life unbearable: the ideal is impossible; dreams are meaningless. Through paradox and even contradiction, she defends her vision with a defense of poetry, for poetry, finally, is what the Roman world would destroy. If she rejects Dolabella's simple negative, she insists on no simple positive ("But *if* there be or ever were"). She leaves open the possibility of realization and goes on to the more important matter of the substance of her vision; for Dolabella, the realist, would "laugh when boys or women tell their dreams." In three lines she gives the essence of Sidney's defense of poetry and Aristotle's justification (by way of Sidney) for the place of poetry in the world of men. Imperfect nature may not be able to compete in strangeness with the fanciful jumblings of dreams—those "strange forms" of the fancy's merely sensual construction. But the poet, because he knows what perfection is, can glimpse through fallen nature the marvelous forms of ideal nature. He

---

[84] Knights, p. 149. For Knights, therefore, Shakespeare makes it clear that the love is finally "discarded or condemned." Derek Traversi also emphasizes Cleopatra's self-deception in her dream and "the origin in unreality" (p. 195).

is not bound like Dolabella or the historian to what has been, but imagines what might have been and what should be.

Cleopatra reaches the universal (*an* Antony) through the aid, but not the limitation, of the specific (*the* Antony), as the highest art works to perfect nature, not to compete with it. She therefore implies the important distinction between two Renaissance conceptions of art—conceptions morally opposed to one another—that Spenser shows us in the Garden of Adonis and the Garden of Acrasia. Cleopatra is poetically restoring nature to its original perfection, not concealing truth but revealing it. Her art here, as Goddard has suggested,[85] is in marked contrast to that which Enobarbus describes in his famous passage; there fancy had striven with nature to deceive, to appeal only to the senses:

> O'erpicturing that Venus where we see
> The fancy out-work nature.
>
> (II.ii.204–5)

Now Cleopatra insists that her art is nature's art, as Polixenes assures Perdita in *The Winter's Tale:*

> Yet nature is made better by no mean
> But nature makes that mean; so over that art,
> Which you say adds to nature, is an art
> That nature makes.
>
> (IV.iv.89–92)

Cleopatra convinces Dolabella. He swears by his world's highest value, "pursu'd success," that he is in perfect sympathy. He observes, incidentally, what we now feel for the first time, that Cleopatra has risen to the moral stature of Antony and is capable of responding to his love and aspiration in kind:

> Your loss is, as yourself, great; and you bear it
> As answering to the weight.

Her vision has condemned shadows quite—the shadows of fancy, the shadows of nature, and the shadows of death.

Because her dream is real, the sleep of death, where she might see "such another man," is now filled with life. Because she is defeating Caesar in death as well as reconciling the tragically comic contradictions, there is neither jarring nor relief when a clown helps her bring about the happy ending.[86] His comic

---

[85] Goddard, pp. 589–90.

[86] For Bradley (*Shakespearean Tragedy*, p. 62) Shakespeare's bringing on the clown at this point was "the acme of audacity."

confusions of sexuality with death, death with life, and life with immortality laugh the complexities of the play into affirmation. Will the worm eat her? Cleopatra wants to know:

You must not think I am so simple but I know the devil himself will not eat a woman. I know that a woman is a dish for the gods, if the devil dress her not. But truly, these same whoreson devils do the gods great harm in their women, for in every ten that they make the devils mar five.

Daniel Stempel, who sees Cleopatra as the villainess in a political play, hears the traditional misogynic voice of antifeminist satire;[87] but by the clown's calculation that is only half correct. A woman has potentiality for evil so great that even the devil is in awe of her. Nevertheless, woman was created by the gods to be worthy of the gods if the devil does not corrupt her. The odds are fifty-fifty. If on one hand is the traditional condemnation of women, on the other is the traditional glorification. Shakespeare's point of view is not unlike that of Robert Burton, who could likewise stress the very worst dangers of passionate love and who also triumphed over the caveat that the topic "is too light for a divine, too comical a subject":

So Siracides himself speaks as much as may be for and against women, so doth almost every philosopher plead pro and con, every poet thus argues the case (though what cares *vulgus hominum* what they say?); so can I conceive peradventure, and so canst thou: when all is said, yet since some be good, some bad, let's put it to the venture.[88]

Cleopatra's snare is finally a "toil of grace." Her desire to call Antony husband is a reconciliation of flesh with spirit and, though belatedly, of the lovers with the world. In the pagan environment of the play, however, their tragedy is inevitable because they demand the perfection of new heaven and new earth without the real means of grace and hope of glory. The peace of Augustus, however ironic and limited, will offer the occasion for the nativity that will clarify the significance of man's ability to love and his desire for honor. But for these pre-Christians, in a world where the lovers can have no other means to rise but the flesh and earthly glory, these means, with their possibilities of substance and worth, are not rejected, just as the

[87] "The Transmigration of the Crocodile," p. 70.
[88] *The Anatomy of Melancholy*, ed. Holbrook Jackson (London: Dent, 1932), III, 253 (III.2.v.5).

Renaissance did not reject them. The ability to transcend the clay is still the distinction between beast and man. The grandest irony of *Antony and Cleopatra* is that even the member of the audience who approaches it with Christian expectations is forced, finally, to approve the lovers. With a comic spirit beyond tragedy, the poetic imagination can at least point them upward and suggest that time, space, and death are not the final realities.

V

Conclusion

SHAKESPEARE very likely read the following in
Thomas Wilson's *The Arte of Rhetorique*, one of the
most popular and important of the Elizabethan rhetorical
treatises; at any rate, the idea was commonplace:

He that mindeth to perswade, must needes be well stored with
examples. And therefore much are they to be commended, which
searche Chronicles of all ages, and compare the state of our Elders
with this present time. The Historie of Gods booke to the Christian
is infallible, and therefore the rehearsall of such good things as
are therein conteined, moue the faithfull to all vpright doing, and
amendment of their life. The *Ethnicke* Authours stirre the hearers,
being well applied to the purpose. For when it shalbe reported
that thei which had no knowledge of God, liued in a brotherly
loue one towards an other, detested aduoutry, banished periuries,
hanged the vnthankful, kept the idle without meate till they
laboured for their liuing: suffered none extortion, exempted bribes
from bearing rule in the Commonweale, the Christians must needes
bee ashamed of their euill behauiour, and studie much to passe
those which are in calling much vnder them, and not suffer that
the ignorant and Pagans life, shall counteruaile the taught children
of God, and passe the Christians so much in good liuing, as the
Christians passe them in good learning.[1]

Sir Thomas North, in the dedication of his Plutarch to Queen
Elizabeth, was no doubt drawing upon this rhetorical principle of
historical *exempla* when he made what was also the Augustinian
point about the persuasiveness of "unegall examples." Shakespeare's conception of Roman history could therefore have been
shaped not only by the biblical and Augustinian exposition of
"ethnicke" history but also by this common rhetorical tradition.
Of course this popular view of classical history could in the
hands of lesser playwrights inspire only negative, didactic moral-

[1] *Wilson's Arte of Rhetorique* (*1560*), ed. G. H. Mair (Oxford: Clarendon,
1909), pp. 190–91. This work—first published in 1553, significantly revised in
1560—was frequently reprinted during Shakespeare's lifetime.

izing. But with Shakespeare's humanistic genius the attitudes of Christian historiography generated a vision more encompassing and more tragic than the self-consciously classical historicism of Ben Jonson, George Chapman, or Philip Massinger in their efforts at stately Roman tragedy.

Perhaps the most impressive evidence that Shakespeare was preoccupied with the crucial factors of Christian historiography lies beyond a study of the Roman tragedies and in the complex of motivations that led Shakespeare, uniquely, to fix his attention upon the reign of King Cymbeline. *Antony and Cleopatra*, as we have seen, anticipates "the time of universal peace"; but in *Cymbeline* Shakespeare's interests in the histories of England and Rome converge on the achievement of that peace as the necessary condition for this all-important moment in history. Once more Shakespeare turns to Holinshed, although clearly he brought to his reading more than he found. The only un-equivocal evidence about Cymbeline to be picked up in Holinshed was that not much is known "except that during his reigne, the Sauiour of the world our Lord Jesus Christ the onelie sonne of God was borne of a virgine, about the 23 yeare of the reigne of this Kymbeline, and in the 42 yeare of the em-perour Octauius Augustus, that is to wit, in the yeare of the world 3966, in the second yeare of the 195 Olympiad, after the building of the citie of Rome 750 nigh at an end."[2] There again, even in a single phrase anticipating the fall of Rome, history is shaped in the way that most captured Shakespeare's imagination. With that shape in mind, the other data in Holinshed clearly generates momentous possibilities. Although most of the chroni-cler's sources report an uneventful reign—"all nations content to obeie the Romane emperors and consequentlie Britaine" (p. 32)—Holinshed offers Tacitus' account of the British refusal during this period to pay the tribute established with Rome by Cassibellane. Holinshed sums up the matter:

But whether this controuersie which appeareth to fall forth betwixt the Britans and Augustus, was occasioned by Kymbeline, or some other prince of the Britains, I haue not to auouch: for that by our writers it is reported, that Kymbeline being brought up in Rome, & knighted in the court of Augustus, euer shewed himselfe a friend to the Romans, & chieflie was loth to breake with them, because the youth of the Britaine nation should not be depriued of the benefit to be trained and brought vp among the Romans,

---

[2] *The Chronicles of England, Scotland, and Ireland* (London, 1587), I, 32. And see Robin Moffet, "*Cymbeline* and the Nativity," *SQ*, 13 (1962), 207-18.

whereby they might learne both to behaue themselues like ciuill men, and to atteine to the knowledge of feats of warre.

But whether for this respect, or for that it pleased the almightie God so to dispose the minds of men at that present, not onlie the Britains, but in manner all other nations were contented to be obedient to the Romaine empire. (p. 33)

Given the significance of this movement in history from darkness to light and the providential necessity of universal peace, the dramatic potentialities of a possible controversy with Rome become apparent. Such a controversy would stand in the way of the benefits not only of classical humanism but, more importantly, of divine revelation. Only with the essentials of Christian historiography accepted as the cosmic background of *Cymbeline* can we understand why Shakespeare joyfully leaves us with Rome at its height, commanding the tribute of Britain:

> Never was a war did cease,
> Ere bloody hands were wash'd, with such a peace.

Patriotic sentiments of the earlier English history plays are now voiced by the evil queen and her gross son Cloten, as the insular world of English history must give way to divine providence and the Roman peace. But being at its height means also that Rome is "nigh at an end." The future belongs to England.

Shakespeare at the end of his career was thus clearly absorbed, to an impressive degree never fully recognized, by the historical significance of pagan Rome. We should not forget, furthermore, that his first essay in tragedy was also, as the entry in the Stationers' Register specifies, "a Noble Roman Historye."[3] *Titus Andronicus* might well have been included for discussion in this study except that, with all the tragic possibilities of the play, Shakespeare floundered finally in the wealth of potentiality, and the uncertainties of structure, plot, and character awkwardly obtrude upon consideration. But despite the immaturity of the play and the nonhistorical nature of the material, Shakespeare is already treating Rome distinctively, as the city of man struggling against the opposing forces of barbarous nature.[4] The tragedy of Rome, moreover, is already evident; for it is Titus, the exemplar of Roman honor and piety, who in a rigid excess of

[3] For an appreciation of *Titus Andronicus* as a Roman play, see T. J. B. Spencer, "Shakespeare and the Elizabethan Romans," *Shakespeare Survey*, 10 (1957), 27–38.
[4] Alan Sommers, "'Wilderness of Tigers': Structure and Symbolism in *Titus Andronicus*," *Essays in Criticism*, 10 (1960), 275–89.

Roman virtue paradoxically unleashes the forces of barbarism. Just as clearly as in *Coriolanus*, the hero of *Titus Andronicus* follows false gods. Honor and the Roman rites demand the destruction of children, and, ironically, the naked forces of diabolic evil and lust can do no more in return. Already Shakespeare is anticipating the juxtaposition of procreation and destruction that allies Lady Macbeth and her husband with Volumnia and her son.

In *Titus Andronicus* only Aaron, the evil representative of brute nature, cares truly for his offspring; and, at the moment he begins to protect his son, he must leave Rome. To gain a moral stature rather higher than that of Aaron the Moor requires a coign of vantage from which nature is seen to be an instrument of God. But this requires a perspective in which history too can be seen as revelation. I hope the preceding chapters have shown that Shakespeare viewed Roman history in such a perspective and that the ironies and tragedies of his pagan world are finally to be placed within this comic vision.

Appendix

The Moral Environment
in Shakespeare's
English History Plays

IF WE OMIT from consideration the two rather special cases of
Henry V, in which the moral attitude toward the hero is an
affirmative one with qualifying irony, and of *Richard III*, in
which the moral conflict shows absolute evil scourging evil and
then itself being destroyed by a minister of absolute good, we
are left with plays dealing with conflicts in which absolute right
has been confused and each side can claim only a limited right.[1]
The result, as in the Roman plays, is a dialectic allowing both
sides to assert a positive value. A merely de facto king is never
absolute. Although order demands the support of such a king,
tensions in the play dramatically question what is of limited and
relative stability. Opponents to this king can gain qualified sympathy when they seize upon the limitation and appeal to the
ultimate sanction that the king lacks. They in turn, however,
are flawed by the act of rebellion.

Through an examination of *King John* and the two tetralogies
(particularly the tragic *3 Henry VI* and *Richard II*), we can
see the historical perspective that determines and then resolves
this dialectical conflict. I emphasize *King John* for several reasons. First, it is free from the interlocking tendencies of the
other histories; it opens with the ideal in abeyance, presents conflicting sides of right, and progresses to the peace and restoration
of the ideal in the youthful, innocent, and absolute Henry III.
Second, the play's single source offers an unencumbered opportunity to watch Shakespeare transforming flawed material to
achieve the coherence of this distinctly Shakespearean conflict.
Third, in the conflict of this play, despite all its deficiencies,
are found tragic potentialities that will be realized in the Roman

[1] See A. P. Rossiter, "Ambivalence: The Dialectic of the Histories," in
Angel with Horns (New York: Theatre Arts, 1961), p. 45. This important
essay was first published in *Talking of Shakespeare*, ed. John Garrett (London:
Hodder & Stoughton, 1954).

plays. But the sanction of a moral and political absolute for England and its ideal restoration at the conclusion keep *King John*,
as well as the two tetralogies, in the genre of history and,
loosely, of comedy.

I

The source of *King John* is generally agreed to be the anony-
mous *Troublesome Raigne of King John*, published in 1591 in
two parts.[2] Shakespeare follows the earlier play almost scene
by scene in its very skillful conflation of various crises in
Holinshed's account of the reign. But despite this uncomplicated
and unique relationship between play and source, a critical comparison of *TR* and *King John* has not been fully exploited to
resolve what one commentator describes as "the problem of
King John," the widely divergent opinions regarding its unity,
structure and, most importantly of late, its reflection of Tudor
political and historical thought.[3] We need to question what
thematic and artistic considerations motivated Shakespeare to

[2] E. A. J. Honigmann's argument that Shakespeare's play is the earlier
of the two has been discounted. See his *King John*, Arden Shakespeare,
4th edition (London: Methuen, 1954), pp. xiff. For reviews of Honigmann's
thesis, see T. M. Parrott, *JEGP*, 55 (1956), 297–305; and Robert A. Law,
"On the Date of *King John*," *SP*, 54 (1957), 119–27. For convenience of
reference I have cited the text of *The Troublesome Raigne of King John*
(hereafter referred to as *TR*) from Geoffrey Bullough, ed., *Narrative and
Dramatic Sources of Shakespeare* (London: Routledge & Kegan Paul, 1962),
IV.
[3] F. M. Salter, "The Problem of *King John*," *Trans. Royal Society of
Canada*, 43 (1949), 115–36. John R. Elliott, in "Shakespeare and the Double
Image of King John," *Shakespeare Studies*, 1 (1965), 64–84, treats *TR* and
King John in his final section (pp. 72–81), but he does not really pursue
"a fresh comparison" beyond the initial issue of John's and the Bastard's
illegitimacy. The most thorough comparison of *TR* and *King John*, one
exactly opposed to my findings, is in Virgil K. Whitaker, *Shakespeare's
Use of Learning* (San Marino, Calif.: Huntington Library, 1953), pp. 123–42:
Whitaker considers that Shakespeare, working with *TR*, did not develop
"his own interpretation of events" (p. 124). The finest discussion of *King
John* is in M. M. Reese, *The Cease of Majesty* (London: Arnold, 1961),
pp. 260–86. Reese makes frequent reference to *TR* in regard to the papal
issue, John's usurpation, and general characterization. My emphasis, however,
is on the structural and thematic coherence of the two plays. Also, as will
be seen, I regard the affirmative nature of the conclusion as an integral,
inescapable part of *King John;* I would therefore disagree that the play
is, finally, "cynical and disillusioned" (p. 280).

take a recent, respectable dramatic work and, in Pembroke's words concerning John's second coronation, "strive to do better than well" (IV.ii.28).

"Shakespeare's sources are worth studying," asserts Hardin Craig, "because they have significance, value, meaning; Shakespeare chose them for that reason."[4] *TR*, specifically, is in many ways remarkable; of the known contemporary dramatists, only Shakespeare and Marlowe show the structural powers for handling such sprawling events from the chronicles. But whatever its origins and despite its relative impressiveness, *TR* is flawed by dramatic and moral incoherence, a flaw far more serious than the mediocre verse. The source is worth studying in this case not only for its significance but for its limitations as well. A critical examination of the relationship between *King John* and its source will reveal that Shakespeare, with a coherent pattern of changes, resolves all the structural and thematic dissonances of his material. It is not tenable to think of him as engaged in "hack work" or as forced by the nature of the conflict to stand back and admire "the fine confusion," unable to make any "dramatic sense."[5]

There is, however, confusion in the source play. The author, surely not inadvertently, incorporated into *TR* conflicting material and attitudes from two contradictory readings of the history of John and his troubles, two strains that refused to cohere.[6] The medieval chronicles were unanimous in depicting John as a despicable king who by his own willful failures brought England to the point of ruin. He alienated not only the clergy and the Pope but his own nobles and subjects. Holinshed points to this tradition: "Verelie, whosoeuer shall consider the course of the historie written of this prince, he shall find, that he hath beene little beholden to the writers of that time in which he liued: for scarselie can they afoord him a good word, except when the trueth inforceth them to come out with it as it were against

[4] "Motivation in Shakespeare's Choice of Materials," *Shakespeare Survey*, 4 (1951), 33. For the rationale of the critical method employed in this section—and generally in my treatment of Shakespeare's sources—see also Charles Tyler Prouty, "Some Observations on Shakespeare's Sources," *Shakespeare Jahrbuch*, 96 (1960), 64–77.

[5] E. K. Chambers, *Shakespeare: A Survey* (London: Sidgwick & Jackson, 1925), p. 100; John Palmer, *Political Characters of Shakespeare* (London: Macmillan, 1945), p. 323.

[6] The most recent and significant account of King John's reputation in the sixteenth century is that by John R. Elliott, "Shakespeare and the Double Image of King John."

their willes."⁷ The reason for their hostility was, of course, that John "was no great freend to the clergie." But after Henry VIII successfully defied the Pope, the attitude changed drastically. Bale's *Kynge Johan* represents the extreme form of a new perspective: John has become the Moses of the Reformation's promised land, the virtuous proto-Protestant who almost succeeded in breaking the tyranny of Rome. His responsibilities for the revolt of his barons and for the death of Arthur, as well as all defects of his moral character, are expunged as "suggestyons of the malicyouse clergye."⁸

This Anglican propagandizing was, however, infiltrated by the Roman view from the very start. Polydore Vergil's history of England, published in 1534, included the traditional picture of John's reign and made the charge that John had usurped the throne from his nephew Arthur after the death of Richard I.⁹ Although Holinshed does not include this latest accusation, he gives most of the information accumulated in both hostile and friendly traditions. He does not attempt to reconcile the two points of view but nevertheless inclines toward a generous, Protestant evaluation: "Certeinelie it should seeme the man had a princelie heart in him, and wanted nothing but faithfull subiects to haue assisted him in reuenging such wrongs as were doone and offered by the French king and others" (p. 196). This generosity is not unreasonable since so many details could not be definitely established as factual. For example, Holinshed offers several versions of Arthur's death as possibilities, and the uncertainty carries an honest weight of extenuation: "It is not throughlie agreed vpon, in what sort he finished his daies: but verelie king John was had in great suspicion, whether worthilie or not, the lord knoweth" (p. 165). Holinshed's refusal to judge without God's omniscience has, through *TR*, an important effect on *King John*. Questions of innocence and guilt, of right and wrong, are helplessly posed by the chronicler; and that honest and simple presentation generates a more profound vision than any interpretation, necessarily biased, could have done.

The author of *TR*, unlike Shakespeare, did not have the imaginative power to encompass the two extreme interpretations

⁷ *The Chronicles of England, Scotland, and Ireland* (London, 1587), III, 196. Subsequent page references, given in the text, are to this edition and volume.
⁸ *John Bale's "King Johan,"* ed. Barry B. Adams (San Marino, Calif.: Huntington Library, 1969), p. 134 (l. 2196).
⁹ See John R. Elliott, Jr., "Polydore Vergil and the Reputation of King John in the Sixteenth Century," *ELN*, 2 (1964), 90–92.

172 *Appendix*

of Holinshed's material.[10] But his was no simple failure. Although the author happily indulges in Protestant hysterics, he
has taken for the play's central action the most heinous episode
that the Roman tradition charged against John. The author very
deliberately contrives a situation of moral complexity found
only in the best plays of the period. He makes Arthur's death
the dramatic turning point in the structure, whereas the event
in Holinshed results in only a very minor crisis. Nor does the
playwright shun the moral effect of his hero's criminal intention.
Only after John's repentance can his ideal reemerge, still untarnished, the ideal of a throne and church free from papal control and clerical abuse. He can then be entirely affirmed once
more by his vision of

> a Kingly braunch
> Whose armes shall reach unto the gates of *Rome,*
> And with his feete treade downe the Strumpets pride,
> That sits upon the chaire of *Babylon.*
>
> (II.1084–87)

The failure of *TR* is that the plot does not bear out the moral
significance that the author places on John's defiance of the
Pope. Although this defiance comes at the dramatic peak of the
scenes in France, the subsequent political events make the
Protestant cause irrelevant to the two genuine moral conflicts—
the one between the king's and the rebel forces and the one
within John himself. Unlike Shakespeare, the author cannot use
this irony because he cannot see it. John, after a real moral struggle, finally yields to Pandulph when the messenger reports that
the barons and the French have joined forces. As in Shakespeare,
Pandulph then cannot effect the peace that was the papal bar-
gaining condition. It is true that the author allows John clear
sight at this turn:

> Accursed *John,* the divell owes thee shame,
> Resisting *Rome,* or yeelding to the Pope, alls one.
> The divell take the Pope, the Peeres, and *Fraunce*:
> Shame be my share for yeelding to the Priest.
>
> (II.704–7)

[10] I am aware that the author of *TR* probably consulted sources other
than Holinshed (see John Elson, "Studies in the King John Plays," in *Joseph
Quincy Adams Memorial Studies* [Washington, D.C.: Folger Shakespeare
Library, 1948], pp. 183–97). Certainly the Protestant bias is in the line
of Bale and Foxe. The fact remains, however, that the author has imposed
this bias onto Holinshed, and matters of detail perhaps added from other
sources do not affect the argument that follows.

But after John's repentance the author tries to impose a significance that the facts have not supported:

> My tongue doth falter: *Philip*, I tell thee man,
> Since *John* did yeeld unto the Priest of *Rome*,
> Nor he nor his have prospred on the earth:
> Curst are his blessings, and his curse is blisse.
>
> (II.1074–77)

John's yielding has in fact nothing to do with the outcome one way or the other. Dramaturgically it is a spurious issue, underlined by Pandulph's busy part as peacemaker in the happy close. Thus the moral value that has been placed upon the papal conflict is extraneous and jarring not because one should be tolerant of Roman Catholics but because it is irrelevant to the genuinely dramatic moral vision.

Shakespeare did not allow John's defiance of the Pope to represent an unqualified appeal. This omission, when taken in conjunction with Shakespeare's most important addition to his source, seems at first to remove us altogether from the Tudor and Protestant view of King John. For Shakespeare adds the charge of John's usurpation and indeed makes it the central element in the conflicts of John's reign. One may doubt whether Shakespeare had to depend upon Polydore Vergil for this issue: even if Holinshed and *TR* accept the legality of the will that made John the legitimate successor to Richard, they cannot avoid representing Arthur as having the genealogical precedence. Such a precedence might well have been sufficient for one recently immersed in the tragic lineages of York and Lancaster, for one contemporaneously treating Richard's suicidal act of disinheriting Bolingbroke. There is ample evidence that a will barring lineal descent must fail as an absolute appeal; since disinheritance necessarily breaks those charters of time that uphold order, the law in such a case would be unnaturally turned against itself. Ironically confirming that such a will can never be legally valid, Shakespeare's King John undermines the basis of his own right to the throne by denying that the elder Faulconbridge had the legal power to disinherit a son—even though the man knew that son to be none of his own begetting. The comic argument is not in the parallel scene in *TR*.

Even though Shakespeare takes the potentially proto-Protestant and heroic king and turns him into a usurper, *King John* nevertheless remains securely within the Tudor tradition, but comprehensively so, without partisan hysterics. The Pope's influence is still inimical to England's welfare; but because the facts make no correlative for a spiritual issue, the conflict remains strictly political. Denied this false spiritual affirmation, John has left only the fact of the crown to support him, a considerable support but not an absolute one. Shakespeare goes still further and develops in Arthur's claim, in those who support it, and in the barons' motivation for revolt a positive appeal that directly exposes John's political and moral limitations. Neither side receives an absolute sanction; each side fails by the standard of that ideal to which each makes a claim.

The justification and reality of the ideal are shown by the return to peace and unity at the conclusion, a resolution possible only because Henry III can without further disruption reconcile the duality of fact and right, reality and ideal: he is both the son of the usurper and next in line of true descent. *King John* becomes a microcosm of the sequence of plays dealing with the aftermath of Richard II's deposition, but Bolingbroke's confusion of right cannot be resolved within the generation. Until Richmond comes along, with both providential and genealogical sanctions, there is no one like Henry III with an unchallenged claim de facto and de jure.

Shakespeare establishes John immediately as a usurper. Instead of using the French challenge to elicit a naive response from the audience, Shakespeare emphasizes John's "borrowed majesty" and allows Elinor to confirm the French charge:

> K. John. Our strong possession and our right for us!
> Eli. Your strong possession much more than your right,
> Or else it must go wrong with you and me;
> So much my conscience whispers in your ear,
> Which none but heaven and you and I shall hear.
> (I.i.39–43)

The English position is thus undercut: the fact of kingship has been severed from the right of it. We are in another moral world altogether from that in *TR*, where the initial conflict between England and France is patriotically without ambivalence. John's decision that "Our abbeys and our priories shall pay / This expedition's charge" for the war in France is removed from the end of a scene in *TR*, where it is given five emphatic lines, to a merely parenthetical observation (I.i.48–49). Shakespeare very skillfully avoids provoking in his audience a simplistic response that would overthrow the moral balance. Of course the fact that France charges the usurpation will assure that the Englishman's "strong possession" maintains its positive value.

This drastic realignment of forces naturally changes the conflict in the French scenes. In *TR*, without the Bastard's piercing soliloquy on commodity, the peace between France and England through the marriage of the Dauphin and Blanche gains the author's approval. John at least understands what price he must pay:

> my brother got these lands
> With much effusion of our English bloud:
> And shall I give it all away at once?
>
> (I.832–34)

But his mother, who is not a dissembler as in Shakespeare, argues that peace and stability are well worth the territorial loss (I.768–71, 835–36). The arrival of Pandulph with the papal intervention that will destroy the truce provokes John's lengthy invective against Rome; the proto-Protestant receives complete moral affirmation. This issue also simplifies and rejects King Philip in a single line: "I must obey the Pope." John is without qualification England's hero; King Philip, a moral straw man.

Shakespeare makes of the same material a situation of profound moral complexity. Philip, Lewes, and Austria are fighting for Arthur's clear lineal right to the throne. Lewes's tribute to Coeur-de-lion jars all patriotic expectations. They claim their absolute authority

> From that supernal judge that stirs good thoughts
> In any breast of strong authority,
> To look into the blots and stains of right.
>
> (II.i.112–14)

This claim is duplicated in John's view of himself as "God's wrathful agent" (II.i.87), backed by his de facto possession of the crown and an otherwise peaceful England. Thus the indecisive battle that the two forces wage before Angiers has a dramatic cogency absent in *TR*. Though each is fighting for "God and our right," the trial by combat, which traditionally ought to prove God and right, must fail. If John is a usurper, the true heir is hopelessly involved in foreign intervention and the inevitability of dissension.

The impasse is broken by the Citizen's suggestion of marriage between Lewes and Blanche. But instead of accepting peace as a value worth the compromise, Shakespeare allows the truce

to expose the moral vulnerability of both parties. Yet he gives
each side a voice of moral awareness that prevents either from
collapsing into sheer hypocrisy. The Bastard recognizes that
both sides, finally, are governed by commodity. And even King
Philip, while he can no longer lay claim to his divine agency,
maintains if only wistfully a concern for principle:

> Brother of England, how may we content
> This widow lady? In her right we came;
> Which we, God knows, have turn'd another way,
> To our own vantage.
>
> (II.i.547–50)

The following scenes develop the issue already at the heart
of the conflict, the failure of absolutes in a world where right
and wrong have been confused. When kings break faith upon
commodity, when all guidelines fail except the relativity of self-
interest, what happens to truth and justice? The railing of Con-
stance suggests, but rather absurdly, an ultimate nihilism:

> when law can do no right,
> Let it be lawful that law bar no wrong.
>
> (III.i.185–86)

The arrival of Pandulph complicates the situation even further.
Already the conflict is morally too ambiguous for the issue
suddenly to become right versus wrong, England versus Rome.
Upon Pandulph's order for Stephen Langton's bishopric, John
indignantly evokes the absolute and divine right of kings even
though the moral environment in the play is so complex and
uncertain precisely because of his inability to offer that absolute
and divine right:

> What earthly name to interrogatories
> Can task the free breath of a sacred king?
>
> (III.i.147–48)

John's attack upon the Pope's "usurp'd authority" recalls his
own liability. (The word *usurped* and its cognates have been
declaimed eight times before, all in relation to John.) Even the
most avid Protestant would have difficulty ignoring the irony
of the king's position.

The moral implications are equally keen in King Philip's situation. Instead of the simple acquiescence to Pandulph's demand
that Philip makes in *TR*, Shakespeare's French king recognizes
a genuine moral dilemma. Having taken an oath with John and

being called upon to break that oath, Philip desperately seeks advice from the one man who, according to France's light, should be able to give it:

> Good reverend father, make my person yours,
> And tell me how you would bestow yourself.
> This royal hand and mine are newly knit,
> And the conjunction of our inward souls
> Married in league, coupled and link'd together
> With all religious strength of sacred vows.
>
> (III.i.224–29)

The situation dazzles with irony. While we agree that the peace, described by Philip with passionate sincerity, should not be broken, we remember that the truce itself was made only by his playing "fast and loose with faith"; an oath was made with John only by breaking the one with Arthur. Pandulph, even so, refuses to sympathize. For the papal legate the matter is absolute—Rome against England:

> All form is formless, order orderless,
> Save what is opposite to England's love.
>
> (III.i.253–54)

Pandulph's argument, releasing Philip from his oath, may have reminded the audience of the hated doctrine of equivocation and the subtleties of Jesuitical casuistry, but Dr. Johnson was correct in insisting that the logic is flawless, granting "the propositions, that the 'voice of the church is the voice of heaven,' and that 'the Pope utters the voice of the church.' "[11] "It is religion that doth make vows kept," Pandulph says. Both sides can agree with this premise. But since the next logical step for England is Erastian, the king over religion ("we under heaven are supreme head," John proclaims), the absoluteness of the crown "doth make vows kept." When that crown's integrity fails, then, where is the appeal? Certainly not to Rome: Pandulph and the Roman Church prove themselves worshipers of commodity like the other earthly forces.

The final section of the play, proceeding from the turning point of Arthur's death, presents an ironic resolution to this thematic search for a moral landmark "Among the thorns and dangers of this world." For this resolution Shakespeare focuses on the one character who has, in his soliloquy on commodity, seen

[11] *Johnson on Shakespeare*, ed. Arthur Sherbo (New Haven, Conn.: Yale Univ. Press, 1968), I, 419.

the fundamental basis of the dilemma. The Bastard rises above boisterous, satirical irony to tragic apprehensions. The earlier conflict had involved a unified England, no matter what her imperfections. The Bastard loses his spirited detachment when the new conflict suddenly finds England turned against herself.

As in the previous points of tension, Arthur's fate in *King John* generates an entirely different moral conflict from the corresponding one in the source. The centrality of Arthur's death in *TR*, as already noted, gives that play a remarkable complexity, and the author took some pains to achieve it. He establishes Arthur's death in 1203 as the immediate occasion for the barons' revolt in 1216. John's submission to the papal legate in 1213 is also linked causally by the author to this conflation of crises.[12] As a motivation for rebellion, Arthur has no place in Holinshed: upon the rumor of his death, the people of the English provinces in France worked "all the mischeefe they could deuise" (p. 165), but the death had the desired effect of ending France's disputes in behalf of Arthur's claim. *TR*, therefore, makes a crux out of an event in John's career that could be taken to reveal his greatest capacity for evil but that was not at all decisive politically.

The discontented barons, however, have other motives:

> This hatefull murder, *Lewes* his true discent,
> The holy charge that wee receivde from *Rome*,
> Are weightie reasons, if you like my reede,
> To make us all persever in this deede.
>
> (II.88–91)

The author has provided the rebels with the combined motivations of all of John's various enemies throughout his reign. "The holy charge" was given to English subjects as well as to King Philip after 1208, and John was forced to yield in 1213. The barons supported Lewes's claim after the signing of Magna Carta (1215) when John showed no intention of abiding by the agreement and the barons had to look to France for help.

Such compression is masterly. The plural motivation, an intermixture of good and evil, strikes one indeed as Shakespearean. But Shakespeare deliberately cuts away all except the nobles' genuine indignation over Arthur's death as motivation for their rebellion, a simplicity he could not have derived directly from Holinshed. In the chronicle Arthur's death was not an English concern at all, and only *TR*'s conflation made it so. The priority

---

[12] See Bullough, IV, 9–10.

of *TR*, incidentally, therefore appears indisputable: in what is the structural crux for both plays, *TR* is recognizably close to Holinshed, but *King John's* relationship to the chronicle is hardly comprehensible without the intervening accentuation of Arthur's death in conjunction with more strictly historical motivations.

Clearly, as Geoffrey Bullough observes, Shakespeare "wished to show [the nobles] in a terrible dilemma, as good men rebelling against an erring monarch for a righteous reason, yet in so doing putting themselves in the wrong."[13] The author of *TR* permits little or no sympathy for the nobles. By giving them a papist loyalty, he keeps the focus on John as the proto-Protestant. Shakespeare not only gives his nobles a single, sympathetic motive for rebellion; he develops in them—particularly in Salisbury—a moral vision that reflects the thematic confusion of right and wrong:[14]

> But such is the infection of the time
> That, for the health and physic of our right,
> We cannot deal but with the very hand
> Of stern injustice and confused wrong.
>
> . . .
>
>   O nation, that thou couldst remove!
> That Neptune's arms, who clippeth thee about,
> Would bear thee from the knowledge of thyself,
> And grapple thee unto a pagan shore,
> Where these two Christian armies might combine
> The blood of malice in a vein of league,
> And not to spend it so unneighbourly!
>
>   (V.ii.20–39)

The concluding image is remarkable in both its poetic and its historical aptness: Salisbury yearns for a conflict in which the morality is without ambivalence—a Christian crusade against the pagans, such as the absolute King Richard had led.

After dramatizing a cynical, disillusioned world in which self-interest determines all political behavior, Shakespeare gives us English noblemen motivated by the simplest moral feeling of revulsion from evil. There is no commodity in their action;

[13] IV, 21. See M. M. Reese, p. 276, n. 1: "Shakespeare takes great pains to show that the rebels have a very serious case."

[14] Honigmann (p. lx) notes "that the word 'right' occurs more times in *John* (28 times) than in any other play of Shakespeare (*3 H 6* is next: 21 times)." See the following section for the similarity of thematic concern in *3 Henry VI*.

they have nothing to gain. They soon discover, in fact, that they have everything to lose, for Lewes plans to put them to death after the conquest of England is effected. This ironic discovery leads to the resolution of the play's moral perplexities. Shakespeare has examined the springs of political action and discovered that, while self-interest is the cause of evil and confusion, it is also, rightly understood, the mainstay of the whole framework.

This structural and thematic paradox is a familiar one in sixteenth-century political thought based on natural law. "The destruction of all true common weals" is a consequence of those who "so highly exteem their own private pleasure and weal," explains Reginald Pole in Thomas Starkey's *A Dialogue Between Reginald Pole and Thomas Lupset* (1533-36). True common weal, he immediately continues, paradoxically lies "in the very same thing wherein standeth the wealth and prosperous state of every particular man by himself." Lupset then observes that "that thing which you noted before to be the destruction of every common weal, now by this reason and ground should maintain the same."[15] Ideally, as in Alexander Pope's version, "God and Nature link'd the gen'ral frame, / And bade Self-love and Social be the same."[16] This eighteenth-century view, though optimistically strained as a compensation for Hobbes, comes from a much older world picture of natural order and stability. Richard Hooker and Sir Thomas Elyot are the convenient spokesmen:

For we see the whole world and each part thereof so compacted, that as long as each thing performeth only that work which is natural unto it, it thereby preserveth both other things and also itself.[17]

And in thynges subiecte to Nature nothynge of hym selfe onely may be norisshed; but whan he hath distroyed that where with he dothe participate by the ordre of his creation, he hym selfe of necessite muste than perisshe, whereof ensuethe uniuersall dissolution.[18]

[15] Thomas Starkey, *A Dialogue Between Reginald Pole and Thomas Lupset*, ed. Kathleen M. Burton (London: Chatto & Windus, 1948), p. 45.

[16] *An Essay on Man*, ed. Maynard Mack (New Haven, Conn.: Yale Univ. Press, 1951), p. 126 (III.317-18).

[17] *The Works of Richard Hooker*, ed. John Keble (Oxford: Clarendon, 1865), I, 237. (*Of the Laws of Ecclesiastical Polity* I.ix.)

[18] *The Boke Named the Governour* (1531), ed. Foster Watson (London: Dent, 1907), p. 3.

Even though the nobles follow a genuine moral light, it leads toward dissolution. Vengeance belongs to God not only because He alone can punish a king but also because He alone can determine, especially in this ambiguous case, the degree of guilt. Critics generally consider that *King John* concludes by offering in opposition to commodity the Bastard's selfless patriotism. But commodity and honor are not "two antagonistic ethical principles."[19] Shakespeare extends the narrow frame of cynical self-interest to show that the individual's true interest, the highest commodity, demands the unity and integrity of the commonwealth.

King John's central experience, his dilemma in the disposal of Arthur, has prepared us for this paradoxical resolution. The most commodious action, thinks John, will be the child's murder. So Pandulph neatly projects this necessity to Lewes:

> A sceptre snatch'd with an unruly hand
> Must be as boisterously maintain'd as gain'd.
> (III.iv.135–36)

But the short-term profits are delusive and self-defeating. As Pandulph proceeds to show, immoral cause and effect insist upon moral cause and effect:

> For he that steeps his safety in true blood
> Shall find but bloody safety and untrue.
> This act, so evilly borne, shall cool the hearts
> Of all his people and freeze up their zeal,
> That none so small advantage shall step forth
> To check his reign but they will cherish it.
> (III.iv.147–52)

John's repentance upon seeing his nobles' reaction to Arthur's supposed death is thus bluntly juxtaposed with his recognition that the action has not been politically wise:

> They burn in indignation. I repent.
> There is no sure foundation set on blood,
> No certain life achiev'd by others' death.
> (IV.ii.103–5)

One must approach the problem of the play's hero, or lack of hero, in line with the thematic development. John is prominent at the beginning, the Bastard at the end, and efforts to

[19] James L. Calderwood, "Commodity and Honour in *King John*," *Univ. of Toronto Quarterly*, 29 (1960), 341. See also William H. Matchett, "Richard's Divided Heritage in *King John*," *Essays in Criticism*, 12 (1962), 231–53.

bolster the weaker end of either character are not convincing.[20] In the first three acts the Bastard stands choruslike outside the central conflict. He satirizes the English courtier and the world of commodity while his energetic actions proceed in the background on an entirely simplistic moral level—England against France, Rome, and the clergy. In the last two acts, however, this same simplistic willingness to fight for England moves him into the center of the plot; and he saves England from defeat. The Bastard of the last two acts still knows that the reality of the situation offers nothing as a moral absolute. With the death of Arthur,

> The life, the right, and truth of all this realm
> Is fled to heaven; and England now is left
> To tug and scamble, and to part by th' teeth
> The unowed interest of proud-swelling state.
>
> (IV.iii.144–47)

This tragic disillusionment is a heightening of the satiric disillusionment in the commodity soliloquy, but the reality that he perceives can no longer be the final appeal. While England was unified, the Bastard might cynically observe, even revel in, the absurdities of imperfection. Upon the withdrawal of the nobles, he must make a choice between an imperfect England or no England at all. The disillusionment becomes the measure of the Bastard's greatness at the same time that it must become, practically speaking, an irrelevancy.[21]

The king-subject relationship connects John and the Bastard as dual protagonists as much as love creates dual protagonists in *Antony and Cleopatra*. The Bastard has no identity apart from his connection with John. It was surely a very serious critical mistake to speak of him as "an early Henry V" who replaces the king in the last act and "proves to be himself the natural ruler that John had ceased to be."[22] The Bastard is not an image of

[20] Adrien Bonjour's view, that the pattern is "decline of a hero—rise of a hero," is a little more satisfactory. See his "The Road to Swinstead Abbey: A Study of the Sense and Structure of *King John*," *ELH*, 18 (1951), 270.

[21] See J. Middleton Murry, *Shakespeare* (London: Cape, 1936), p. 159: "The Bastard is a cynic, and not a cynic at all. He is realist and idealist at once, yet he is not divided."

[22] John Dover Wilson, ed., *King John* (Cambridge: Cambridge Univ. Press, 1936), p. lxi; Bonjour, p. 272. See also E. M. W. Tillyard, *Shakespeare's History Plays* (London: Chatto & Windus, 1944), pp. 226–29. Only Julia Van de Water ("The Bastard in *King John*," *SQ*, 11 [1960], 143–44) objects strongly to this view: "Actually, in the last two acts the Bastard comes much closer to epitomizing the loyal follower than he does the regal leader."

the true king, but of the ideal subject with a vision of the true king. It is a vision that John, to be sure, cannot embody; but to that vision the Bastard is absolutely loyal.

The relation between the Bastard's imaginative vision and John's reality is similar to that between Cleopatra's vision, in her final scene, and Antony's reality. Since the Bastard is without illusions, he can be capable of that vision which, while untrue to actuality, is not delusive. Shakespeare's emphasis in the play has been on this actuality, exposing "the bare-pick'd bone of majesty" (IV.iii.148), and he does not, with the growing affirmation, turn away from the facts. After the Bastard's imaginative representation of the king, the appearance of John, weak with fever, is a powerful irony; but the irony does not negate the appeal to a higher reality and loyalty. In the light of the Bastard's vision, John as a man becomes an irrelevancy, and his quick removal is artistically and thematically just. Because the ideal of kingship is victorious, the Bastard can give a final tribute to John with little intrusive, questioning irony. But this happy conclusion is possible only because the ideal is finally capable of full realization—as Cleopatra's vision is not. When the Bastard transfers his loyalty to Henry III, the gap between the real and the ideal closes. With this confirmation of history, all irony is dispelled.

II

One cannot too strongly insist that the affirmation with which *King John* concludes is possible only because Henry III has the unchallenged claim de facto and de jure. Even the off-stage proximity of Pandulph, belatedly helping to arrange the truce between England and France, cannot spoil the effect:

> This England never did, nor never shall,
> Lie at the proud foot of a conqueror,
> But when it first did help to wound itself.
> (V.vii.112–14)

The de facto nightmare is over. In the *Henry VI* trilogy, however, there is no waking; each play concludes with only a temporary cessation of conflict that anticipates more chaos. We have a situation, as in *King John*, in which neither side, Lancaster or York, can offer the absolute right to establish an undisputed order:

> For though usurpers sway the rule a while
> Yet heav'ns are just, and time suppresseth wrongs.
>
> (*3 Henry VI* III.iii.76–77)

Margaret's indignation, unwittingly ironic, indicates the inevitable doom of both sides. To her plea for French aid against the recent usurper Edward IV, Warwick can effectively counter: the Lancastrians "tell a pedigree / Of threescore and two years—a silly time / To make prescription for a kingdom's worth" (III.iii.92–94). York's claim looks back to the violated line of Richard II; but in asserting their claim the Yorkists again violate the order of descent and the order of England, limited though those orders have become.

For one who insists upon absolute sanction, the only recourse is to retire from the battle, like Henry VI, in tragic contemplation. Everyone else, in the third part of the trilogy, is motivated by a narrow selfish interest, the vicious individualism that quintessentially emerges with Richard Crookback. Love, as the divinely creating and ordering principle, dissolves and with it all loyalty except that to the sanction of self:

> I have no brother, I am like no brother;
> And this word "love," which greybeards call divine,
> Be resident in men like one another,
> And not in me! I am myself alone.
>
> (V.vi.80–83)

Richard III is poetically appropriate as the scourge, for he epitomizes England's moral condition: this morality figure represents allegorically the vice of Margaret, Warwick, York, Clarence, Edward, Clifford, and everyone except Henry. Henry alone can prophesy upon the appearance of the silent Richmond: the future Henry VII is the absolute that God will reestablish with the new dispensation of the Tudors.

The prominence of oath-breaking in *3 Henry VI* has behind it the same failure of absolutes as in King John's reign. In the opening scene of the play, immediately following upon the battle of St. Alban's, the two forces attempt an impossible reconciliation, York swearing to allow Henry to rule in peace until his death, Henry swearing to disinherit his son in favor of York. Richard's equivocation, justifying York's renewal of the conflict, has the same thematic function as Pandulph's advice to France:

> An oath is of no moment, being not took
> Before a true and lawful magistrate

> That hath authority over him that swears.
> Henry had none, but did usurp the place;
> Then, seeing 'twas he that made you to depose,
> Your oath, my lord, is vain and frivolous.
>
> (I.ii.22–27)

This argument approximates an Erastian version of Pandulph's "It is religion that doth make vows kept." If York is the true king, his oath to deny himself the crown is as much against absolute right as was King Philip's oath, if one grants the absoluteness of the Roman Church. Henry's oath, in turn, is broken by Margaret, and she can likewise claim, with some face-saving, an offense against order. For Henry to disinherit his own son is "unnatural." It is with tragic irony, then, that both sides can at the same time violate oaths and scorn the other side for perjury. In addition to the instability of the two sides, individuals fluctuate disloyally between them, particularly Warwick and Clarence. All make oaths and break them, and the only one who shows remorse is Henry, whose oath should never have been made at all:

> Withhold revenge, dear God; 'tis not my fault,
> Nor wittingly have I infring'd my vow.
>
> (II.ii.7–8)

No scene more clearly shows the failure of a merely de facto claim than the one in which Henry, returning secretly from Scotland after Edward's usurpation, encounters the two Keepers who arrest him:

> *2 Keep.* You are the king King Edward hath depos'd;
> And we his subjects, sworn in all allegiance,
> Will apprehend you as his enemy.
> *K. Hen.* But did you never swear, and break an oath?
> *2 Keep.* No, never such an oath; nor will not now.
> *K. Hen.* Where did you dwell when I was King of England?
> *2 Keep.* Here in this country, where we now remain.
> *K. Hen.* I was anointed king at nine months old;
> My father and my grandfather were kings;
> And you were sworn true subjects unto me;
> And tell me, then, have you not broke your oaths?
> *1 Keep.* No;
> For we were subjects but while you were king.
>
> (III.i.69–81)

If all loyalties are chained completely to the temporal condition, there can be no order. The secular rules. As Andrew S. Cairncross observes, the reality of an eternal stability exists only in that "the overwhelming prevalence of disorder and perjury . . . implies reference to order and faith."[23]

The lovely hawking scene in *2 Henry VI* shows with symbolic cogency the conflict between traditional hierarchical values, in which the divine order infuses the natural order, and the new secularism of pride and rapacious individualism:

> *King.* But what a point, my lord [Gloucester], your falcon
>   made,
>   And what a pitch she flew above the rest!
>   To see how God in all His creatures works!
>   Yea, man and birds are fain of climbing high.
> *Suf.*   No marvel, an it like your Majesty,
>   My Lord Protector's hawks do tow'r so well;
>   They know their master loves to be aloft,
>   And bears his thoughts above his falcon's pitch.
>   (II.i.5–12)

The King and his faithful counselor do not catch the perversion that Suffolk and the venal Cardinal make of this basic Neoplatonic doctrine. They are describing their own seditious aspirations, not Gloucester's. If the wicked prelate and Margaret's lover are removed after hurrying on the more disastrous contention, the houses of York and Lancaster are no less guilty of this worldly view. Their "heaven is on earth" (II.i.19). Temporal values have been severed from eternal ones. The contestants would establish an earthly order without any reflection of divine order, with the individual as the ultimate and absolute law. The resulting chaos is the same as that which Donne describes in his *Anniversaries:*

> 'Tis all in pieces, all cohaerence gone;
> All iust supply, and all Relation:
> Prince, Subiect, Father, Sonne, are things forgot,
> For euery man alone thinkes he hath got
> To be a Phoenix, and that there can bee
> None of that kinde, of which he is, but hee.[24]

The oath-breaking in *3 Henry VI* can therefore carry the thematic and the structural weight it does. When the basic order is destroyed, no basis for loyalty or integrity exists beyond per-

[23] *The Third Part of King Henry VI*, Arden Shakespeare, 3rd edition (London: Methuen, 1964), p. liv.

[24] *John Donne: The Anniversaries*, ed. Frank Manley (Baltimore: Johns Hopkins Press, 1963), pp. 73–74. (*FA*, ll. 213–18.)

sonal expediency. An oath indeed depends upon some personal ideal of order that relates to some order outside the individual. Without that relationship oaths are as vain and frivolous as the Machiavel insists.

As king, Henry VI bears a great responsibility for the wounds of civil war, but he as well as England cannot avoid the guilt of history. To suggest that Henry simply needs might to enforce his right is to miss the irony underlying the entire conflict. One can scarcely consider York a kingly foil to Henry—as Boling-broke is to Richard—when the Duke is implicated in the deaths of Talbot and Gloucester, and is directly responsible for the Cade anarchy. The only possibility of salvation for England lay in Talbot and Gloucester who, like the Bastard, maintained the ideal subject-king relationship even when the king could not sup-port them. Unlike the situation in *King John*, however, an abso-lute king is beyond the events' providing; Talbot's and Glouces-ter's ideal loyalty is not sufficient to survive protracted realities of imperfection.

In the first two plays of the trilogy, it is true, Shakespeare emphasizes the king's political failure. In Part One, Henry does nothing to prevent the rivalry of York and Somerset; he even puts them in the position to fail to support Talbot. In his deadly marriage to Margaret, Henry disregards a previous commitment as well as good advice. In Part Two, by failing to support Gloucester against his enemies, the king loses the only power that is above the struggling factions. These failures prevent his absolutely passive Christianity from winning sympathy. He ac-cepts the loss of France: "God's will be done!" (*2 Henry VI* III.i.86). And upon Gloucester's death he refuses the most im-portant task of God's viceroy:

> O Thou that judgest all things, stay my thoughts—
> My thoughts that labour to persuade my soul
> Some violent hands were laid on Humphrey's life!
> If my suspect be false, forgive me, God;
> For judgment only doth belong to Thee.
>
> (III.ii.136–40)

Such blatant failure to govern, sanctioned by Christian senti-ment, foreshadows unsympathetically the problem of *Measure for Measure*. But in the first scene of *3 Henry VI*, the king's moral capacity to recognize the justness of York's lineal claim and the weakness of his own lifts him above the factions; whereas in the earlier plays he was removed from the conflict because of weakness, now his moral awareness distinguishes him. Shakespeare for the first time places his titular hero in the moral and dramatic center and endows him with the accompanying pathos of England's tragedy. He is still weak, of course; but it is superficial to see him merely as "ineffective virtue."[25] He is virtue that must of necessity be ineffective. Though circumstances trap him on the Lancastrian side, he inclines toward neither. "To whom God will, there be the victory!" he prays at Towton. The important thing, as he sees it, is that one side unequivocally win, that order be restored at any price:

> Wither one rose, and let the other flourish!
> If you contend, a thousand lives must perish.
>
> (II.v.101–2)

God's providence, however, is not so arbitrary. The Yorkists thrive at the end of the trilogy, the Lancastrians having been punished. But in *Richard III* punishment is given in equal measure to the Yorkists, a point specified by the choric Margaret. More importantly, England has expiated her sins, and so God restores order with the absoluteness of Henry VII at the Battle of Bosworth Field.

The role of providence does not obviate human responsibility; that would be not only dramatically but theologically unsound. God's providence, for Shakespeare as for Milton, involved a rational sequence of moral cause and effect and was therefore amenable to dramatization in secular terms. The sixteenth-century conception of history fused a providential and a humanistic view and taught "that while God ordains human affairs after a pattern that is rational and inevitably good, secondary causes may be found in the behaviour of men."[26] Edmund Bolton's position is typical in his criticism of both pagan and Christian histories, one for omitting the role of providence and the other for eliminating the role of free will.[27] The reconciliation of both attitudes is the most impressive achievement of Shakespeare's histories through *Richard II*, and one must reject as insufficient a view that would deny the relevance of either: "The plays of *Henry VI* are not, as it were, haunted by the ghost of Richard II, and the catastrophes of the civil wars are not laid to Boling-

[25] Ernest William Talbert, *Elizabethan Drama and Shakespeare's Early Plays* (Chapel Hill, N.C.: Univ. of North Carolina Press, 1963), p. 223.

[26] Reese, p. 15. See his Chapter One, "The Uses of History."

[27] Edmund Bolton, *Hypercritica*, in J. E. Spingarn, ed., *Critical Essays of the Seventeenth Century* (Oxford: Clarendon, 1908), I, 84–85.

broke's charge; the catastrophic virtue of Henry and the catastrophic evil of Richard are not an inescapable inheritance from the distant past but are generated by the happenings we are made to witness."[28] This ghost operates, however, as the controlling moral environment for "the happenings we are made to witness"; it lurks in the limited rightness of, and sympathy for, York's cause, in the qualification of Henry's regal title, and in the supernatural implications of Richard's evil and Richmond's goodness. The characters are not only making history, they are circumscribed by it.

III

In many ways *Richard II* is a prototype of the moral conflict to be found in *Julius Caesar*. Like the conflict between Caesar and Brutus, that between Richard and Bolingbroke invited biased interpretations in Shakespeare's age: the historical accounts that the sixteenth century inherited could corroborate a simple ethical dichotomy of good versus evil from either side's point of view. Most commonly, however, Tudor historians viewed the moral nature of Richard's deposition as paradoxical; in Brents Stirling's words, "as a kind of secular fall of man which tainted generations unborn until England was redeemed from consequent civil war by appearance of the Tudor Messiah, Henry Earl of Richmond."[29] This fall, like Adam's *felix culpa*, could ultimately be considered a fortunate one, as is seen, eulogistically, in Samuel Daniel's *The Civil Wars:*

> Yet now what reason haue we to complaine?
> Since hereby came the calme we did inioy;
> The blisse of thee *Eliza;* happie gaine
> For all our losse: when-as no other way
> The heauens could finde, but to vnite againe
> The fatall sev'red Families, that they
> Might bring foorth thee: that in thy peace might growe
> That glorie, which few Times could euer showe.[30]

Even if we omit consideration of this ultimate good fortune, however, the event suggested moral complications when one con-

[28] J. P. Brockbank, "The Frame of Disorder: *Henry VI*," in *Early Shakespeare*, Stratford-upon-Avon Studies III (London: Arnold, 1961), p. 98.

[29] "Bolingbroke's 'Decision,'" *SQ*, 2 (1951), 27.

[30] *The Civil Wars*, ed. Laurence Michel (New Haven, Conn.: Yale Univ. Press, 1958), pp. 71–72. (I.3.)

sidered only more immediate climactic results. The deposition
of Richard confused the lineage of English kings, thus producing
the environment for the chaotic War of the Roses and the
tyranny of Richard III; but Bolingbroke's usurpation also gave
England its heroic King Henry V. Thus from the seeds of time
planted in 1399 spring both good and evil. The judgment of
providence, as confirmed by the events, seems to be ambivalent.

These two climaxes, an integral part of the history as structured by Edward Hall, concerned Shakespeare not merely historically but dramatically. This concern can be obscured by
forcing the history plays into the procrustean beds of two
tetralogies: "The cycle of plays which begins with the deposition of Richard II does not culminate in the bloody tyranny
of Richard III; it culminates in the glorious victories of Henry
V. Out of Richard's deposition immediately proceeds, not the
cruelest of England's tyrants, but the greatest of English
kings."[31] Ribner is justified in attempting to reduce Tillyard's
extravagant claim that Shakespeare had a unified, epical
conception of the eight plays in 1590 or even earlier;[32] but a
clear modulation into the glory of Henry V does not begin until
after *Richard II*. In *1 Henry IV* Mortimer's title, derived directly from Richard II, does not claim either our sympathy or
Shakespeare's dramatic interest as did York's title in *Henry VI*;
in *2 Henry IV* the Mortimers are dropped altogether. Even so,
Henry IV has a severely limited sanction, and the dramatic focus
is upon Hal's emergence from a decidedly tainted environment.
His father's death, however, "changes the mode." The brief in-
trigue that Hal quells in *Henry V* is deliberately obscured as
a questioning of his legality, though Shakespeare is honest
enough to wink at the omission:

> *Cambridge:* For me, the gold of France did not seduce,
> Although I did admit it as a motive
> The sooner to effect what I intended.
>
> (II.ii.155–57)

Henry's prayer before Agincourt, while it insists upon the larger
scheme, enforces rather than questions the fact that God is on
his side, short-lived though His sanction will be. It is almost
impossible to imagine Shakespeare's dramatically carrying the
forebodings of disaster or the challenging of Lancastrian legality

[31] Irving Ribner, *The English History Play in the Age of Shakespeare*
(Princeton, N.J.: Princeton Univ. Press, 1957), p. 160.
[32] Tillyard, pp. 148–49.

into the triumphs of Henry V, though he allows a questioning irony. We have no answer to why Shakespeare wrote the history plays in the order he did; but I think it quite evident that if the earlier plays, *Henry VI* and *Richard III,* had not been written before *Henry IV* and *Henry V,* they would not have been written at all. In the case of *Richard II,* however, while Shakespeare was looking forward to the three following plays, necessitating some moral justification for Bolingbroke's usurpation, he was also anticipating, in terms of history, the disasters he had already dramatized, disasters originating morally in Bolingbroke's confusion of absolute right.

In addition to the ambivalence of the deposition in its historical outcome and in Shakespeare's dramaturgic requirements, the event had been further complicated by its topical associations with Elizabeth and the conditions of late sixteenth-century England. As M. M. Reese points out, "no writer who chose to handle this reign can have been unaware of the contemporary immediacy of his theme."[33] Malcontents of various kinds had seen in King Richard a mirror for magistrates; but, as with *Julius Caesar,* the events could argue for either side of the conflict depending upon a bias neither historically nor artistically relevant. If Shakespeare's play was the one shown on the eve of the Essex uprising, Ernest Schanzer has proof that there were indeed many liberal John Dover Wilsons around to attend *Julius Caesar* in 1599. At the same time, conservatives must have seen in the moral paradox of *Richard II* a satisfying reconciliation, for Shakespeare escaped the fate of Sir John Hayward, who invited trouble and got it when he dedicated his prose history of Henry IV to Essex in 1599.

My oblique reference to Schanzer's work is appropriate here. Ernest Talbert, for one, considers that *Richard II* is "a problem drama as purposeful as any of Shakespeare's 'problem comedies.' "[34] Talbert's analysis of the play, showing the complex presentation of both Lancastrian (anti-Richard) and Yorkist (pro-Richard) views, is similar to Schanzer's demonstration of the medieval and Renaissance views of Caesar balanced in the Roman play. The result, according to Talbert, is a conflict be-

[33] Reese, p. 228. And see Lily B. Campbell, *Shakespeare's "Histories": Mirrors of Elizabethan Policy* (San Marino, Calif.: Huntington Library, 1947), pp. 168–212.
[34] Talbert, p. 321. His extensive treatment of *Richard II* is found here (pp. 300–22) and in *The Problem of Order* (Chapel Hill, N.C.: Univ. of North Carolina Press, 1962), pp. 158–200.

tween Elizabethan commonplaces, a conflict generated by the problem of order. Both Tillyard's affirmation and Ribner's skepticism regarding the divine right of Richard II fall short. The ideal and the reality must face each other. Bullough clarifies the requirements:

The play must fit into the scheme of British history according to which misrule brings condign punishment, and political plotting, civil war and usurpation bring destruction on crown and people. Hence there is a twofold aim; the king is to be shown as bringing about his own downfall; yet his forced abdication and death must not be justified.[35]

In having it both ways, as it were, Shakespeare was following a well-established ambivalent judgment:

[In 1399] happened the strange and also the lamentable deposing of this king Richard II. aforesaid, from his kingly sceptre: strange, for that the like example hath not often been seen in seats royal: lamentable, for that it cannot but be grievous to any good man's heart, to see him either so to deserve, if he were justly deposed, or if he were unjustly deprived, to see the kingly title there not able to hold its right, where, by force, it is compelled to give place to might.[36]

Shakespeare did not, in his dramatic medium, have Foxe's expository advantage of authorial explicitness. The contradictions had to be reconciled in a dramatic fusion of opposites, and this reconciliation prevents *Richard II* from being, finally, a problem play. Both Richard and Bolingbroke disturb the foundation of order on which the structure of majesty is built, a foundation that gives the moral conflict an absolute frame of reference. Richard and Bolingbroke are mutually guilty because each violates, in their confrontation, a divinely sanctioned order by annulling the charters of time.

Shakespeare is careful not to develop any of Richard's specific political weaknesses, follies, or crimes so that they unequivocally justify his overthrow. Though the king is clearly implicated in the death of his uncle Woodstock, Shakespeare does not allow what is a potentially villainous association to align Richard with evil. Shakespeare achieves the ambiguity of history by withholding information. Virgil Whitaker has charged, however, that the murder of Woodstock, as puzzlingly reflected in *Richard*

[35] Bullough (1960), III, 378.
[36] *The Acts and Monuments of John Foxe*, ed. Josiah Pratt (London, 1877), III, 216.

II, argues Shakespeare's lack of interest in history;[37] John Dover Wilson urges that Shakespeare neglected an important thread in a lost source play.[38] But Shakespeare knew that there was no unbiased information to give. The Woodstock episode itself allowed a pro- or anti-Richard interpretation, and Shakespeare rather proves himself the better historian by calculating a dramatically realistic sense of confusion. He omits a simplistic consideration of the cause and confines himself to the effects—the exiling of Bolingbroke, the use of Woodstock's death as one of the Lancastrian justifications for Richard's fall, and the generation of personal antagonism between the two protagonists. As for the audience's identification with either side, an observation by E. E. Stoll, taken from another context, is just: "To sympathize you must know the facts; when you don't know them, your interest is of another sort."[39]

Shakespeare does not deny Richard's part in the murder or his other faults; but if they were confirmed to the extent that the Lancastrians charged, the voice in the play expressing the absolute of kingship would have little force in a dramatic conflict of good versus evil that would patently justify his removal. Perhaps Shakespeare had the cautionary example of *Woodstock* before him, a play that does present such a negative treatment of Richard, justifying York and Lancaster's rebellion by the ghostly sanction of Henry III and the Black Prince. The voice of Woodstock, refusing to sanction rebellion against his king though he is viciously murdered by Richard's order, becomes dramatically incoherent lip service to orthodoxy while the main thrust of the drama continues on its amazingly unorthodox course. One has only to compare *Richard II* with *Woodstock* and Marlowe's *Edward II* to see how the relations between Richard and his flatterers have been underplayed. We see Richard refusing the sound advice of York and Gaunt, and that is enough. The scenes with Bagot, Bushy, Green, and Aumerle are quite restrained, and their firm loyalty, except in the case of Bagot, seems admirable. That they received the profits from Richard's farming of the realm is not evident in the least, and it was a point made quite clear in the chronicles. The chronicles do not mention that the purpose of the farming was to pay for the Irish war, and in creating this motive Shakespeare cer-

[37] Whitaker, pp. 143–77.
[38] *Richard II* (Cambridge: Cambridge Univ. Press, 1939), pp. lxiv–lxxvi.
[39] *Shakespeare and Other Masters* (Cambridge, Mass.: Harvard Univ. Press, 1940), p. 14.

tainly makes that act less offensive than it would otherwise have been.

The tragic richness of *Richard II* results from Shakespeare's transmuting politics into the profound ambiguities of poetry. The responsibility for Woodstock's death is obscured, but Richard has definitely shed royal blood. That physical act itself of course can be medicinal or destructive, sacrificial or murderous. As in Gaunt's dying speech to Richard, the potential absolutes are poetically established against which the king is found miserably wanting:

> O, spare me not, my brother Edward's son,
> For that I was his father Edward's son;
> That blood already, like the pelican,
> Hast thou tapp'd out, and drunkenly carous'd.
>
> (II.i.124–27)

In shedding royal blood, Richard has suicidally shed his own. In degrading the land of England by farming out the realm ("Landlord of England art thou now, not king"), Richard ironically secularizes those spiritual qualities that would mystically support him:

> This earth shall have a feeling, and these stones
> Prove armed soldiers, ere her native King
> Shall falter under foul rebellion's arms.
>
> (III.ii.24–26)

In rejecting the wisdom of England and of the past and embracing instead the foreign and the new, Richard cancels the charters of time and in the pursuit of the modern brings about, to his dismay, the new world of Bolingbroke.

The turning point of the play is Richard's direct attack upon the temporal order that sustains him, his seizing Bolingbroke's inheritance. The suicidal nature of this act is in Holinshed's account of York's alarm: "He thought it the part of a wise man to get him in time to a resting place, and to leaue the following of such an vnaduised capteine, as with a leden sword would cut his owne throat" (p. 496). Shakespeare's York is not so pragmatic or so trite. He appeals to the hierarchical stability, to those charters of time that control the temporal flux and impose order upon mutability. The political and the poetic brilliantly fuse:

> Take Hereford's rights away, and take from Time
> His charters and his customary rights;
> Let not to-morrow then ensue to-day;

> Be not thyself—for how art thou a king
> But by fair sequence and succession?
>
> (II.i.195–99)

As Elyot and Hooker warn, a man destroys himself by destroying order. Richard's subsequent experience is the tragedy of a king who, not being himself, can be nothing. It is the profoundest irony of the play that Bolingbroke's advance, with Northumberland's determination to "make high majesty look like itself" (II.i.295), makes Richard for the first time the image of highest regal appeal. And Shakespeare manages to keep that image untarnished while it dramatizes Richard's weakness; the now impotent appeal accents Bolingbroke's superior managerial power while it reveals what ideal sanction the usurper can never gain.

Nevertheless, Bolingbroke's greatest justification is that Richard uncrowns himself, morally and literally. Bolingbroke is portrayed in such a way that in a later play he can offer two versions of his actions:

> Though then, God knows, I had no such intent
> But that necessity so bow'd the state
> That I and greatness were compell'd to kiss.
>
> (*2 Henry IV* III.i.72–74)

> God knows, my son,
> By what by-paths and indirect crook'd ways
> I met this crown.
>
> (IV.v.184–86)

The second version, from the king's dying words to Hal, gets the greater dramatic emphasis. And even if one is reluctant to translate Bolingbroke's silences into explicit motives, Brents Stirling is certainly correct in insisting that "Bolingbroke's use of force to gain just concessions from his sovereign has committed him to the destruction of sovereignty."[40] Like King John's nobles, he finds out his right with wrong, as York insists; and the most generous verdict on Bolingbroke cannot preclude his and England's guilt, a guilt borne out by the political necessity for Richard's death. The play ends, as it began, with a king guilty of shedding royal blood.

Even references to the future—the Bishop's and Richard's prophesies of disaster, the promise of a reformation for Hal—confirm the paradoxical nature of the events in *Richard II;* the

[40] Stirling, p. 32. And see Peter Ure, ed., *Richard II*, Arden Shakespeare, 4th edition (London: Methuen, 1956), p. lxxiv.

two morally opposed climaxes of the historical cycle are thus prepared. Henry IV is a king for whom might must make right as best it can, a limited right being the only possible result of the confusion of absolute right. But the reference to the lost ideal remains to enable us to judge and to blame both sides. The reference, however, intimates an affirmation as well. England is now a fallen world, but the absolute is still there beyond the tragedy. Although Bolingbroke's personal hope is illusory, England can trust in the historical inevitability not of decline and fall but of God's forgiveness.

Index

Index